Olafimihan S. Oladejo-Babalola

Sanctity of Human Life in the Old Testament and Yoruba Worldview

Studying Human Worth in Ancient Israel and African Context

CW00684096

LAP LAMBERT Academic Publishing

Imprint

Any brand names and product names mentioned in this book are subject to trademark, brand or patent protection and are trademarks or registered trademarks of their respective holders. The use of brand names, product names, common names, trade names, product descriptions etc. even without a particular marking in this work is in no way to be construed to mean that such names may be regarded as unrestricted in respect of trademark and brand protection legislation and could thus be used by anyone.

Cover image: www.ingimage.com

Publisher:
LAP LAMBERT Academic Publishing
is a trademark of
International Book Market Service Ltd., member of OmniScriptum Publishing Group
17 Meldrum Street, Beau Bassin 71504, Mauritius

Printed at: see last page
ISBN: 978-620-0-48619-6

Zugl. / Approved by: A comparative understanding of Numbers 35:9-34 and Yoruba worldview of the sanctity of human life can serve as a veritable tool to identify and correct defiant practices among the modern-day Yoruba people.

Olafimihan S. Oladejo-Babalola

Sanctity of Human Life in the Old Testament and Yoruba Worldview

SANCTITY OF HUMAN LIFE IN THE OLD TESTAMENT
AND *YORÙBÁ* WORLDVIEW:

Studying Human Worth in Ancient Israel and African Context

Rev. Olafimihan Solomon Oladejo-Babalola, PhD

1

DEDICATION

To

My wife,

Mrs. Dele Esther Oladejo-Babalola

ACKNOWLEDGMENTS

I give Almighty God all the glory for the success of this academic journey. His faithfulness was great, love was unfathomable, and care was adequate throughout my studies. He was always available for me, my family and the local church committed to my attention. I appreciate His surveillance over me during my trips between Lagos and Ogbomoso almost every week. His provisions for all necessities of life at school, in the family, and the church throughout the period are equally amazing. His security over my life was sufficient on the field while conducting interviews with my respondents most of whom were *Ifa* Chief Priests.

I indeed appreciate all members of my supervisory committee. The contributions of Dr O.B. Oladejo my chief supervisor are quite commendable. I will always remember him for his extraordinary expertise, academic prowess, and notable sacrifices, especially towards the end of this journey. His impacts on my life and contributions to my success are indeed significant and unusual! The fatherly role of Dr M.F. Akangbe, my co-supervisor, will not be forgotten in a hurry. His gentle touch has contributed immensely to the success of this research. Both of them gave me sufficient attention and shared with me from their wealth of experiences on how I should go about this study pragmatically. Their interactions with me really shaped my thought and imparted my academic and general life in no small measure.

Moreover, I am indebted to all members of the NBTS Faculty whose relationships have significantly impacted my life and enhanced my studies such as Prof. J.O. Enyinnaya the Dean of the School of Postgraduate Studies, Dr S.A. Kolawole the Dean of the Faculty of Theology, Dr S.O. Akintola the Head of Biblical Studies Department, Dr. Japheth Yaya Seminary Chief Liberian, and Dr. P.O. Oguntoye the former Head of Biblical Studies Department. The immense contributions of Dr. S.F. Kehinde BCT Oyo cannot be forgotten in haste. The efforts of Dr Abraham O. Odeleye are tremendous and appreciable. This is in the areas of structuring my research instrument (interview guide) and validating and certifying its contents.

Indeed, my unreserved appreciation goes to my loving and amiable wife Mrs Dele Esther Oladejo-Babalola and my four children, namely, Wisdom, Rhoda, Luke, and Testimony whose patience and perseverance owing to my frequent absence at home during the period is unquantifiable. My wife's support, especially her numerous counsels and advice have resulted in this giant academic stride.

I also wish to express my gratitude to others whose roles have resulted to the successful completion of all aspects of my doctoral studies, most especially my dissertation writing. In particular, I am indebted to Deaconess Funke Abioye of Victory Baptist Church, Ajaa, Lagos and Mr Adebayo Oladejo-Babalola for their financial contributions. The following scholars and pastors are to be appreciated for their roles in shaping my academic prowess: Rev. Dr Olalekan O. Bamidele, Rev. Dr

Moses A. Adeyemo, Rev. Dr Aderemi G. Fakorede, and Rev. Dr (Mrs.) Aderenle O. Afolabi.

LIST OF TABLES

LIST OF FIGURES

6

LIST OF PICTURES

LIST OF ABBREVIATIONS

AJSIH - America Journal of Social Issues and Humanities
ANE – Ancient Near East
ATR – African Traditional Religion
B.A – Bachelor of Arts
B.Ed – Bachelor of Education
BCT – Baptist College of Theology
CA - Critical Apparatus
CeS – Church & Society Commission
CMDA - Christian Medical & Dental Associations
COLF - Catholic Organization for Life and Family
D.Min. – Doctor of Ministry
DH – Documentary Hypothesis
DNA – DeoxyriboNucleic Acid
EPM - Eternal Perspective Ministries
JBL – Journal of Biblical Literature
JESHO – Journal of the Economic and Social History of the Orient.
JETS – The Evangelical Theological Society
JP – Oyo State Justice of Peace
LXX – Greek Version of the Hebrew Bible, called Septuagint
M.A – Master of Arts
MT – Masoretic Text
Mss - Manuscripts
NBAC – National Bioethics Advisory Commission
NBTS – Nigerian Baptist Theological Seminary
NBTSO – Nigerian Baptist Theological Seminary, Ogbomoso
NCE – Nigeria Certificate in Education
NGO – Non Governmental Organisation
NRLC - National Right to Life Committee
NT – New Testament
PhD – Doctor of Philosophy
SBL - Society of Biblical Literature
TMSJ – The Master's Seminary Journal
UK – United Kingdom
UN – United Nations
UNODC - United Nations Office on Drugs and Crime
US – United States
USCCB - The United States Conference of Catholic Bishops
WAATI - West Africa Association of Theological Institutions
WRS – Western Reformed Seminary

YTR – *Yorùbá* Traditional Religion

ABSTRACT

Globally, the rate at which people violate the sanctity of human life at this time is alarming. Terrorism, assassination, kidnapping, human trafficking, and abortion are a few instances of this phenomenon. This study concerns itself with the inconsistency between the belief system of ancient Israel and *Yorùbá* people on the worth of human life and what the peoples practice in reality. Thus, the study aims at comparing the cultural understanding of the subject matter in Numbers 35:9-34 with that of *Yorùbá* worldview to identify and correct defiant behaviour among the modern-day *Yorùbá* people.

The following five objectives mark the study: to explain the sanctity of human life in the chosen text from the viewpoints of literature, grammar, and exegesis; clarify the concept in *Yorùbá* worldview philosophically, ritualistically, linguistically, socially, and politically; describe some *Yorùbá* practices that support the subject matter; express some *Yorùbá* cultural manifestations that negate the sacredness of human life; and compare the worth of human life in the two contexts to identify areas of nexus and dissonance and draw necessary implications.

Furthermore, the writer employed the analytical research design: using an eclectic technique that consists of the historical-critical and grammatical methods to investigate the worth of human life in Numbers 35:9-34 from the perspectives of literature, grammar, and exegesis. This concentration is with a particular reference to the Hebrew verb רָצַח Also, this writer examined both the context of *Yorùbá* people and the contents of their worldview: covering their philosophy, rituals, vocabulary, social relations, and political life. The researcher conducted oral and written interviews with a representative sample of 22 *Yorùbá* individuals in four states of the Yorubaland; namely, Oyo, Ogun, Osun, and Lagos. Most of these respondents were traditional *Ifa* Chief Priests.

Moreover, this study identified certain areas of nexus and dissonance. First, the understanding of the worth of human life in the two contexts overlaps in these areas: ethnicity with certain common cultural elements, the basis for the sacredness of life, a good ethical standard for the appreciation of human life, availability of records of violations, and punitive measures against the violators. Second, only ancient Israel had distinctive cultural practices of cities of refuge and right of asylum. The system of cultural purging of land from blood pollution is also well-defined in the same context. Only *Yorùbá* people practice enhancement of one's earth-life.

Consequently, the study recommends specific action-plans for governments, religious bodies, and families in Yorubaland. Governments should check the laid-back attitude of their officials and put appropriate mechanisms in place to curtail violations of the sanctity of human life. Also, religious leaders should emphasise post-marital counselling and be exemplary in their approach to life. Finally, parents should embark on the revival of training of children in their cultural languages, values, and practices.

10

The revealed areas of nexus and dissonance and various deviant practices identified and how these could be corrected are some of the contributions this study adds to knowledge.

Keywords: Sanctity, *Yorùbá*, and worldview

TABLE OF CONTENTS

CHAPTER ONE

INTRODUCTION

1. Background to the Study

One of the apparent issues of global concern in contemporary times is the gross lack of reverence for the dignity and sanctity of human life. With the spate of unabated killings and other forms of dehumanisation, it appears that the concept of the sanctity of human life is globally waning. The phenomenon is evident in the rising wave of violations to this belief system of which terrorism, murder, kidnapping, assassination, human trafficking, and abortion are few instances. As the pervasiveness of this trend is apparent in Africa, its reflections also look widespread in some Asian countries. For example, acts of terrorism, violence, bombing, and insurgency in the Middle East are in connection with the ongoing struggles between various terrorist groups and government forces in Iraq, Afghanistan, and Syria.[1] Europe and America are not free from this sad incident owing to the prevalence of racism in many of the member nations.[2]

Two factors motivated the conduct of this study. First, the writer noticed some violations of human worth within the biblical context of the Old Testament and among *Yorùbá* of Southwestern Nigeria. One thing becomes evident each time any of these infringements takes place; there is a violation of the worth of human life very often, and people cast aspersion on the worldviews of the people groups.

In the context of the OT, the political hegemony of the stronger nations like Egypt, Assyria, and Babylonia was a factor to reckon with among their weaker counterparts in the world of the Ancient Near East. In this regard, Daniel I. Block argues that the world in question was a violent type where stronger nations were switching roles, and the weaker ones were disappearing from the scene.[3] Thus, the world powers of the time often devastated the lives of many of the inhabitants and continuously violated the sanctity of their victims. According to Alexander H. Joffe, this was usually by geopolitical competition and constant warfare.[4]

---

[1] National Consortium for the Study of Terrorism and Responses to Terrorism (START), ed., *Global Terrorism Index 2016: Measuring and Understanding the Impact of Terrorism* (Sydney: Institute for Economics & Peace, 2016), 10.

[2] "History of Racism and Immigration Time Line: Key Events in the Struggle for Racial Equality in the United States." *https://www.google.com.ng/url?sa=t&-source=web&rct=j&url=http://cw.routledge.com/textbooks/9780415892940*(accessed April 30, 2018).

[3] Daniel I. Block, "Ezekiel 11:1-21," *The New International Commentary on Old Testament,"* eds., R.K. Harrison, Robert L. Hubbard, Jr. (Grand Rapids, Michigan\ Cambridge, U.K.: William B. Eerdmans Publishing Company, 1997), 9.

[4] Alexander H. Joffe, "The Rise of Secondary States in the Iron Age Levant." *JESHO* 45:4 (2002): 427-28.

Similarly, an increase in the prevalence of life-threatening situations in some parts of Nigeria is worrisome. Their frequency in the North-East and North-Central especially is mind-boggling. Instances of these threats to human worth generally are terrorism,[5] corruption, political killing, human trafficking,[6] drug trafficking, armed robbery, assassination, poverty, insecurity, electoral violence, lousy leadership, poor infrastructure, kidnapping,[7] conflict, and war.

Nonetheless, the concern of this writer is the context of the *Yorùbá* people. There is a kind of lopsidedness and disconnect between what is known to be the people's worldview, most importantly in the area of appreciation of human life, and certain practices among the present-day *Yorùbá* people. Sanctity of human life is mostly believed to be part of the value system of the people. According to Akinbowale Akintola, this value is by *Yorùbá* people's understanding of human life.[8] The people built their cooperative system of living on this understanding. More so, the peaceful co-existence which existed among them in the past was notably by this excellent value. However, the reverse is the case today as those values are vanishing.

The Ishola Oyenusi's armed robbery saga of the 1970s[9] is an example of militant robbery attacks in Lagos and its adjoining cities. The devastation, dehumanisation, and pains the bandit inflicted on people are some of the effects which utter disregard for the sanctity of human life could cause any land. Again, the gruesome killing of Bola Ige, the former Attorney General of the Federation,[10] is an instance of the numerous political murders carried out in Nigeria especially within the territory of *Yorùbá* people. Similarly, the "letter-bomb" murder of Dele Giwa on October 19, 1986, whose mastermind remains a mystery,[11] is another instance of many assassination cases that characterise the nation. Besides, the ritual killings and various kidnapping cases that take place almost on a daily basis are some others.

Festus Adedayo recently pictured the summary of all of these situations in "Nigeria: Fatherland as murderland."[12] The argument is that although not all these

---

[5] START, 12-13.

[6] UNODC, *Global Report on Trafficking in Persons 2016* (Vienna: United Nations Publication, 2016)], 26-31, 46.

[7] NYA International: Crisis Prevention and Response, ed., "Global Kidnap Review 2016," *http://presswire.com/pr/nya/160203-NYA-January-Kidnap-Review.pdf*), 1, 2.

[8] Akinbowale Akintola, *Yoruba Ethics and Metaphysics: Being Basic Philosophy Underlying the Ifa System of Thought of the Yoruba* (Ogbomoso: Valour Publishing Ventures Limited, 1999), 12.

[9] Teslim Opemipo Omipidan, "The Real Story of Ishola Oyenusi-Nigeria's Deadliest Armed Robber,"*https://oldnaija.com/2017/03/23/the-real-story-of-ishola-oyenusi-nigerias-deadliest-armed-robber/* (accessed August 9, 2018. Ishola Oyenusi, whose brutality earned him an appellation 'Doctor rob and kill,' was regarded as the "first celebrated armed robber in Nigeria" who never allowed any of his victims to witness another day. He is reported to be the deadliest armed robber that Nigeria has ever had. He is followed by Lawrence Anini, Babatunde Folorunsho, and Shina Rambo, among others.

[10] Amnesty International, *Nigeria: Impunity for political violence in the run-up to the 2007 elections"* (April, 2007), under "Settings" *https://www.amnsety.org/download/Documents/60000/afr440042007en.pdf*), 13.

[11] Omipidan, "The Death of Dele Giwa on October 19 1986," *https://oldnaija.com/2015/10/30/the-death-of-dele-giwa-on-october-19-1986/amp* (accessed September 11, 2017).

[12] Festus Adedayo, "Nigeria: Fatherland as murderland," *Nigerian Tribune*, September 24, 2017.

cases mentioned were orchestrated and carried out by *Yorùbá* people, they all took place on their land. One of their proverbs is handy in this regard, "*Bi iku ile o ba pani, t'ode o le pani*" (If there are no collaborators within, one cannot die from outside).

Second, the opportunity extended to this writer as a member of the research team set up by the NBTSO in 2015 was another source of motivation. The team was to submit a proposal to the Nagel Institute of America, requesting for a grant to conduct a study on the sanctity of human life about highway automobile mortality. In the process, the writer's horizon became extensive as he gained better exposure to various ways by which people violate human sacredness in Africa.

Studies abound on the subject of the sanctity of human life. However, as related and relevant as these studies are, the writers did not take into consideration the discrepancy and disconnect that exist between the cultural belief of the people groups and their actual praxis of the concept of human sanctity. The apparent dissonance between what the people, in this case the ancient Israel in Numbers 35:9-34 and the 21st-century *Yorùbá* claim to believe and their actual practices is the gap which this study intends to fill.

2. Statement of the Problem

Reading through the Law Codes of the OT, it is apparent that the sanctity of human life is rooted in the worldview of ancient Israel. However, when the reading is taken further to the Prophetic Corpus and Writings, several instances of violations of these codes are equally evident. Similarly, despite the presence of the Christian faith in *Yorùbá* land in addition to the rich cultural value of life enshrined in the people's worldview, practices that are deviant to the cultural heritage of human sanctity are evident among the contemporary people. The problem of this study is, therefore, the irregularity and contradiction of this kind within the two contexts of the people groups.

In other words, the problem of this research is the disagreement, lopsidedness, and contradiction that exist between the belief system of the people groups of ancient Israel and *Yorùbá* on the sanctity of life and what they practice. Thus, both ancient Israel and *Yorùbá* of today appear to have this problem in common. To what extent is this similarity? Hence, there is a need for this comparative study on the sanctity of human life in Numbers 35:9-34 and among *Yorùbá* people.

3. Purpose of the Study

The primary purpose of this study is to compare cultural understanding of the sanctity of human life in the Old Testament, specifically in Numbers 35:9-34, with the worldview of *Yorùbá* people on the same subject matter. However, to achieve this aim, specific objectives are essential to consider. Five of them are considered necessary for this study; namely, To:

1. Explain the concept of the sanctity of human life in Numbers 35:9-34 from the viewpoints of literature, grammar, and exegesis.

2. Clarify the idea of the sacredness of the presence of humankind in the worldview of the *Yorùbá* from philosophical, ritualistic, linguistic, and socio-political perspectives.

3. Describe certain practices of the *Yorùbá* people which support the sanctity of human life.

4. Express some of the practices of the *Yorùbá* people which negate the sacredness of human life in their society.

5. Compare the concept of the sanctity of human life in Numbers 35:9-34 with that of *Yorùbá* to identify areas of nexus and dissonance and to draw necessary implications.

4. Thesis Statement

The thesis of this study is that a comparative understanding of Numbers 35:9-34 and *Yorùbá* worldview of the sanctity of human life can serve as a veritable tool to identify and correct deviant practices among the modern-day *Yorùbá* people.

5. Significance of the Study

This study aims to promote the value and worth of human life among contemporary Yorùbá. The writer believes that the step would generally benefit all *Yorùbá* people and their host communities in identifying and correcting deviant practices on the worth of human life among them. This understanding would foster unity among them and enhance their relationships with other peoples of different worldviews. The study would also promote a better appreciation of the Great Commission among *Yorùbá* Christians as they partner with God in missions. Thus, the research would benefit various *Yorùbá* churches within their host communities as they gain appreciations for missions and evangelism and better ways of carrying out the Great Commission pragmatically.

Moreover, the work also aims at benefitting religious institutions, especially those within the Nigerian Baptist Convention (NBC). The benefit of this kind is to make the study become a biblical basis for a theology of the sanctity of human life in the curriculum of these institutions. This would, in turn, significantly contribute to the training of pastors as they impact the worth of human life to their various congregations. Not only this, this appreciation would equally help various churches where these pastors function to become potential agents of transformation to their host communities. Finally, the work would ultimately transform the cultural heritage of the *Yorùbá* people of Southwestern Nigeria.

The writer would make these benefits available as he communicates the findings to religious bodies, theological institutions, and different organisations and communities within and outside the context of Yorubaland through workshops, seminars, and conferences. The writer would also make copies of the findings of this research available to the library of the NBTSO. More so, efforts would again be made to ensure that the entire work is published either wholly or in parts.

6. Scope of the Study

The content scope of the study is about the sanctity of human life in the Old Testament, specifically in Numbers 35:9-34, and in *Yorùbá* worldview. In view of this, the following contents are given consideration: sanctity of human life in ancient Near Eastern culture, human sacredness in OT literature, pro-life and pro-choice arguments, and recent and current issues on sanctity of life.

The writer also investigates the contextual meaning of the sacredness of human life in the Hebrew grammar with emphasis on related Hebrew verbs translated as "to kill." The writer later exegetes Numbers 35:9-34. The writer equally examines meaning of the sanctity of human life generally among the *Yorùbá* people by investigating various aspects of the people's cultural experience and manifestations in their philosophy, rituals, vocabulary, and social and political life. Additionally, the geographical scope of the study is the duo of the context of the OT and *Yorùbá* people of Southwestern Nigeria.

7. Method of the Study

The need to study the world of the writer of the Book of Numbers is pertinent to this study. Taking this step would help in gaining a better understanding of the original intention of the writer which necessarily influences the meaning of the passage of the book among the original audience of the biblical literature. Given this, the writer employs historical-critical and grammatical methods of biblical hermeneutics[13] to investigate the sanctity of human life within the context of biblical language and literature of the OT in Numbers 35:9-34.

These methods became necessary in biblical hermeneutics since the culture and worldview of the authors that produced biblical literature and the audience to whom the writings were sent are quite different from the culture and worldview of the contemporary readers. Therefore, it becomes imperative to consider the meaning of Numbers 35:9-34 in the light of the original audience with specific attention to the literary form of the book, genres, authorship, historical situation surrounding the writing, dating and the situation that informed the writing.[14]

The writer also investigates the sanctity of human life in some critical aspects of the *Yorùbá* worldview; namely, their philosophy, rituals, vocabulary, politics, and social life. Additionally, the writer again conducts a comparative study on the two contexts to bring various harmonious and dissonant elements of the sacredness of human life to the fore for possible implications on the contemporary *Yorùbá* people. Moreover, the writer considers it necessary to conduct interviews with certain representative elements of the *Yorùbá* people. The writer made this effort of looking

---

[13] Historical-critical method is a critical apparatus or exegetical tool devised by a German scholar, called Hermann Gunkel, to investigate the world of the authors of biblical literature for the purpose of interpreting biblical literary works correctly. According to Olugbenga Olagunju in "The Relevance of Historical-Critical Method of Biblical Interpretation for the Church in Africa," (*American Journal of Biblical Theology, http://www.biblicaltheology.com/Research/Olagunju005.pdf*), "Thus, historical-critical approaches discuss the world of the author vis a vis the culture, the language and the social background of the Biblical world" (1).

[14] Ibid.

at the sanctity of human life in *Yorùbá* worldview critically and sufficiently to have a comprehensive understanding of the value and gain correct perspective of how the people appreciate human being within the context.

8. Operational Definition of Term

Essentially, the word "sanctity" connotes the idea of importance attached to something, as a result of which such must be respected and preserved. Thus, "sanctity of human life" brings the ideas of "human worth" and "value of human life" to the fore. Nonetheless, the idea of "human sacredness" or "sacredness of human life" is also employed in this study. The reason for this action is that the editor of the Longman Active Study Dictionary pictures the adjective word "sacred" as something significant as a result of relating to a god or religion and is as such made holy.[15] Since it is common knowledge in biblical studies that man is a carrier of God's image, the life of man thus has a close affinity with God. The writer, therefore, regards human life as being sacred and must be given adequate attention, respect, and protection.

In addition to all this, three terms are employed synonymously for "sanctity" by David P. Gushee; namely, "sacredness," "worth" and "dignity." The fact is evident in Gushee's operational definition for the sanctity of human life:

> The conviction that all human beings, at any and every stage of life, in any and every state of consciousness or self-awareness, of any and every race, color, ethnicity, level of intelligence, religion, language, nationality, gender, character, behavior, physical ability/disability, potential, class, social status, etc., of any and every particular quality of relationship to the viewing subject, are to be perceived as sacred, as persons of equal and immeasurable worth and of inviolable dignity. Therefore they must be treated with the reverence and respect commensurate with this elevated moral status, beginning with a commitment to the preservation, protection, and flourishing of their lives.[16]

In the same way, these three terms are equally expressed synonymously for sanctity in the study.

---

[15] Longman Active Study Dictionary, ed., s.v. "Sanctity."

[16] David P. Gushee, "The Old Testament and the Sanctity of Life," *Bioethics & Human Dignity, Trinity International university,* https://cbhd.org/content/old-testament-and-sanctity-life&ved (February 5, 2008) (accessed September 21, 2016), 1.

CHAPTER TWO

REVIEW OF RELATED LITERATURE

Studies abound on the sanctity of human life. However, scholars have not given necessary consideration to a comparative understanding of Numbers 35:9-34 and *Yorùbá* worldview of human life. In this review, the writer considers existing works in the following areas: ancient Near Eastern Culture, OT literature, and pro-life and pro-choice arguments. The writer also considers studies on previous and current issues on the subject matter, especially in the fields of philosophy, culture, law, socio-economic growth, medicine, and bioethics.

1. Sanctity of Human Life in ancient Near Eastern Culture

Rational understanding of the concept of the sanctity of human life in Numbers 35:9-34 requires looking at the general culture that influenced the OT in ANE. Stuarts A. West examines the cultural influences of the Hurrian upon Nuzi people during the patriarchal period with the claim that there is every reason to believe that Hurrian culture had an impact upon Nuzi cultural life and practices during this period. The basis of this claim lies upon more than 4,000 archaeological findings which involve written documents such as clay tablets.[17]

As a result of these discoveries, a better understanding of the specific actions taken and practices performed by biblical patriarchs in the light of the cultural traditions of Nuzi people is available. First, the act of "wife-sistership" displayed by the duo of Abraham and Isaac (Gen. 20:1-20 and 26:6-12) is an example. One needs these findings to understand that this cultural practice was commonplace in Nuzi custom for double protection of the wife from possible molestation. It was also for superior benefits in this society where the patriarchs lived. This evidence dispels the apparent notion of trickery that many OT commentators had against the patriarchs.[18]

Second, it was also the custom of Nuzi people for a brother to give his sister away in marriage. This practice was informed by Hurrian societal culture, evidence of the system called "fratriarchy" within the empire. A biblical example of this custom is the role which Laban played in the giving away of Rebekah his sister to become Isaac's wife. In this instance, Laban acted as the chief negotiator (Gen. 24:29-51). They also consulted Rebekah before the marriage deal was finally sealed. All this reflects Nuzi culture which had it basis in the custom of the Hurrian people.[19]

Again, another biblical example of Nuzi cultural influence is the case of Abraham asserting that Eliezer would become the possessor of his house-will (Gen. 15:2-3). Stuart, reflecting on the Nuzi tablets' report says, "Under Hurrian law (sic) a

---

[17] Stuart A. West, "The Nuzi Tablets: Reflections on the Patriarchal Narratives," *Dor Le Dor* Vol. VIII No.1 (Fall 1979): 12.

[18] Ibid, 13-14.

[19] Ibid, 14-15.

man's heir could be either his natural born son – a direct heir – or, in the absence of any natural born son, an indirect heir, who was an outsider adopted for the purpose."[20] Similarly, the issue of concubinage is another. According to one Nuzi tablet, "Kelim ninu has been given in marriage to Shennima.... If Kelim-ninu does not bear children, Kelim-ninu shall acquire a woman of the land of Lulu (i.e., a slave girl) as (sic) wife for Shennima." This statement reflects a provision in the marital custom of Nuzi for those who could not bear children by natural descent. This situation is in agreement with the case of Sarai giving Hagar to Abram as a wife (Gen. 16:1-4), a repeat of which happened to Rachael and Jacob in Genesis 30: 1-5.[21]

Furthermore, the stolen household gods' story between Jacob and Laban (Gen. 31:19) is another biblical practice that reflects the culture of the Hurrian people of keeping household gods. The significance of stealing them lies in one of the disclosures that whoever was in possession of the household gods was the right heir of the family.[22] However, the emphasis placed on Rachael hiding these gods is a clear indication of biblical contempt for the practice.

Lastly, sharing of inheritance under Nuzi custom was by what is termed "testamentary disposition," which, more often than not, was carried out orally at that time. In one of the tablets, there is a story of a lawsuit between brothers concerning the possession of their deceased father's slave girl, called Sululi-Ishtar. In this narrative, the youngest of three brothers, named Tarmiya, was responding to his elder brothers' claim to Sululi-Ishtar. His testimony goes thus, "'My father, Huya, was sick and lay on a couch; then my father seized my hand and spoke thus to me, "My other sons, being older, have acquired a wife; so I give herewith Sululi-Ishtar as your wife.'" In the end, the Court ruled in favour of Tarmiya on the ground of his father's oral testamentary disposition. This practice is similar to the situation of Isaac's desire to give his elder son Esau his testamentary blessing (Gen. 27:2).[23]

Furthermore, given the ongoing debates on the problem of identity between the Habiru of the Amarna Letters and Hebrew of the OT, Nadav Naaman argues against specific claims which are erroneous on the distinctiveness of the Habiru. This argument is by anthropological study in the field of tribal society of the antiquity and aims at contributing to the ongoing discussion that seeks clarification of the ambiguous identities of the Habiru of the Amarna letters and Hebrews of the Bible. The description made in this study was by recent archaeological discoveries at Mari and Palestine, specifically in the hill country where the Israelites settled before the period of the Monarchy.[24]

Naaman's idea of human life within the socio-political and economic environment of the time gained the interest of this writer. Usually, the Habiru were uprooted from their original socio-political setting and thereby forced to adapt to new

---

[20] Ibid, 15.
[21] Ibid, 16-17.
[22] Ibid, 17.
[23] Ibid, 18.
[24] Nadav Naaman, "Habiru and Hebrew: The Transfer of a Social Term to the Literary Sphere," *Journal of Near Eastern Studies* Vol. 45, No.4 (Oct.1986): 272.

environmental conditions in another social context. Commenting on factors which generally resulted to this situation, Naaman advances, "The different traits and social behavior of the Habiru in each area of Western Asia are the outcome (sic) of this adaptation to new circumstances. Among the various reasons for breaking off their former political and social ties were wars, disasters, famine, debt, heavy taxes, prolonged military service, and so on."[25]

Moreover, while studying the nature of migration and diffusion during the Palaeolithic Age, Pal Fejes identified a "'lingua franca'" which existed a long time ago called *HUN*. This scholar claims that the language belonged to the Eessa people who populated the then habitable parts of the world. Fejes idiomatically referred to this language as "Earth Mother's Sacred Language." This writer identified that the sanctity of human life was betrayed even at that ancient time by Eessa People. The argument is from Fejes' analysis that the people usually migrated to a different occupied part of the then world. According to the revelation and interpretation of the Tamana toponyms, Eessa people killed and maimed human lives in the process of conquering the original occupants of their newly acquired land.[26] Examples of Eessa people were the Indra's soldiers, named Aryans, who invaded India around 1984 B.C. Also, the earlier inhabitants sent away into the southern region of the sub-continent were Dravidian population.[27] This situation is another form of violation of the sacredness of human life in antiquity.

More so, Joffe investigated the formation of the Levantine states during the Iron Age with particular emphasis on the lands of Israel, Judah, Ammon, and Moab. Joffe claimed that the structure of secondary states was radically different from that of previous countries in Mesopotamia and Egypt. The scholar declared that the difference was similar to the secondary states in the Levant which did not lead to the creation of any new bureaucracy. Instead, it resulted in a modern society regarding a new form of identities called, "novel ethnic categories and boundaries." Joffe employed both archaeological and textual proofs to justify this claim. This choice was with the intent that archaeology could immensely demonstrate the emergence of "polities integrated by means of identity," which was brought about by the long-standing integration of both imperial domination and the city-state system. As a result of these social forces, new forms of local identity and organisation emerged with relative dislocation. This phenomenon manifested again and again between more massive empires.[28]

The basis of Joffe's argument is that sanctity of human life was significantly impaired during this period of political hegemony of the World Powers like Egypt, Babylonia, and Hittites, leading to a complete breakdown of society. This situation usually resulted in a new culture. Some of the leading factors at the root of this

---

[25] Ibid.
[26] Pal Fejes, "The Eessa-Exodus in the Paleolitic Age (An Epigraphic and Historical Study)," *Migration & Diffusion* Vol. 1, Issue No. 5 (2001): 6.
[27] Ibid, 23.
[28] Joffe, 425-26.

situation are; namely, an organisation of the second millennium Levant around rival city-states headed primarily by mayors and by councils of elders in a minimal proportion, Egyptian taxation, and corvee, geopolitical competition, and warfare.[29] An instance of war of this kind was the constant invasion of the Sea Peoples.[30]

Furthermore, William M. Schniedewind and Joel H. Hunt studied the language, culture, and literature of the Ugarit. These scholars claimed that life in ANE was an unbalanced type. To justify this, they advance that the welfare of human beings was unstable by the conflicting interests of their world powers. Although the people of Ugarit thrived as their land became a melting point for ancient Near Eastern peoples, their economy was a dominated type. This situation was argued to be the general state of life at the time. Ugarit was a vassal to the Hittite kingdom and a combination of many cultures –the Syrian, Canaanite, Egyptian, Mediterranean, and Mesopotamian, among others. As a result, an imbalance developed between these conflicting interests.[31]

Moreover, Schniedewind and Hunt also described life in the family as an unstable type. Since family life in Ugarit was patriarchal, a man could marry to as many wives as possible; thereby subjecting women to second-class citizens. Sons born to the same man were also not of the same status and daughters were regarded as servants. This situation affected the inheritance of female children in the family, although women could still rise to prominence especially in the royal family.[32] All this describes the nature of life within the city of Ugarit. According to Ian Shaw, Ugarit was one of the significant Canaanite sites located on the Levantine coast during the Bronze Age which got destroyed probably by the sea people around c. 1200 BC.[33] Thus, human lives could be so devastated by gender inequality within the family line and wide-scale destruction by the large nations during the Bronze and Iron Ages.

Furthermore, Ann E. Killebrew and Gunnar Lehmann studied the world of the Philistine and other Sea Peoples and set out to debunk the general ugly portrayal of the "Sea Peoples" who were believed to have emerged from "Islands." These people, especially the Philistines, appear severally in New Kingdom Egyptian writings and were described as the principal enemy to the people of Yahweh. They were also often presented as assailants from the north in their previous appearance during Merenptah and Ramesses' reigns.[34]

Killebrew and Lehmann argue that the origins of the Sea Peoples are fading away with their material manifestations and role in the eastern Mediterranean world during the 13th and 12th centuries B.C. This argument is said to remain despite the

[29] Ibid, 427-28.

[30] Ibid, 429.

[31] William M. Schniedewind and Joel H. Hunt, *A Primer on Ugaritic Language, Culture and Literature* (New York: Cambridge University Press, 2007), 15-16.

[32] Ibid, 18.

[33] Ian Shaw, "Ugarit," *A Dictionary of Archaeology*, eds., Ian Shaw and Robert Jameson (Cowley Road, Oxford: Blackwell Publishers Ltd, 1999), 593.

[34] Ann E. Killebrew and Gunnar Lehmann, "'The World of the Philistines and Other 'Sea Peoples,' The Philistines and Other Sea Peoples'" in Text and Archaeology, *Society of Biblical Literature (SBL)*, eds., Ann E. Killebrew and Gunnar Lehmann No. 15 (2013): 1-2.

explosive archaeological discoveries and record. The Hittites and Egyptians were the dominating political powers of the time. However, there was an experience of a major crisis by these large nations as the Mediterranean world was transiting from the Late Bronze to Iron Age. This crisis eventually severed their power, eventually leading to their decline. Gradually, some other peoples began to surface. These are called "'ethnically' defined groups" in contemporary and later texts. Among them were the Philistines with others such as Phoenicians, Israelites, Aramaeans, and Moabites.[35]

Again, the Mediterranean world was a complex type during the Late Bronze Age. The experience of diverse fates marked this situation. The complexity was also characterised by some regions in the eastern part of the then world, witnessing both continuity and changes. In addition to all this, some sites also saw large-scale destruction during the final century of the period or its transition to Iron Age. Examples of these sites are Mycenae, Hattula, Troy, Ugarit, Hazor, Megiddo, Lachish, and Ashdod.[36] Thus, people of the Mediterranean world indeed significantly violated the sanctity of human life during the Late Bronze Age.

Similarly, Geza Vermes investigated the nature of the Dead Sea Scrolls unearthed around Khirbet Qumran. This site is located almost eight miles south of Jericho on the western shore of the Dead Sea. Vermes claims that individual members of an ancient Jewish religious community ran out one day and hurriedly climbed the nearby mountains in search of places to secure their precious documents. Incidentally, Khirbet Qumran was made to be their city centre. They invariably deposited their all-important materials in eleven caves and did not come back for them. The scrolls remained there for about 2,000 years without getting destroyed.[37] Citing Sukenik, Vermes disclosed that the people were the religious community called the Essenes. By their writings, they were discovered to be very ascetic and well known to Philo, Josephus, and Pliny, the Elder. Thus, violation of human life in the ANE did not only thrive during the Stone-Iron Ages, but the same record of a breach persisted in Palestine until the intertestamental period. This writer's submission was by the final plight of forceful ejection of the Essenes possibly as a result of a war.

2. Sacredness of Human Life in Old Testament Literature

The need to give necessary considerations to the meaning of the sacredness of human life within the three sections of the OT literature is excellent to this study. Without this, there will be a disappointment in the focus of investigating the similar meaning of sanctity of human life between Numbers 35:9-34 and *Yorùbá* worldview and necessary appreciation of the worth of human life in the exegesis of the chosen text will also be difficult. Given this, there will be an investigation of the sanctity of human life in the Pentateuch, Prophets, and Writings.

---

[35] Ibid, 5-6.

[36] Ibid, 6.

[37] Geza Vermes, *The Complete Dead Sea Scrolls in English*, Revised Edition (New York: Penguin Books, 2004), 25.

According to Robert Ray Ellis, Pentateuch is a Greek derivative of the Hebrew OT books called תּוֹרָה (*Torah*, meaning "Law").[38] In other words, it is the first five biblical books of the OT; namely, Genesis, Exodus, Leviticus, Numbers, and Deuteronomy. Similarly, the section of the Prophets is named נְבִיאִים (*Nᵉbhiim*, meaning "Prophets"). The section comprises two main sub-divisions: "Former Prophets" (Joshua, Judges, Samuel and Kings) and the "Latter Prophets" (Isaiah, Jeremiah, Ezekiel and the Twelve: Hosea, Joel, Amos, Obadiah, Jonah, Micah, Nahum, Habakkuk, Zephaniah, Haggai, Zechariah, and Malachi).[39] Finally, the last section is called כְּתוּבִים (*Kethubhim*, meaning "Writings"). It is made up of the following biblical books: Psalms, Job, Proverbs, Ruth, Song of Songs (Canticles), Ecclesiastes, Lamentations, Esther, Daniel, Ezra, Nehemiah, and Chronicles.[40]

a. Pentateuchal Estimation of Human Life

Walther Zimmerli, in his analysis of the Decalogue, argues that Yahweh enacted the sixth law to protect the life that He has given humanity from indiscriminate attack.[41] He then posits that human sacredness in the OT is by God's image in man, the murder of which demands atonement.[42]

Moreover, while analyzing the semantics behind אָדָם ("Adam"), Leland Ryken, James C. Wilhoit, Tremper Longman III, Colin Duriez, Douglas Penney and Daniel G. Reid argue that Adam is literarily and theologically a leading figure in the Western thought. These scholars presented this Hebrew word as an essential vocabulary whose imagery is fundamental to the understanding of the concept of the sanctity of human life in the OT. The word is also regarded as a paradox because the man was initially innocent and is archetypally a sinner.[43]

In their analysis of the imagery to support their claim, the scholars argue that אָדָם is both a proper name and generic term inclusively employed for humanity. The scholars also viewed the imagery in some other ways. First, Adam is advanced to be a divine image presented as the creative and divine word fleshly formed in the first creation narrative (Gen. 1). The term is equally viewed as a form shaped by the holy hands with the divine breath in the second creation narrative (Gen. 2). Hence, they depict Adam as a means by which God relates to His created order, human beings especially. Again, these scholars also present this designation as the divine image in man; the living image of the living God. Similarly, they also view it as the image that received the divine commandments which have universal application.[44]

---

[38] Robert Ray Ellis, *Learning to Read Biblical Hebrew: An Introductory Grammar*, Revised Edition (Texas: Baylon University, 2003), 166.

[39] Ibid.

[40] Ibid.

[41] Walther Zimmerli, *Old Testament Theology in Outline*, trans., David E. Green (Edinburgh: T & T Clark Ltd, 1978), 134.

[42] Ibid, 135.

[43] Leland Ryken, James C. Wilhoit, Tremper Longman III, Colin Duriez, Douglas Penney & Daniel G. Reid, "Adam," *Dictionary of Biblical Imagery* (England: InterVarsity Press, 1998), 75.

[44] Ibid, 75-76.

Likewise, scholars also depict Adam as the earthly man. He was shaped from the dust of the ground (Gen. 2:7), having the colouration of אָדָם ('*ādām*) which means "human" and that of אֲדָמָה (*ᵃdāma*) which implies "ground." In Genesis 1: 26-28, the imagery of Adam as הָאָדָם (*hā'ādām*, 'the man/human'), in the form of both male and female in gender and sexuality, rule and dominate as active bearers of the creative power of God-divine vice-regent to preserve God's creation order.[45]

Similarly, the work of Daniel Simango concerns how the concept of *imago Dei* (Gen. 1:26-27) was developed in the Pentateuch, most importantly from early Jewish interpretation to the contemporary time. This scholar employed a biblical-theological approach from the standpoint of a Reformed tradition of the chosen text. Simango investigated the selected text in the context of the larger pericope of Genesis 2-11. On this basis, the scholar discovered that *imago Dei* is both moral, having a likeness to God, and relational as a result of the relationship between God and man which it signifies.[46]

Furthermore, the study conducted by Richards S. Hess relates to cultural influences within the OT from extra-biblical context with the claim that the OT is a record of various forces of the ancient Near Eastern countries on the people of Israel. According to Richards, these influences were in categories and great. They were especially from Egypt in the south, the Hittites and Aramaeans in the north, and Babylonia and Assyria in the east. In addition to these were the influences of Israel's immediate neighbours like the Canaanites, Philistines, Ammonites, Edomites, and Moabites. As part of these influences made on the people of Yahweh, the Hebrew writing system was also inclusive. All of these influences were claimed to be on the level of transformation, and the situation is quite evident in the Hebrew Bible.[47]

Hess presents certain instances of influences of this kind to elucidate the claim within the context of the Pentateuch. The operational mode of Yahweh's covenant with ancient Israel was the first of them. This covenant was on the style of repetition and reaffirmation by the people. According to Hess, this mode was introduced to Israel from other cultures like Hittite, Ugaritic, and Emar (Exod. 20-24; Josh. 8:30-35; 24). Again, the structure of this covenant is another. Citing Kenneth A. Kitchen, it resembles legal codes and treaties of the second millennium BC[48] which establishes priority placed on the sanctity of human life in the Bible.[49]

Furthermore, the operational definition of the sacredness of human life in light of the OT by Gushee is on the imperative to consider. According to this scholar, the sanctity of human life is:

---

[45] Ibid, 77.

[46] Daniel Simango, "The Image of God (Gen 1:26-27) in the Pentateuch: A Biblical-Theological Approach" (Ph.D. Dissertation, North-West University, 2006), iii.

[47] Richard S. Hess, "Cultural Relationships in the Old Testament Period," *Dictionary of Biblical Criticism and Interpretation*, Porter, Stanley E., ed. (London: Routledge: Taylor and Francis Group, 2007), 63-64.

[48] Kenneth A. Kitchen, "Egypt, Ugarit, Qatna, and Covenant," *Ugarit Forschungen* 11 (1979): 453-64.

[49] Hess, 64.

The conviction that all human beings, at any and every stage of life, in any and every state of consciousness or self-awareness, of any and every race, color, ethnicity, level of intelligence, religion, language, nationality, gender, character, behavior, physical ability/disability, potential, class, social status, etc., of any and every particular quality of relationship to the viewing subject, are to be perceived as sacred, as persons of equal and immeasurable worth and of inviolable dignity. Therefore they must be treated with the reverence and respect commensurate with this elevated moral status, beginning with a commitment to the preservation, protection, and flourishing of their lives.[50]

Two things are worthy of note in this definition. Certain character traits, on the one hand, are inherent in all human beings. These are the substantive qualities of the *imago Dei* in humankind. Given this intrinsic worth or value inherent in every human being, on the other hand, respect, reverence, honour or dignity must be accorded to all human beings.

In another development, Gushee worked on the nature of OT creation theology about the subject of the sacredness of life. In this study, Gushee claims that the implicit universality of this theology is one of its contributions which receive less attention from biblical scholars. In the Book of Genesis 1:26, all humanity is implied in being made in God's image — both male and female carry God's image. Similarly, God also forbids shedding human blood in chapter 9:5-6 of the same book. According to Gushee, this prohibition in the context of the latter text is on the premise that everyone carries the status of God's image with God's delegated responsibility which Gushee termed, "Delegation dominion." William P. Brown similarly pictures this responsibility, "Democratization of royalty in the creation account."[51]

More so, the honour and glory crowned humankind in Psalm 8 also applies to all regardless of status, colour, and race. Gushee described all of these as mere human distinctions in history which also crept into biblical law and narrative, weakening the implicit democratic and universality of creation theology. Because of this, one God making one humanity is a profound element of biblical creation theology of the OT. The scholar presented this as an underline factor for the sacredness of human life.[52]

Moreover, apart from the making of man by one God, implicit universality of OT creation theology also extends to the oneness of humanity in "one shared ancestor." This reality is a profound truth implied from the creation narrative expressed by the Yahwist that one man, called Adam, was the starting point of God's creation of the entire humanity (Gen. 2).[53] Given this, Genesis 1 is about "the *universality* of the imago Dei," while Genesis 2 is that of "a primal human unity" that all humanity comes from one shared ancestor.

One major threat to the implicit universality of biblical creation theology, however, is the hierarchical worldview of humankind. An example of this is the ideology of the Nazi championed by Adolf Hitler and characterised by non-Semitism.

---

[50] Gushee, "The Old Testament and the Sanctity of Life," 1.
[51] William P. Brown, *The Ethhos of the Cosmos* (Grand rapids: Eerdmans, 1999), 43.
[52] Ibid.
[53] Ibid.

27

This ideology posits that another god creates the Jews and this god is against humanity.[54]

Besides, Shaun Lewis investigated the nature of God's image in humankind with the claim that the concept of *Imago Dei* is fundamentally basic to the understanding of all biblical doctrines. The author justifies this by conducting a historical survey of significant views on the idea. Lewis' discussion of these views consulted on the concept aimed at working towards a biblical understanding.[55] The author, therefore, categorises these views into three; namely, the substantive view, the relational view, and the functional view.

First, some people view *imago Dei* substantively throughout church history with the understanding that it is an inherent quality of God's capacity in man. While relating this image to the fall of humankind in Genesis 3, some of the adherents of this view opine that this Fall destroyed God's image in man. However, there are objections to this position from others. Irenaeus is a prominent adherent of this view.

Irenaeus was among those who made a distinction between צֶלֶם (*tselem* meaning "image") and דְּמוּת (*Demuth,* meaning "likeness") as obtained in Genesis 1:26. According to this scholar, image, on the one hand, is God's physical features in humankind, involving the mind and human volition. The likeness of God, on the other hand, has to do with man's spiritual part. Tertullian's position on this is similar, positing that the Fall had little or no effect on God's image while God's likeness in man was greatly impaired. As a result of this impairment, humanity lost "his 'robe of sanctity." Tertullian regards this robe as an original gift given by God's Spirit. Therefore, the destruction left humanity in a state of incommunicado with God. Clement of Alexandria and Origen are two others with the idea of image-likeness separation.[56]

During the Medieval Age, various theologians continued in the image-likeness distinction. They all viewed *imago* as the mind and will of man. The claim that the Fall did not affect God's image in man also dominated their views. They also held to the destruction suffered by the likeness of God in humankind, but the quality of God's likeness was claimed to be unimportant to the being of man.

However, the Reformers' views are somewhat different from their predecessors' positions. They are of the opinion that both image and likeness are synonymous. One prominent scholar among these theologians is Martin Luther who regarded the *imago* as the original righteousness of man completely lost to sin at the Fall. John Calvin also related the *imago Dei* to all that distinguishes humanity from animals – man's original righteousness with specific natural resources. Nonetheless, these two differ in their conclusions. Luther argues for the complete loss of the *Imago*

---

[54] Ibid.

[55] Shaun Lewis, "What is Man? Or, The Image of God," eds., Christopher B. Cone, Ron J. Bigalke, and Gary E. Gilley, *Journal of Dispensational Theology,* Volume 16, Number 48 (August 2012): 13-14.

[56] Ibid, 15.

Dei since humanity was dead by sin while Calvin posits that the effect of crime on the image was not cataclysmic. It was only marred by sin, leaving its spiritual part dead.[57]

Second, the relational view of the concept of *Imago Dei* in man prevailed in the 20th century. This view is by the "Trinitarian plurality" in Genesis 1:26-27. Scholars argue that there is an underlining factor of plurality both within the Godhead and humankind. With this provision, both parties can relate together pragmatically. Among these scholars are Karl Barth, Emil Brunner, Bonhoeffer, G.C. Berkouwer, and John Sailhamer.[58]

Third, the last of these three is the functional view of the concept of *imago Dei*. Unlike the substantive view that regards the idea as an ontological part of man, functional view differs. This view sees God's image as something God-like which expresses itself in humanity. Adherents of this view oppose the image-likeness distinction and perceive a close connection between the two. They view the image as man's activity of ruling over creation, making humankind God's representatives or agents on earth. All this is pictured as the mandatory role given man to exert God's rulership and dominion upon the rest of God's creation. In addition to Genesis 1:26-27, adherents of this view cite Psalm 8:5-6 in support of their position.[59]

Similarly, the focus of Daniel J. Denk's study on the concept of the *imago Dei* in man is the context of Genesis 1-3. Denk interprets the narratives as the primary account of man's origins. This interpretation is with the story that human beings are designed for good but were, however, impaired by evil. Genesis 1:1-26 accounts for the progression of God's created order using His divine wisdom and power. Again, Genesis 1:26-31 shows the unique nature of man's creation in God's image and likeness. By implication, man is an intelligent, moral, and creative being with the responsibility of being co-rulers or co-regents with God which many refer to as "Creation or Cultural Mandate." Therefore, being made in God's image has a tremendous impact on man, and there is every need to respect the inherent dignity and value thereof.[60]

The study of Matthew Rowley aims at discouraging today's violent-approach to the reading of the Bible. Rowley engaged the readers with epistemological scriptural interpretation. The study reveals some of the claims often cited to justify religious violence carried out in the name of God at this modern time. These claims are not limited to biblical perspective but extend to other faiths including the atheists. Notable among the arguments are commands from Muhammad, Osama bin Laden, and Moses. The first half of the Rowley's study is by the epistemology of sacralised violence in the exodus and conquest accounts. By this footing, the latter part of the

---

[57] Ibid, 16.
[58] Ibid, 17-18.
[59] Ibid, 18-19.
[60] Daniel J. Denk, "Created in God's Image (Genesis 1-3)," *Intervarsity Christian Fellowship* (2013), 1.

29

survey was established; critiquing various claims of religious leaders who invoked God's will to justify violence today.[61]

The position of Rowley on questions bothering on atheism, ethics and the will of God is unique. Rowley advances that there can be no real foundation for right and wrong when a man is without the awareness of God's existence. Rowley regards this 'right and wrong' as human rights. The scholar eventually justified this biblical claim by positing that "In a biblical worldview, ethics are founded on the character of God and are made known to man through revelation. Man is not permitted to do anything *per se* since God has decreed that man *ought to do* some things and *ought not to do* other things."[62]

Nonetheless, Rowley, citing Meredith Kline, argues that God could issue another command different from the standard ethics whose effects bind on all humanity since obedience to Him is the ultimate ethics. Instances of these commands appear in the instruction given to Abraham when instructed to sacrifice Isaac. The killing of the Canaanites is another. Rowley argues that God employs miracles to validate new knowledge in guarding against a possible misunderstanding of His will.[63]

According to this writer, Rowley's interpretation of God's instruction to Abraham on the supposed sacrifice of Isaac, his son is not sufficient. The scholar would have done better if the argument had taken the previous context of Genesis 12-21 into consideration. This context explains what had taken place in Abraham's covenant relationship with Yahweh. In this context, Abraham's loyalty to God, the Giver of the promised child, was tested. Therefore, it was never in God's intention to make human sacrifice a new ethical standard and was never after that.

From the preceding, the sacredness of man is by the concept of *Imago Dei*. Therefore, the Pentateuchal estimate of the sanctity of human beings is by God's image in humankind which could be viewed substantively, relationally and functionally. On account of the presence of this image in man, humanity receives significant attention and care from God (Gen. 1:26-28; Psa. 8) and shares certain qualities in common with God which make man God's vice-regent. Thus, termination of the life or shedding the blood of any man is tantamount to destroying these God's deposits. This destruction is a gross violation of the divinely endowed rights and privileges of such an individual which always attracts punishments.

b. Human Life in the Prophets

Understanding the sacredness of human life and how human beings fared within the Bible World can also be obtained from various revelations given to the writers and editors of the Prophetic Corpus. This revelation could be understood better by critically investigating extra-biblical accounts relating to the books.

---

[61] Matthew Rowley, "The Epistemology of Sacralized Violence in the Exodus and Conquest," *JETS* 57/1 (2014): 63-64.

[62] Ibid, 65-66.

[63] Ibid, 66.

Robert I. Bradshaw investigated the city of Tyre. This city was one of the ancient towns of Canaan which located on two islands 600-700m from the mainland and about 40 km south of Sidon. Looking at this city in light of the concern of this paper and according to extra-biblical accounts, this writer could identify certain atrocities committed. Revelation from *Amarna Letters* disclosed that the entire Canaan of that time was characterised by constant war for some reasons, most of which were political and economic. This process often jeopardised the lives of people and always violated their dignity. Bradshaw declares, "We know from the *Amarna Letters* that as Egyptian power declined during the 12th-century BC the King of Tyre repeatedly appealed to Pharaoh for assistance against his rival the King of Sidon. No help came from Pharaoh, and Tyre fell victim to the invasion of the Sea Peoples."[64]

Similarly, internal crises which often endangered the lives of people were another form. Disasters of this kind had their appearances in the city of Tyre on many occasions about a coup in the palace. Hiram I of Tyre, who assisted the duo of Kings David and Solomon in constructing the castle in Jerusalem (2 Sam. 5:11-12) lost his grandson to a palace coup around 919 BC. It was the same Hiram I who aided David and Solomon in the supply of timber for temple construction in ancient Israel (1 Kings 5:1-11). Again, Asermymus was murdered by his brother Pheles in the same city and Pheles, in turn, became assassinated by Ethbaal, priest of Astarte. Violations of this kind against the sanctity of human life were argued to be a common phenomenon to the Mediterranean World.[65]

William P. Brown analysed the life in Palestine before the patriarchal age. Brown claims that any attempt to understand the religion and history of Israel will amount to an exercise in futility without a proper understanding of the culture of the ancient Near East. In this regard, Brown argues that shortly before the period of the patriarchs, the region of Israel was in a struggle as the political hegemony of the Sumerian people had just waned and Egyptian people just entered into a time of chaos. All these situations had cumulative effects on the people as the socio-economic life of the land of Palestine was utterly devastated.[66]

Again, John Bright analysed the origin of Israel in Canaan. In this study, Bright argues that one thing remains evident regarding the place of the worth of human life in the ancient world: "Israel's advent begins at the end of the Late Bronze Age, when the power struggle among the empires of the Fertile Crescent had 'ended with the death or exhaustion of all the contestants.'" It was this situation that cleared the space for Israel to emerge in Palestine. Among the contestants mentioned were the indigenous Canaanites, Amorites, Indo-Aryans, and Hurrian people who populated the entire landscape.[67]

The work of Beth Alpert Nakhai was informed by the perceived lopsidedness which pervaded biblical texts as the primary point of reference for studies of

---

[64] Robert I. Bradshaw, "Tyre," *Biblical Archaeology* (Grand Rapids: Zondervan, 1998), 1.

[65] Ibid, 2.

[66] John Bright, A *History of Israel: With an Introduction and Appendix by William P. Brown*, Fourth Edition (Louisville, Kentucky: Westminster John Knox Press, 2000), 7.

[67] Ibid, 8.

Canaanite and Israelite religions despite advances in the field of archaeology. In view of this, Nakhai sought to correct this anomaly by making archaeological data a strong and independent witness to the studies of these religions in the second to mid-first millennia B.C.E.[68] As part of the analysis, Nakhai related Israelite religion (1 and 2 Sam.) and the pre-Temple passages (I Kings 1-4) together. The nature of this religion was discovered to depict a "richly variegated cult in Israel's late pre-monarchical and early monarchical periods" to the sanctity of human life.[69] In this direction, Nakhai argues that apart from the need for sacrifice, the sanctity of human life, as well as that of an object, was paramount important in the administration of the ceremonies. Only the Levites had the exclusive right to administer the rituals. The people also had to preserve themselves before the LORD as they prepared to enter God's presence. There is a record of this instance in I Samuel 16:1-13.[70]

Elizabeth Bloch-Smith studied ethnicity of ancient Israel. In the process of dating the period of Israel's settlement in Palestine and the contention between them and the Philistines, Block-Smith argues that 12th to 10th centuries B.C.E. has been established by archaeologists as the period of struggles between the early Israelites of the highland and the Philistines. This position was by the sudden appearance of quantities of Myc IIIC:Ib pottery relating to Sea Peoples' Settlement of whom the Philistines were formidable. Based on this also, one could reasonably conclude that the migrants (both early Israelites and the Philistines) settled in the southern Levant in the 12th-century B.C.E ranging from ca. 1185 B.C.E. to late 12th-century B.C.E.[71] According to this scholar, this dating is in line with biblical accounts of Israelites' fight against Philistine's invasions during the periods of Samuel the Prophet, King Saul, and King David. This time was between the late 12th and early 10th centuries B.C.E. in conformity with the archaeological evidence.

These battles were of different dimensions within this period in question. Hostility towards the so-called "uncircumcised" Philistines was the basis by the time of Samson (Judg. 14:1-3; 16:1, 4). This situation later metamorphosed to a full-blown war by the time of Samuel (I Sam. 4:9; 17:9) and further degenerated into a territorial fight at the time of King Saul (I Sam. 4:1-11; 7:7-14). The national fight continued after the coronation of David over the United Kingdom of Israel (2 Sam. 5:17-25).[72]

There is every possibility that ancient Israel exhibited violations of the sacredness of human life in the second part of their history. This is evident in a link between violations of this kind and the deportation of the people to exile as God-sanctioned punishment. This situation is apparent in the study conducted by this

[68] Beth Alpert Nakhai, *Archaeology and the Religions of Canaan and Israel*. Vol. 7 eds., Victor Matthews (Boston: The American Schools of Oriental Research, 2001), 1-2.

[69] Ibid, 53.

[70] Ibid, 56.

[71] Elizabeth Bloch-Smith, "Israelites Ethnicity in Iron I: Archaeology Preserves What is Remembered and What is Forgotten in Israel's History," *JBL* 122/3 (2003): 413.

[72] Ibid, 414.

writer on leadership failure in Ezekiel 11:1-15.[73] Yahweh deported Israel and Samaria in the north to Assyria in 722 B.C while He sold Judah and Jerusalem in the south to Babylon in 586 B.C.

From these analyses, it is a fact that the sanctity of human life was betrayed by the peoples of the ancient Near East, most especially the people of Israel. This fact is attested to by the Prophetic Corpus of the biblical literature. Extra-biblical materials like archaeological findings are also in support of this claim. The world of the Bible was that of constant war. This situation often kept the inhabitants of the city-states in perpetual fear of humiliation, degradation, mutilation, and murder. Again, migration and territorial expansion were two significant causes of violations of the sacredness of life at that time. This expansion could be evident in the constant war between the Israelites and Philistines as a result of occupation and territorial expansion. Also, the Bible world encouraged the promotion of the demonstration of the hegemony of the stronger nations at the expense of the weaker ones. This violation became noticed as various city-states lived at the mercy of their political overlords for safety and welfare of their people. More so, the violations also took the form of internal crisis within each of the nations. The palace coup in the city of Tyre is an example. Besides, there were struggles for power among empires. This situation often claimed many lives among the armed forces.

c. The Writings and the Worth of Life

The sacredness of human life in the Bible World also has its reflection in the Writings. The situation is just like the previous section of the Hebrew Bible; namely, the Prophets. Editor of the Church Educational System wrote from the perspective of the impacts of the OT on certain individuals in human history. The editor claims that this impact was enormous. An instance of this is the tremendous influence which Christianity, Islam, and Judaism exert the world over. These are three great religions of Abraham's descent, referred to as "the world's great religions," which had their roots from the fertility of OT soil. The writer, therefore, argues that the recorded messages of the OT are of great value, especially to those living in the dispensation of the fullness of times.[74]

Moreover, the editor also argues that the period of Assyrian conquest greatly betrayed the sacredness of human life. This betrayal reflected in the various acts of violence that permeated the region such as the following: killing, enslavement, devastation, and wretchedness which depict the depravity of humankind. The Assyrian army was said to be gullible and greedy for power. The ten tribes of Israel in

---

[73] Olafimihan Solomon Oladejo-Babalola, "Leadership Failure in Ezekiel 11:1-15 and Its Implications for the Nigerian Context" (M.Th. Thesis, NBTSO, 2015), 102. Yahweh indicted the leaders of His people in Jerusalem of certain crimes which could be regarded as various ways by which the sacredness of the lives of the masses were violated at the time of King Zedekiah. These violations were five-fold according to the writer and are the following: corruption, evil counsel, perverse thoughts, murder, and worldliness (96-100). As a result, Yahweh rolled out His punishments which culminated in the final destruction of Jerusalem and people's deportation to Babylon (102).

[74] Church Educational System, ed., *Old Testament Student Manual: I Kings –Malachi* (Utah: The Church of Jesus Christ of Latter-day Saints, 2003), v.

the north were part of the victims of their cruelty. They took these people into captivity in the late eighth century B.C: "In 721 B.C. Assyria swept out of the north, captured the Northern Kingdom of Israel, and took the ten tribes into captivity. From there, they became lost to history."[75] This situation is evident in the following books of the Writings: 1 Chronicles 5:26; Ezra 4:2 and Psalm 83:8. Similarly, a further expression of the brutality of the Assyrian army goes thus:

> The most vital part of the Assyrian government was its army. Warfare was a science to the leaders of Assyria. Infantry, chariots, cavalry (introduced by Ashurnasirpal to aid the infantry and chariots), sappers, armor made from iron, siege machines, and battering rams were all developed or perfected by the Assyrians. Strategy and tactics were also well understood by the Assyrian officers.[76]

If one were to analyse the life expectancy of the people within the ancient Near East, there might not be any visible difference from that of Africa, Nigerian people in particular. This claim is because the two settings have the following in common: war of varying types, greediness, the wickedness of the leaders and wanton destruction.

Furthermore, Olusayo 'Bosun Oladejo worked on the concept of life and death in the OT and *Yorùbá* worldview with specific attention on the misreading of the language and message of the Book of Qoheleth by the *Yorùbá* Christians.[77] This scholar advances that only God has the right to give and take life while analysing this concept within the context of the Writings. More so, dying at an old age is considered a great blessing. Oladejo cited an example of Job who lived 140 years more after his travail (Job 42:16-17). The scholar recognised this as one of the values which OT people had in common with the Yorùbá.[78]

Similarly, indecent burial is a sign of dishonour to the deceased in the Writings, especially in Wisdom literature (Psa. 72:9; Eccl. 6:3). Again, the idea that life is common to both human and animal is apparent in the context (Job 12:10). However, the scholar, citing Illman K.J. and H.J. Fabry, argues that human beings place more value on their personal lives than on any other thing and are ready to sacrifice anything for its preservation (Job 2:4).[79] The basis of this value in Writings can be explained by its complex nature which Oladejo observed by the various terms employed. This complexity is on the imperative to express different possible meanings which life connotes in Qoheleth.[80] Given the concluding message of the Qoheleth, therefore, this scholar submits that God would bring all human activities to judgment whether good or bad.[81]

---

[75] Ibid, 113.

[76] Ibid.

[77] Olusayo B. Oladejo, *Life and Death in the Old Testament and Yoruba Worldview: Reading Ecclesiastes in an African Context* (Saarbrucken: Lap Lambert Academic Publishing, 2012), 11.

[78] Ibid, 71.

[79] Ibid.

[80] Ibid, 201-202.

[81] 206.

Besides, Israel Finkelstein's work was born out of certain perceived injustices done to Northern Israel by various writers of the Hebrew Bible. These injustices cover Israel's continued living in the shadow of Judah in the south, especially in the manner the OT tells their story. These become more evident when consideration extends to the supremacy of the kingdom over Judah regarding population, military dominance, and economic buoyancy before their deportation to exile. In addition to all this is the inadequate attention given to the north by modern scholarship.[82] Correcting this anomaly, therefore, Finkelstein tells the story of the Kingdom essentially in its cradle from the archaeological viewpoint. This effort made is in addition to biblical texts with available extra-biblical documents from ANE.[83]

Analysing this situation, Finkelstein argues that the world of the ANE was primarily that of survival of the fittest. The reason for this argument is that the world was characterised by the political dominance of the stronger empires to the detriment of the weaker ones. Understanding this situation would enhance the perception of how human lives fared within the various cultures which informed the culture of the Bible. In this regard, the scholar describes Canaan of the Late Bronze II as a divided type, marked by a system of city-states dominated by the administrative and military giant of the time, most especially the Egyptians. Each of these city-states consisted of the central city which was of the ruling power. It also included a system of villages around it.

These city-states, however, varied when consideration extends to certain elements; namely, the size of their hub-cities, the extent of the territories within their domain, and the number of villages in their hinterland. They were also different in the volume of their populations, and their sedentary/pastoral nature.[84] Among these city-states was the Shechem Coalition which included the city-states on the coastal plain. It also contained the city-states in Jezreel and the Jordan Valleys.[85] According to Finkelstein, most of these city-states, especially those in the northern valleys under Egyptian hegemony, were ruined by some destructions in the late 12th century B.C.E. Given this, the collapse of Egyptian domination in Canaan marked the fall of the Late Bronze city-states.[86] The worst example of violations of the political supremacy of the giants over the weaker cities was that of the Assyrian empire over Northern Israel. The situation resulted in the captivity of God's people in 722–720 B.C.E. It also led to their complete disappearance from the scene while the armies deported the elites among their captors to Mesopotamia and foreign groups settled in their territories instead.[87]

Given the analysis of the various views considered, two main deductions are evident. On the one hand, the cruelty, gullibility, and insatiability of the Assyrians are

---

[82] Israel Finkelstein, *The Forgotten Kingdom: The Archaeology and History of Northern Israel*, eds., Ehud Ben Zvi & Roxana Hammini (Atlanta: Society of Biblical Literature, 2013), 1.

[83] Ibid, 5.

[84] Ibid, 15.

[85] Ibid, 17.

[86] Ibid, 21-22.

[87] Ibid, 153.

equally attested to by the Writings just as obtained from the studies of the Pentateuchal and Prophetic books on the subject of the sanctity of human life. Various elements marked the Assyrians which brought about different degrees of their acts of dehumanisation and devastation they caused within the world of the Bible. Without any doubt, the effects of these were capable of polluting the political atmosphere of the entire region in no small measure for denying their numerous victims the right to enjoy the God-given image.

On the other hand, the value or worth accorded to human life in the Writings is all-encompassing. The claim is on account of various words employed to depict the concept and a variety of meanings these terms connote. This all-inclusive nature also reflects in the extent to which an average Jew could go for the preservation of one's life to enjoy the blessing of old age.

3. Pro-Life and Pro-Choice Arguments

Sanctity of human life is within the established framework of pro-life and pro-choice arguments in this study. The concern of this section is primarily to identify certain definitive elements of these two movements and bring some of their cases to the fore.

John Clapper identified some of the primary arguments of these movements about the sanctity of human life. On the one hand, the Pro-Choice Movement, which equally implies the Pro-Abortion Movement, argues that every person was once part of one's mother's body at conception. And so, abortion does not mean killing of the unborn child for it was the blood of the mother that is shed, not that of the baby. Clapper objects to this principle based on Psalm 139 with the argument that individual genetic makeup is distinct and that of a child is a combination of the DNA of both parents. Therefore, it is the blood and DNA of the child in the womb that lay bare on the ground, meaning that the child is bleeding to death. On the other hand, Clapper analysed history in support of the Pro-Life Movement. The scholar took this step to establish the fact that issues on the sanctity of human life have not just started. It has been a historical one far before the second century A.D. [88]

Clapper, citing Saint Benedict Center which is an internet publication of 1997, provides certain opinions of the early Church Fathers and Reformers whose views are all in support of pro-life arguments.[89] Some of these personalities are; namely: the Didache, circa AD 120; Clement of Alexandria, circa AD 150-180; Tertullian, circa AD 160-240; St. Jerome, circa AD 342-420; St. John Chrysostom, circa AD 340-407; and John Calvin. Feminist foremothers in the US and their advocacies were also considered, citing Feminists for Life of America, 1996. Susan B. Anthony; Mattie Brinkerhoff; Sarah Norton; and Victoria Woodhull, the first female candidate vying for the office of the president are few of these individuals.[90]

The scholar also examined the opinions of medical experts such as C.S. Bacon in 1906 and Joseph Dele in 1938 and analysed the views of certain politicians, among

---

[88] John Clapper, "The Sanctity of Human Life and Abortion," *WRS Journal* 5/2 (August 1998): 34-35.

[89] Ibid, 34-35.

[90] Ibid, 35.

whom are these: Senator Edward Kennedy in 1971, Reverend Jesse Jackson in 1977, Rep. Richard Gephardt in 1984, President Ronald Reagan of 1984, and President Bill Clinton. Many of these figures regarded abortion as a criminal sin.[91] Clapper's claim on the sanctity of human life is that the lopsidedness and advancement in any given society is a function of its disregard or reference to the doctrine of the sanctity of human life. Given this, people should provide an adequate reference to the fact that human life is offered only by God and He alone has the right to its termination. However, this fact is except capital punishment for it is ordained by God and sanctioned by scripture. It is to be carried out by the state on God's behalf against those who demonstrate utter disregard to the life of humankind. Again, the killing of an enemy by members of the army in what the scholar refers to as "a 'just' war" is equally an exception.[92]

On the issue of abortion as a disregard to the sanctity of human life, Clapper, citing Philo of Alexandria, the philosopher, and Josephus, the Church historian, and apologist argues that abortion is the same as murder and infanticide. The author posits that human life begins right from conception. Any termination of such from this stage is abortion, a complete violation of the sacredness of life.[93] The rate at which people commit abortion in the United States alone is alarming and worrisome. The claim is on account of statistical data analysis on abortion, citing the "World Almanac and Book of Facts" (New Jersey). Specific facts are evident from the data. First, the number of abortions (1,528,930) done in all of 1992 was far above one-third of the total number of live births (4,065,014) while deaths from firearms in all of 1994 and deaths from motor vehicle accidents within the same year are 39,720 and 43,000 respectively. Second, the total number of abortions since 1973 amounts to 37 million while the percentage of abortions performed for social reasons alone was 93%.[94]

Furthermore, Randy Alcorn presents factual and analytical reasons in support of the Pro-Life Movement. The efforts of this scholar became necessary because of the scarcity of information about the position of the movement and the culture of the moral relativism of this postmodern society. Alcorn's effort was mainly from the perspective of medical science and psychological studies.[95] According to this author, the reasons for the movement are of five sections, each of which is about an aspect of what the group is. Part one is mainly about the basics of pro-life movement, while both two and three deal with the elements of the child and woman respectively. The fourth section is about other important issues such as the disabled and unwanted children, and chapter five is on spiritual perspectives and opportunities.

More so, Cathy Cleaver Ruse and Rob Schwarzwalder concerned themselves with the best pro-life arguments. The focus of this study is to identify and analyse what is called "the best pro-life arguments" against abortion. The focus is claimed to

---

[91] Ibid, 35-40.

[92] Ibid, 32-33.

[93] Ibid.

[94] Ibid.

[95] Randy Alcorn, *Why Pro-Life? Caring for the Unborn and Their Mothers* (Sandy: Eternal Perspective Ministries (EPM), 2004), 14-15.

be an issue at the front-burner of the debate today. The scholars considered these arguments from the perspectives of science, law, and women's rights to promote pro-life case against abortion. It is to nullifying various justifications of abortion coming from millions of women, together with their loved ones, who have aborted at least a child and are facing the consequences of the attendant pain, loss, and emotional need. These various justifications from pro-choice scholars are what Ruse and Schwarzwalder refer to as "an invisible thumb on the scale so that even the best logic will fail to persuade."[96]

Arguments from science against abortion are the first writers' consideration. One of the strong claims in support of abortion is that no one knows the beginning of life. The scientific argument that refutes this pro-abortion's claim is the discovery which establishes the fact that life begins before birth. This discovery explains the nature of zygote, the first cell formed at conception upon the penetration of a human egg. A zygote is formed generally in the upper portion of the Fallopian Tube using human sperm. Against this pro-abortion claim, science has confirmed that zygote is made up of human DNA and every human molecule. Thus, it is undoubtedly that the zygote is a full human being.[97] A few abortion defenders later agreed that life indeed begins in the womb. However, their argument remains that zygote is not yet a person forgetting that humanness is either persons or property.

Similarly, the objective response against the claim of pro-choice defenders that pregnancy does not commence "until the embryo implants itself in the lining of the uterine wall, which occurs about a week later," is another argument. The writers describe this as an interplay of politics of definition to justify various forms of contraceptives in use today. However, pregnancy begins upon fertilisation, and this definition is said to subsist till date in different current medical dictionaries.[98]

The third argument relates to the law against abortion. Given the various rulings of the Supreme Court of the US, most especially that of *Roe v. Wade*, the writers argue that Roe created an unlimited right to abortion for it gives parents and doctors emotional reasons. Lydia Saad's data analysis, however, establishes the fact that most Americans prefer legal restrictions on abortion.[99]

The last of these arguments is that which came from women's rights. According to the writers, women have started coming out of their shell in ever increasing number to speak out boldly about the devastating effects of abortion. Against pro-choice proponents' claim that abortion is an act of empowerment, "They speak out about how abortion was not an act of empowerment but the result of abandonment, betrayal, and desperation, and how it has negatively affected their lives."[100]

---

[96] Cathy Cleaver Ruse & Rob Schwarzwalder, "The Best Pro-Life Arguments for Secular Audiences," *Family Research Council* (2011):1.
[97] Ibid.
[98] Ibid, 2.
[99] Ibid, 3-4.
[100] Ibid, 5.

Furthermore, an unverified source presents specific information on the pro-life organisation. Pro-life is an organisation that consists of all beliefs and political affiliates which vehemently oppose abortion. Pro-life opposition to abortion is on account of its conclusion that life begins at conception. It, therefore, advocates that all human beings have the right to protection from conception to death. It also argues that death should occur naturally. Again, its supporters also support the right of the child within the womb whether or not it is wanted. On this basis, they oppose the deliberate killing of an unborn child. An unborn child should be adequately protected by law just like any others. Summarily, the claim of pro-life is that abortion is evil.[101]

Moreover, other information about Pro-Life Movement arguments from this source is available. Some issues are pertinent to this Movement; namely, the right to terminate, kill or murder any man is not within anybody's prerogative, and the foetus is a potential human being with equal rights to its mother's rights. Also, late abortion can be life-threatening and wasteful, and abortion can cause emotional distress to the mother immediately and health problems in the future. More so, medical practitioners argue that saving human life is more satisfying than destroying it. Similarly, some of the other arguments are the these: since contraceptives are readily available, abortion is then not an option; disabled individuals have the potential to live; abortion of a foetus is murder because an embryo is a potential life, and the foetus is innocent, and the mother has to protect it. Again, whoever does not want a baby can give others the chance to adopt instead of killing. Also, life is sacred, including the foetus and so it must be protected.[102]

4. Previous and Current Issues on Sanctity of Life

Investigation of the sanctity of human life in light of various recent and current issues is relevant to this study. The work of Catherine Bel is on rituals with the argument that ritual is more interestingly understandable as a strategy, a culturally planned way of getting things done in the world. Approaching this subject within this framework, Bel claims that it raises good questions about the origins, purposes, and power of ritual strategy than when approached through current models.[103] The use and efficacy of the ritual itself are one area of interest which reveals a possible reason why the sanctity of human life is violated especially at this postmodern time. In Bel's review of various theories about rituals, Bel's cites Henri Hubert and Marcel Mauss who demonstrate the power of ritual activities in sacralising things, people, or events.[104]

Furthermore, the study of M.H. Abrams focuses on the development of humanism from the 16th century to this contemporary time. This movement began in the 16th century with the concept coined to imply one who taught in humanities for "grammar, rhetoric, history, poetry, and moral philosophy." Also, it is a separate

---

[101] "The Sanctity of Life," *Religion and Early Life*,
http://www.whitworth.lancs.sch.uk/userimages/website/Mock%2501%2520Revision/RS/Early%2520
Life.pdf (accessed August 23, 2017), 5.

[102] Ibid.

[103] Catherine Bel, *Ritual Theory, Ritual Practice* (Oxford: Oxford University Press, Inc., 1992), vii, xv.

[104] Ibid, 15.

discipline from moral and imaginative fields of which mathematics, natural philosophy, and theology are examples. In its cradle, humanism focused on classical culture with a great emphasis on learning to speak and write good Latin. As a result, scholarly humanists were instrumental to the storage of materials and ideas in the European Renaissance. They were also able to write many works related to educational, moral, and political themes following the patterns of classical philosophers and writers like Aristotle, Plato, and Cicero.[105]

Humanism was given prime attention and place in ordering human life at the time of Renaissance. Scholars of this age characterised this subject of humanism by the primacy of reason against the instinctual appetites and animalistic passions that often betrayed the dignity of human life. Many of its proponents also gave rapt attention to the development of the powers, physical, mental, artistic, and moral faculties of an individual.[106] Renaissance humanists were devout Christians who brought the ancient pagan concepts and ideas to bear on Christian creed, leading to their emphasis on values achievable by humans to the neglect of earlier Christian focus on the innate corruption of humankind, the ideals of asceticism and preoccupation with the world to come. This situation is typical of the following writers: Sir Philip Sidney, Edmund Spenser, and John Milton.[107]

In addition to all this, humanism has assumed a new status today as its adherents often connote those thinkers who establish truth on the premise of human experience, reason, and value on the assumption of human nature and culture. They perform this to separate the field from religion which uses revelation as the basis of truth and value. Similarly, around the 18th century, the rapid development and advancement of the natural science and technology after the Renaissance deepened the need to prevent the encroachments of science and practical arts from the role of humanities in liberal education.[108]

Moreover, J. Kerby Anderson studied the possible effects of cloning and stem-cell on the sanctity of human life. These writers argue that although there is a powerful new genetic technology for cloning and stem-cell study with provision for the great promise, cloning and stem-cell portend danger to the sanctity of human life. Therefore, there is a need for careful evaluation of these practices biblically, drawing necessary moral and theological implications.[109]

An ethical debate which relates to the subject of the sanctity of human life has been on the ground since the 1970s. It is on whether or not scientists should clone a human being. Despite this debate, scientists moved on with great passion in Scotland and came up with the cloning of an adult sheep called "Dolly" in 1997. Two legislators among the Republicans sponsored two central bills against cloning in its

---

[105] M.H. Abrams, *A Glossary of Literary Terms*, Seventh Edition (Australia: Heinle & Heinle, 1999), 116.

[106] Ibid, 116-17.

[107] Ibid.

[108] Ibid, 117-118.

[109] J. Kerby Anderson, "Cloning, Stem-Cell Research, and the Bible," *Bibliotheca Sacra* 159 (October-December 2002): 462.

entirety. Representative Dave Weldon in Florida sponsored the first of these bills. The bill passed the House and went to the Senate. Senator Sam Brownback in Kansas sponsored the other one.[110]

Similarly, stem-cell research is the second genetic technology with close affinity to cloning. Although the possibility of directing stem cells to produce particular forms of cells is a welcomed medical advance, this technology raises specific moral issues bothering on pro-life questions. The basis of these issues is that for scientists to gain stem cells, the killing of the embryo is inevitable. Cloning is another way to obtain embryonic stem cells.[111]

Whenever scholars evaluate cloning and stem-cell research in the light of the Bible, ethical questions on threats to the sanctity of life always come up. The basis of these questions is that since human beings are created in God's image (Gen. 1:26-27), it is on the imperative to protect such life right from its conception to death, which should come naturally. According to Anderson, one of the main scriptural passages in support of this argument is Psalm 139. Other scriptures depicting the divine involvement in the formation of the unborn child are the following: Genesis 2:7-8; 29:31-35; 30:17-24; Judges 13:7-8; Ruth 4:13; I Samuel 1:19-20; Psalm 51; Isaiah 49:1; Luke 1:41-44.[112] Given these biblical passages, scientists undermine the sacredness of human life whenever they destroy human embryos for stem cells. An inefficient and wasteful form of reproduction is one of these concerns against cloning.[113]

Furthermore, John Alan Cohan worked on Homicide by Necessity. The research question of this study is philosophical, "How should we act in the midst of a calamity, disaster, or other danger if it is apparent that we can save our own life by the destruction of another's?" What is homicide by necessity? Cohan expressed it as, "The killing of innocents in order to produce a greater good or avert a greater evil - usually to save a greater number of lives."[114] A case study of Edward, the driver of a trolley, is an instance. Edward had his brakes failed and had the options of turning to the right and kill one innocent person or moving ahead to kill five people. The action is intentional homicide which Cohan argues that there is no provision for it under the necessity defence.[115] Cohan identified elements of the necessity defence, which, citing Joseph J. Simeone,[116] states that, "Certain conduct, though it violates the law and produces a (sic) harm, is justified because it averts a greater evil and hence produces a net societal gain."[117]

---

[110] Ibid, 462-64.

[111] Ibid, 464-65.

[112] Ibid, 468-69.

[113] Ibid, 470.

[114] John Alan Cohan, "Homicide by Necessity," *COHAN.DOC* Vol.10, No.119 (2006): 119.

[115] Ibid, 119-120.

[116] Joseph J. Simeone, "Survivors" of the Eternal Sea: A Short True Story, *ST. LOUIS U.L.J* 45 (2001): 1123, 1140-41.

[117] Ibid, 123.

The case of the Nazi holocaust is of more significant interest to this writer. It was about a situation involving the killing of an innocent child who portended danger to the safety of a group of Jews hiding from the Nazis. The cry of this baby would betray them if they did nothing about the situation. Given this, the group smothered the baby to death for the safety of many. A rabbi was then asked to analyse the facts to justify the action. In his response, the rabbi said the move was not necessary but excusable. However, it would have been an act of purity on the part of the group if they had spared the baby in that circumstance.[118]

The two instances presented are indeed dangerous situations which put human lives at risk. However, what justification is defensible enough to explain the intentional killing of innocent human life in an attempt to save one's life or many other lives? Again, how justified is one on the scale of God's standard to smother an innocent child to protect fellow beings from the Nazis' threat irrespective of their number? All of these are ethical issues that bring the need for the comparative study of Numbers 35:9-34 and *Yorùbá* worldview of the sanctity of human life to the fore to identifying and correcting deviant practices among *Yorùbá* people.

Moreover, the study of William Payne was on the claim that the sanctity of human life is about the sacredness of humanity. To this end, Payne presented three underline reasons as evidence. First, humankind is a product of the creative power of the divine and God's image as evident in Genesis 1:26-27. This declaration conflicts with humanistic and non-Christian belief.[119] Payne, quoting Matthew Henry, posits that the image of God in human is about three critical constructs: in the constitution and nature of human soul with its faculties of understanding, will and active power; in man's position of dominion and authority over the earth; and in knowledge, righteousness and true holiness.[120] Second, it is about dignifying humanity using the incarnation of the Son of God in Jesus Christ. Third, humanity has "an eternal future" through the resurrection of the spiritual aspect of man.[121]

Payne, therefore, brought out three implications from the biblical truths about the sanctity of human life. First, the life of man has God-imputed dignity or worth upon it, and this must be acknowledged no matter the living standard and despite the Fall. Second, the killing of any human life without God's sanction is a crime that brings terrible consequences. This claim is in the light of Genesis 9:6. Lastly, the Gospel of Jesus Christ is the only solution capable of meeting human needs pragmatically.[122]

Sean Adams's study was on feminist interpretation. In this study, Adam claims that this method is one of the recent approaches to biblical hermeneutics. The technique was developed during the late 1960s and early 1970s with a shared focus on equality for women in the social, economic, political, and religious aspects of their

---

[118] Ibid,138.
[119] William Payne, "Sanctity of Human Life," *Message Preached at Trinity Baptist Church, Burlington, ON,"* 2007, 1.
[120] Ibid, 2.
[121] Ibid, 3.
[122] Ibid, 3-4.

lives. The approach also has advocated for women's rights. Again, one central presupposition of this approach is that gender discriminations against women from their male-counterparts abound. The violation is especially prevalent in a patriarchal cultural system of Africa in at least some of the following forms: domination, exploitation, and oppression.[123]

Likewise, the work of F. Daniel Davis is on the background of the various issues on Bioethics, beginning from American ethicist Ruth Macklin's claims against the work of the President's Council on Bioethics that sanctity is a useless concept and that the idea merely connotes "respect for autonomy." Davis presented this retort to what he calls "provocation implicit in Macklin's critique."[124] In this, Davis made some possible responses to the questions raised against Macklin's ideas and reflects on the role that concepts of this kind have played in the work of national concerns in public bioethics from a historical viewpoint.

Furthermore, the concern of The President's Council on Bioethics is not only to inform the President of the United States on the nature of this anthology but also to create awareness of the necessity to explore the understanding of the sanctity of human life and the profundity of its contents.[125] While doing this, the council viewed the sanctity of human life as a fundamental and crucial concept, generally to the modern day's discourse in law and ethics and specifically to the dialogue in bioethics. While explaining the necessity for this material, the council claims that the subject of the dignity for human life has frequently been figuring in many of its reports since 2001 when it began functioning.[126]

While commenting on the meaning of sanctity of human life among scholars, the committee argues that a lot of confusion beclouds this concept since there is no consensus on its definition. Some say that the dignity of human life has lost its traditional sense while others object to this view by positing that the concept is "an essential identiifying and irreducible element of human nature." There are others which the committee categorised their understanding can serve as more biological than philosophical or theological.[127]

Similarly, the work of Christian Fuchs concerns whether or not scholars can categorise the contemporary society as a new form of the Marxist idea of imperialism and informational/media imperialism. Following his investigation of the effects of globalisation on the sanctity of human life, Fuchs, citing Tomlinson, defines globalization as: "the rapid (sic) developing and ever-densening (sic) network of

---

[123] Sean Adams, "Feminist Interpretation," *In Dictionary of Biblical Criticism and Interpretation*, ed., Porter, Stanley E. (London: Routledge: Taylor and Francis Group, 2007), 107.

[124] F. Daniel Davis, "Human Dignity and Respect for Persons: A Historical Perspective on Public Bioethics," *in Human Dignity and Bioethics: Essays Commissioned by the President's Council on Bioethics*, ed., The President's Council on Bioethics (Washington, D.C: The President's Council on Bioethics, 2008), 19-20.

[125] The President's Council on Bioethics, ed., "Letter of Transmittal to The President of The United States," *in Human Dignity and Bioethics: Essays Commissioned by the President's Council on Bioethics*, ed. (Washington, D.C: The President's Council on Bioethics, 2008), xi.

[126] Ibid, xii.

[127] Ibid.

interconnections and interdependencies that characterise modern life." Fuchs, therefore, advances that the contemporary world has come to be known for persisting inequality which widens the gaps between the rich and the poor. Given this, the sanctity of human life that characterise humanity is impaired owing to the various socio-political and economic forces such as new imperialism and global capitalism (informational capitalism).[128] From the preceding, the effects of globalisation also contribute to multiple ways by which people undermine human sacredness at this time in question.

Moreover, Committee on Doctrine of the USCCB concerns itself with a reaffirmation of the commitment to health care ministry of the Catholic Church and the unique Catholic identity of the institutional health care services of the Church. The concern became necessary with American health care facing severe changes at this time. The purpose of the directives on ethics and religion of the Catholic Church are of a two-fold; namely, "First, to reaffirm the ethical standards of behavior in health care that flow from the Church's teaching about the dignity of the human person; second, to provide authoritative guidance on certain moral issues that face Catholic health care today."[129]

While writing on the nature of changes in the American health care system, USCCB argues that the changes came to light by new medical discoveries, rapid technological developments, and social change. However, they could either be an opportunity for real advancement in human culture or could lead to policies and actions detrimental to the true dignity of human life. Given this, the Church had to consult with several bodies of professionals in the field of medicine, and ecclesiastical rank to review these developments and judge them in the light of the principles of right reason and the real standard of God's Word.[130]

Similarly, the study conducted by Gushee clams that the sacredness of life is a new moral norm which emerged in Catholic thought in late 20th century Christian ethics. The conservative Protestants and much of the western world later borrowed this norm. The two factors that motivated the implementation of this moral norm were the full legalisation of abortion and "mercy killing." Members of the anti-abortion group, like Pope John Paul II, cited the sanctity of human life as the reason for their position. However, members of the pro-abortion group, like an Australian philosopher Peter Singer, questioned the validity of this ethic. After a while, these ethics witnessed a decline in term of supports even among Christians. This situation still subsists till date among "most politically progressive Christians."[131]

Gushee's current scholarship in Christian ethics attempts to reclaim the concept of the sanctity of human life. It also makes efforts to dissociate the subject

---

[128] Christian Fuchs, *A Contribution to Critical Globalization Studies, Working Paper (CSGP)* 09/8 (Peterborough: Centre for the Critical Study of Global Power and Politic, 2009), 2-5.

[129] Committee on Doctrine of USCCB, ed., "Ethical and Religious Directives for Catholic Health Care Services," *USCCB*, Fifth Edition (November 2009): 3-4.

[130] Ibid, 8.

[131] Gushee, "Can a Sanctity of Human Life Ethnic Ground Christian Ecological Responsibility," *Notre Dame Journal of Law, Ethics & Public Policy* Vol. 23:2 (2009): 473-74.

from abortion fight and culture of wars. In this direction, Gushee argues that the ethics of the sanctity of human life is both old and new. On the one hand, it is as old as Genesis account of the concept of the image of God and the demand to love one's neighbours as oneself.

On the other hand, it is as new as liberation ethics of the 20th century. Equally, it is as fresh as the 20th-century theological personalism which the ethical writings of Martin Buber and Emmanuel Levinas bring to the limelight, "I-Thou relationships and the irreducible Other," among others. All these have a rational sense of the sanctity of human life and sympathetic fight against its dehumanisation. Gushee's current undertaking is against the backdrop of Catholic and conservative Protestants reducing the debate to battle against abortion and assisted suicide which narrows the application of this ethical issue down, instead of broadening it.[132]

Gushee, therefore, proposed to employ the concept of the sanctity of human life as a theological paradigm to the ecological crisis that characterises the contemporary world. The effort will, in turn, be a profound contribution of Christian sanctity-of-life ethics to the ongoing debates at the end. Given this, people must note it that the basis of dignity and sacredness of humans, theocentrically, is *"derived value."* The reason for this is that if not for God's action and an authoritative declaration that all things are good (Gen.1:31), humanity would not have assumed any intrinsic value. Therefore, humankind has a duty to their environment by first of all responding to the needs of their human neighbours and then attend to ecological needs that cripple the lives of fellow humankind. This latter responsibility is on the basis that other creatures are equally sacred but not in the same degree as humans.[133]

Similarly, the primary concern of Emeka C. Ekeke and Ephraim A. Ikegbu is the need to investigate the practice of euthanasia from the Christian point of view. The need becomes inevitable because the scientific advance has become a significant challenge to the sacredness of human life. In their analysis, they etymologically define "euthanasia" as a term which comes from two Greek words: *"eu,"* (meaning 'good'), and *"thanatos,"* (implying 'death'). Therefore, euthanasia means "'good death.'"[134] According to them, scholars classify euthanasia into two types; namely, voluntary/involuntary euthanasia and active/passive euthanasia. This classification is on the level of the physician's participation.

First, voluntary euthanasia implies "A kind of death, which is performed by another with the consent, may be in writing as in the case of a living will or advance directive." Scholars in support of euthanasia of this type do so on the basis that everyone has absolute rights to control one's life. However, some scholars oppose euthanasia in its entirety. The basis of their objection is on the belief that the right to decide when a person dies does not belong to anyone except God. This belief system stands on three things: the inspiration of scripture, the sovereignty of God over His

---

[132] Ibid, 473-74.

[133] Ibid, 486.

[134] Emeka C. Ekeke and Ephraim A. Ikegbu, "The Sanctity of Human Life in the Twenty First Century: The Challenge of Euthanasia and Assisted Suicide," *Educational Research* Vol. 1(9) (October 2010): 313.

creation, and sanctity of life. However, these scholars viewed involuntary euthanasia as "death performed by another without the consent of the person killed." This type of euthanasia, citing Immanuel Kant, is by a loss of previous dignity due to suffering and sickness.[135]

Second, passive euthanasia means a slow kind of death by a patient. It is usually carried out by removing patients from artificial life support systems such as respirators and feeding tubes, or by merely discontinuing necessary medical treatments that sustain life. Passive euthanasia is also called "letting die." Contrastingly, active euthanasia involves taking bold steps to terminate the being of a patient generally by lethal injection.[136] This study also covers the following areas: meaning of euthanasia, its major problem and arguments for/against it.

Ekeke and Ikegbu's position is that all types of euthanasia are murder, suicide, and homicide. This position is on the following reasons: euthanasia ruins societal respect for life; it is against human sacredness, suicide or murder (for the scripture is emphatic in its warning against killing), and not merciful to kill a sufferer.[137]

Moreover, the study of Marcus Düwell is on human dignity and human right. Düwell argues that analysis of violations of human dignity seems to be better resourceful to the subject than giving a theory. Against this background, Düwell's study focuses on the need to develop a positive account of the concept of the dignity of human life. The aims of the writer are of two steps in developing an inductive understanding of one's expectation from an account of the dignity of human life. First, the writer discussed some general features, examples of which are: equality of dignity, emphasis on the inherent worth of the individual, and the main normative claim of the concept. Second, the formulation of specific questions to which each theory must provide answers on the subject matter are of equal importance.[138]

In another development, the aim of the study of Paulus Kaufmann, Hannes Kuch, Christian Neuhauser, and Elaine Webster is to bridge the perceived shortcomings of various debates on human dignity. These inadequacies cover the following areas; namely: features and definitive contents of its role; its limitation to bioethics on such issues as abortion, euthanasia and genetic enhancement; and the abstractness of its values. These scholars claim that all these issues are without any recourse to humiliation and degrading treatment, torture and war, and poverty and slavery which are the focus of the UN and various NGOs in the recent time. Given this, the concern of this anthology is the philosophical notions of dignity violations,

---

[135] Ibid, 314.

[136] Ibid, 314-15.

[137] Ibid, 316.

[138] Marcus Düwell, "Human Dignity and Human Rights," *in Humiliation, Degradation, Dehumanization: Human Dignity Violated,* eds., Marcus Düwell, Paulus Kaufmann, Hannes Kuch, Christian Neuhauser, & Elaine Webster, Library of Ethics and Applied Philosophy Volume 24 (2011): 215-30.

multiple aspects of which the scholars stated above. The effort is called a "'negative approach to human dignity.'"[139]

More so, the argument of Dean G. Blevins, Stanley J. Bodes, John E. Seaman, Terry S. Sowden, and David P. Wilson is that the sanctity of human life is among various subject areas believed to be part of what the Church should uphold as mandated by God. The scholars treated the argument in the manual of the Church of Nazarene under the "Covenant of Christian Conduct." By this belief system, the Church of Nazarene stands against the following; namely, induced abortion, research on embryonic stem cell, euthanasia, and the withdrawal of necessary medical attention to the disabled.[140]

On induced abortion, the Church posits that the sanctity of human life extends to the unborn child. The Church took the position on account of her persuasion that life is a gift from God and this gift continues to the developing child within the womb. Such a child should, therefore, be nurtured, supported, and protected. This belief is by the fact that God created human beings in His image. Given all this, the Church opposes induced abortion by any means. The Church also objects to the laws that support the practice on the basis that people should protect human life from conception to death. However, at the point that doctors discover that the life of the mother or that of the unborn child, or both, is at risk, termination of the pregnancy is inevitable after they had taken necessary medical and Christian counselling.[141]

The Church, similarly, takes positions on the following: genetic engineering and gene therapy, research on human embryonic stem cell and other medical/scientific advancements that destroy human life after conception, human cloning, euthanasia, and allowing to die.[142] On the last issue, the Church of Nazarene supports either the withdrawal or not initiating "artificial life-support systems" at all when death is imminent. The position applies to those in a persistent vegetable state and to those whom the application of life supports gives no hope of returning to health.

To this writer, the position of the Church of Nazarene on the issue of letting die is both conflicting and complicated. It is contradictory because the Church is generally opposed to euthanasia on the basis that God alone has the right to determine when a human life can end. Taking to withdrawing or not initiating artificial life-support systems, therefore, conflicts with this position. Again, it is complicated because no one has an absolute right to determine when the hope of returning to life is completely gone but God alone.

Similarly, the focus of John Victor Enslin's study was an investigation of the notion of the dignity of human life in the thought of Immanuel Kant. Enslin argues

---

[139] Paulus Kaufmann, Hannes Kuch, Christian Neuhauser & Elaine Webster, "Human Dignity Violated: A Negative Approach – Introduction," in *Humiliation, Degradation, Dehumanization: Human Dignity Violated*, eds., Marcus Düwell, Paulus Kaufmann, Hannes Kuch, Christian Neuhauser, & Elaine Webster, Library of Ethics and Applied Philosophy Volume 24 (2011): 1-2.

[140] Dean G. Blevins, Stanley J. Bodes, John E. Seaman, Terry S. Sowden & David P. Wilson, eds., *Church of the Nazarene Manual, 2013 - 2017: History Constitution Government Ritual* (Kansas City: Nazarene Publishing House, 2013), 52.

[141] Ibid, 52-54.

[142] Ibid, 52-56.

that scholars cannot understand Kant's concept of human dignity in isolation of the context of his moral philosophy. To this end, chapter one of Enslin's work is devoted to the work of philosopher Roger Sullivan whose major work, "Immanuel Kant's Moral Theory," involves a robust treatment of human dignity. In this way, Enslin analysed Sullivan's understanding of Kant's thought within the context of his methodology. Enslin also analysed the general approach to Kant's philosophy. Again, Enslin's chapter two is on the work of Susan Shell, "'Kant on Human Dignity.'" Enslin examined human dignity with special consideration of Shell's methodology and some of her work on the early Kant's idea where the concept of human dignity is rooted. The term dignity in Oliver Sensen's novel interpretation and integration of the views of the three Kantian philosophers is made in chapter three and four respectively.[143]

Besides, the work of Rillo Thomas is on the encyclical of Pope Francis. Encyclicals are letters written by Popes to both the clergy and laity of the Catholic Church. The Church regards these letters as very authoritative. This one in particular written in May 2015, titled "*Laudato Si'*" or "*Praise Be*," is regarded as completely overwhelming and historical. This remark is by its address on how people should care for all animals and their environment. It also concerns itself with the impacts that inequality in the distribution of resources, food waste, and exploitation of natural resources have on human lives. In this encyclical, the Pope also considered the health of the poorest of the people. Similarly, the cleric addressed the ecological crisis, such as climate change, and its effects on human activities. In this way, the Pope accused the industrial countries and challenged them to come to the aid of the Third World countries[144]

Furthermore, Danielle Margaret Ramsey Benyon-Payne investigated the degree at which some authors of late-Victorian Gothic fiction engaged certain concerns, fears, and suppositions. These concerns covered the perceived increase in the rates of suicide in the latter part of the 19th-century Western society, essentially in Britain. Benyon-Payne expressed this concern by way of examining how the authors of this fiction brought to bear the ideas of suicide in their texts at the face of wide-reaching fears and anxieties of the late-century. In the end, Benyon-Payne found out that suicide was strongly linked with strong emotion, not minding its cause or motivation. Given this, Benyon-Payne places emphasis on the stronger effects of the emotion of this kind on an individual's passions, thoughts, emotions, and pathological state than the effects that any other forms of death could have. The author also found out that the factor of inheritance was very common to all of the novels investigated and consistent with the 19th-century theories about the inherited nature of suicidal propensity. Similarly, other factors like the consequences of a lack of willpower and self-control were also common among the physicians and psychologists at the end of

---

[143] John Victor Enslin, "Kant on Human Dignity: A Conversation among Scholars" (Ph.D. dissertation, Graduate School of Arts and Sciences, Boston College, 2014), n.p.

[144] Rillo Thomas, "Pope Francis' Encyclical asks for Environmental Stewardship," *Benedictine Oblate*, ed., Mary Jeanne Schumacher Vol. 21:4 (Fall 2015): 4.

the century. Given this, suicide is viewed, "As the alleged end (sic) result of a degenerate nature."[145]

More so, the study of Vani Kesari A. focuses on the sanctity of human life within the context of "human genetic research." Given the various advances within this field, the author claims that the need for a global concern to come up with common criteria to evolve legal standards that could take care of individual achievements in this field is evident. This claim takes into consideration the diagnostic and therapeutic benefits of research of this kind on the one hand and its attendant threats to fundamental ideas and assumptions on humanity on the other hand. Scientific advances within human genetic research include the following: genetic mapping, human cloning, application of rDNA technology, embryonic stem cell research, and pre-implantation genetic screening and diagnosis. Therefore, the study aims at analysing the content, scope, extent, and limitation of the sanctity of human life from a legal perspective.[146]

Moreover, the study of Eva Brems is in the area of legal implications of violation of human dignity in term of State's ban of face covering in France. Brems' effort in this study is to further contribute another critical comment to *SAS* in the debate on this nationwide veil bans in Europe called "burqa bans." The scholar did this on the basis that the Grand Chamber judgment of SAS v France of the European Court of Human Rights has become a focal reference point beginning from 1st July 2014.[147] With this comment, Brems aimed at documenting the effects of the ban on the lives of the women involved.[148]

Three legitimate aims were presented by the French government to justify the face covering ban; namely, the protection of public safety, respect for compliance with the minimal requirements of life in society and equality between men and women, and respect for the dignity of the person. Out of these, the court dismissed the first and last grounds. Nonetheless, the Court upheld the justification for the ban based on the last standing ground of minimal requirements of life in society tagged as "the novel concept of 'living together.'"[149]

Upon critical analysis of the field of protection of women's rights, Brems concluded that the justification was not about protection of the autonomy of women's rights but about removing perceived symbols of gender oppression from the public sphere. This paper's contributions, therefore, are the problems associated with the Court's reasoning as identified through empirical evidence concerning the realities of the concerned women in France and Belgium.[150]

---

[145] Danielle Margaret Ramsey Benyon-Payne, "The Suicide Question in Late-Victorian Gothic Fiction: Representations of Suicide in their Historical, Cultural and Social Contexts" (Ph.D. Thesis, University of Leicester, 2015), 222-23.

[146] A., Vani Kesari. Sanctity of Human Life in the Context of Human Genetic Research (Ph.D. Thesis, Cochin University of Science and Technology, School of Legal Studies, 2015), i.

[147] Eva Brems, "SAS v FRANCE: A Reality Check," eds., Helen O'Nions & Janice Denoncourt, *Journal of Nottingham Law School* Vol. 25 (2016): 58.

[148] Ibid, 59.

[149] Ibid, 61.

[150] Ibid, 71.

Similarly, the study of Samantha Knights is on the same ground of perceived inequality with that of Brems. The basis of the study is on *niqab* with its attendant debates on media and in academia in the United Kingdom, especially in France. Knights' primary quest is to ascertain the compatibility of a UK law, similar to the one passed by the Senate in France, with the Human Rights Acts 1998 (protecting freedom of religion and belief). Knights' secondary quest is to determine whether or not there are special situations where face veil may be judiciously forbidden such as at work or in academia.[151] According to Knights, these quests were by the "rights and freedoms of others" in contention on account of the justification given the French law on veil ban in public places in 2010.[152]

All studies and works consulted and reviewed are indeed related to the subject of the sanctity of human life. However, the writers did not put into consideration the disagreement, lopsidedness, and contradiction that exist between the belief system of the people groups on the subject matter and what they practice which stand in opposition to what they believe. It is, therefore, the writer's opinion that the contemporary *Yorùbá* people can correct these practices after gaining a comparative understanding of Numbers 35:9-34 and *Yorùbá* worldview of human life.

---

[151] Samantha Knights, "Face Veils and the Law: A Critical Reflection," eds., Helen O'Nions & Janice Denoncourt, *Journal of Nottingham Law School* Vol. 25 (2016): 98.
[152] Ibid, 99.

CHAPTER THREE

SANCTITY OF HUMAN LIFE IN NUMBERS 35: 9-34

The main focus of this section is to obtain an understanding of the sanctity of human life in Numbers 35:9-34. The need becomes imperative to ensure a similar knowledge of the subject matter in the context of ancient Israel and *Yorùbá* worldview. Given this, critical introduction to the Book of Numbers is carried out. Similarly, the divine Law which informed the worldview of the Israelites about the sacredness of human life is exegetically investigated in Numbers 35:9-34. Also, inferences or deductions from interpretative analysis of the text are subsequently carried out.

1. Critical Introduction to the Book of Numbers

The Book of Numbers is the story of the nation of Israel in the wilderness as they headed towards the Promised Land from Mount Sinai. It is also a record of their successes and failures towards God's test, ascertaining whether or not they would be obedient to the term of the covenant given to them on Mount Sinai where they had their one-year worship in God's presence. Their failures led to Yahweh's judgment, and this resulted in raising a new generation entirely to replace the old one that experienced the Exodus in Egypt. Yahweh did this to bring about His plan. According to Gerald I. Mattingly, Numbers contains many stories, comprehensive analysis of God's laws and dramatic account of Yahweh's nature, His covenant, and His plan for Israel.[153]

  The writer examines the worth of human life in the Book of Numbers using the historical-critical method. Given this, the writer considers a critical introduction to the book with particular emphasis on its authorship and dating, literary form and genre, and historical situations. The argument of this writer, however, is that critical introduction to the book of Numbers in isolation of that of the Pentateuch is not rational. Given this, the writer generally and critically introduces the first five Books of the OT, regarded as Pentateuch, before he gives specific attention to the Book of Numbers.

a. Background to the Book of Numbers

The Book of Numbers belongs to the first division of the OT called Pentateuch. In modern scholarship, authorship and dating of these five books are fundamental to Pentateuchal studies. Various debates essentially marked these two essential tasks. The concentration is given to these debates first before the writer specifically places paramount concern on Numbers itself.

---

[153] Gerald I. Mattingly, "The Book of Numbers." *New Living Translation (NLT) Study Bible*, Second Edition, eds., Sean A. Harrison, et al. (Carol Stream, Illinois: Tyndale House Publishers, Inc., 2008), 246.

The various Books of the Pentateuch are traditionally believed to be written by Moses. This paradigm is the oldest of Pentateuchal studies which advance that Moses is the author of almost the entire corpus. According to Gordon Wenham, Moses is not only traditionally believed to be the leading player in most of these books, but he is also the recipient of all the laws from Exodus to Numbers. Chapter 31:24 of Deuteronomy also attests to it that Moses is the preacher of all of the second law. This position which subsisted from the pre-Christian times to the 19th century also holds that the Pentateuch dated to about 1400 B.C.[154] There is some evidence in support of this stance within the Pentateuch itself and from other OT books. Archaeological findings and NT Books also attest to Mosaic authorship.

According to O.A. Dada, there is internal support for Mosaic authorship in some ways. Moses was commanded to write down what he saw and heard in many instances (Exod. 17:14; 24:4). Also, the Pentateuch has internal evidence of being written by an eyewitness of the Exodus who is believed to be Moses. Dada argues that the author knows the details of the numbers of wells and trees available at Elim (Exod. 15:27) and the exact form and flavour of manna (Exod. 16:31). Again, the author uses old names and an example from Egypt to explain things in Pentateuch (Gen. 13:10; 23:2; Num. 13:22).[155]

Similarly, the writer uses a more significant proportion of Egyptian words than somewhere else in the OT. Again, there are specific references in other OT books establishing the fact that Moses wrote the Books of the law (Josh. 1:8; Exod. 20:25; I Kings 2:3). Even, archaeological evidence also holds that some artefacts and inscriptions unearthed today attest to the fact that the writing was already in existence before Moses' time. Lastly, NT equally recognises Mosaic authorship of the Pentateuch (Matt. 19:8; John 5:46; Acts 3:22).[156]

However, there are a lot of arguments in modern critical biblical scholarship against Mosaic authorship. This paradigm began in the 18th century, a time characterised by scepticism, relativism and religious plurality. In biblical scholarship during this period, there was a great upsurge of critical OT scholars who questioned old claims and postulations about the historicity, genuineness, and composition of the OT. According to an unverified source, it was at this period that the famous Documentary Hypothesis (DH) theory emerged on the composition of the Pentateuch. The age was characterised by rationalism in Europe which exalted human reason at the expense of divine authority. During this period, rational scholars subjected ancient secular literature to thorough scrutiny. Similarly, the critical biblical scholars equally agreed that the OT too ought to be submitted to the same principles[157] and be studied

---

[154] Gordon Wenham, "Pentateuchal Studies Today," *Themelios: An International Journal for Students of Theological and Religious Studies* 22.1 (October 1996): 3.

[155] O.A. Dada, *Critical Introduction to the Old Testament* (Ibadan: University of Ibadan Press, Distance Learning Programme, n.d.), 41.

[156] Ibid.

[157] José de Ribera, "Mosaic Authorship."
https://en.wikipedia.org/wiki/Abraham_in_History_and_Tradition (accessed March 1, 2016).

independently of ecclesiastical authority, religious dogma, or church traditions of any kind.

According to Dada, the DH followed a process marked by five periods.[158] The first of these was carried out by Jean Astruc, a French physician who became interested in the literary analysis of the Book of Genesis. Upon the reading of the book, he discovered that God is referred to as Elohim in chapter 1 and mostly Jehovah or Yahweh in chapter 2. He then concluded that Moses used two diverse written sources within two different creation accounts. Scholars subsequently tagged these as J and E sources.

The second era was championed by J.G. Eichorn who divided the whole Book of Genesis into two by separating Yahwist materials (J) from those of Elohist (E). Thus, Eichorn identified two sources. The same method was subsequently employed for the rest of the Books of the Pentateuch by some other scholars. The third period was that of Wilhem M.L. Dewette whose concern was the Book of Deuteronomy. This scholar proposed that the writers of the Pentateuch had written the materials before the period of David. He, therefore, concluded that the Book of the law discovered by Hilkiah, the high priest in the temple (2 Kings 22) during the time of King Josiah in 622 B.C. was a forgery. According to Dewette, this falsification was with the ultimate aim of restoring the people to Yahweh and the book discovered was believed to be Deuteronomy (D source) because its origin was from J and E.

The fourth epoch was that of Hermann Hupfield. In his work published in 1853, *The Sources of Genesis*, Hupfield subjected document E to a thorough examination and found another source in the process. He named the first material discovered E.[2] This document greatly resembled J materials in style and vocabulary. Similarly, Hupfield named the other discovered materials E[1] which are cultic and ritualistic for they contain issues like sacrifice, priestly ordinances, and conducts. He, then, renamed the latter materials Priestly code (P).

Julius Wellhausen championed the last era. However, certain scholars like Graf had also contributed to the DH before that of Wellhausen. Nonetheless, Wellhausen was the scholar who charted a new course for the "definitive formulation" of the DH. Although he did not contribute any new known innovation to the argument, he restated the theory with great skill and expressiveness - the JEDP sequence. In this way, he answered the questions of when, where and how the different sources developed. Wellhausen believed that J source was the first document written probably around the 10th century B.C. and was followed by E source which perhaps was written after the division of ancient Israel in 922 B.C. Equally, Wellhausen argues the writing of D source material should be around the seventh century B.C. while P (Priestly code) material is post-exilic in writing.

Dada argues that JEDP sources were illegitimately weaved together by a post-exilic editor. This ingenuity is claimed to be evidenced by the apparent tension in the

---

[158] Dada, 41.

text of the Pentateuch which points to differences in style, vocabulary, and perspectives, reflecting varying "socio-political sensibilities."[159]

Furthermore, this fifth stage is referred to as the New Paradigm by Wenham. The paradigm was championed by Wellhausen who discovered that the Books of the Pentateuch had composite authorship in the 19th century. Nonetheless, there was an indirect modification to DH by the first half of the 20th century. The step was necessitated by scepticism to the historical truthfulness of the text and the proof of how the document came into existence - the historical circumstances of the book. The revision was carried out by the following German theologians: A. Alt, Martin Noth, and von Rad. Also involved in this task was the American Albright School. All of them argued that though it took a long time between the events in the text and the times of writing, yet it was possible to get the picture of the time of Moses and that of the patriarchal age. As a result, the rising opposition to DH systematically waned, and DH became generally accepted by the middle of the century.[160]

However, some scholars upturned the acceptability gained in the 1970s over certain agitations and confusions: the challenges concern certain significant areas; namely, the dating of the sources, the historicity of the narratives and principles that explain the source division. The position of Wenham is that although the debates still subsist, their premises are on mere assumptions and speculations.[161]

Wenham employed four models to simplify these various debates on source criticism of the Pentateuch. He also did this to obtain a better understanding of the growth of the materials. Among these models, Radical-Sceptical Model is prime. The Sceptics were the first to challenge the consensus and were of three groups. According to Wenham, scholars like Van Seters and Thompson from North America were the initiator. Following these scholars were their German counterparts, Rendtorff, Blum, and Levin. Those from Britain, such as R.N. Whybray, subsequently joined the debate. These various groups had certain commonalities. They all challenged the traditional criteria employed to make a distinction between sources and the dating of the sources. Their scepticism about the historicity of the material was of equal importance. Their main disagreement is on the composition of the Pentateuch. Hence, Van Seters and Levin advanced for a modified DH, Rendtorff and Blum pushed for the supplementary model while Whybray advocated for the fragmentary model.[162]

Next, to the model of the sceptics is the Jewish Critical Model advanced by most critical Jewish scholars. They objected to the Priestly code (P source) as the latest source, although they accepted the central source division of the DH following the pattern of Y. Kaufmann. According to them, P is a reflection of worship in Solomon's temple and came before Deuteronomy. They also posit that P may be as old as J source. Essential works on this school of thought have come from A. Hurvitz,

---

[159] Ibid.
[160] Wenham, 3.
[161] Ibid.
[162] Ibid, 4.

M. Haran, J. Milgrom, and M. Weinfeld. A new study of the P material also revealed that the document contains many components. The Holiness Code (H) (Lev. 17-26) is an example. It is often dated to the early part of the exile while the bulk of the material may be dated a century later.[163] Another speculation is that there are P insertions or editorial changes to H. Knohl challenged all these speculations.[164]

Final Form Study and New Critical Model later emerged. Final form study is a simpler explanation of the growth of the Pentateuch in modern Pentateuchal criticism. The study is most evident in the work of Whybray and Knohl. A new trend in literary theory, called "New Criticism," supported this study which holds that "the proper subject for literary study is the text itself, not the author or the circumstances of the text's composition." The study is evident in the work of D.J.A. Clines, *The Theme of the Pentateuch*.[165]

This writer objects to the idea of Whybray and Knohl for undermining the necessity for the historical truthfulness of the biblical literature. This argument follows that the understanding of the final form of the biblical text is impossible in isolation of the historical circumstances that led to its emergence. In other words, understanding the historical setting or details behind a document will go a long way to identify and redact possible textual corruption or inherent error in the existing text as a result of copying and recopying.

The last of these hypotheses is the Theological Model whose emphasis is the theology of the text. An example of works in this direction is that of R.W.L. Moberly[166] which argues that the difference in sources (E ['I am that I am'] in Exodus 3:14-15 and P ['I am the LORD'] in Exodus 6:2-3) does not suggest a difference in historical perspective. Instead, God reiterated that He was the same God who spoke to the patriarchs as He was speaking to Moses; He was not a different deity. Again, the use of Yahweh in Genesis is a reminder of the continuity between the religion of the Patriarchs and that of Moses from the perspective of Moses or Mosaic Yahwism.[167] Given this, the theological model uses a dispensational approach to bring about the theology of OT text. In other words, the text of the OT speaks of different theological dispensations without God invalidating His previous revelation given to the Patriarchs. The new revelations bring new insights into God's character and purposes.

b. Authorship and Dating of the Book of Numbers

Debates on the authorship and dating of the Book of Numbers are on the same basis as that of the other Pentateuchal Books. On the issue of authorship, scholars have traditionally acknowledged Moses as the author of the book. Christian scholars and their Jewish counterparts are in agreement on this position. Both OT and NT made the same assumption as well as much of the Jewish literature in antiquity. This position subsisted until the arrival of the modern scholarship and was based upon specific

---

[163] Ibid, 8.
[164] Ibid, 9.
[165] Ibid.
[166] Ibid, 10. The title of Moberly's work is: *The Old Testament of the Old Testament*.
[167] Ibid, 11.

references all through the Pentateuch, especially in Deuteronomy 33:1-21. Thus, Moses cannot be ruled out primarily as the author of the Pentateuch by the literary contents of the materials.[168]

However, when scholars consider certain accounts like Moses' death (Deut. 34), objection to Moses' authorship is bound to be raised. Nonetheless, Mattingly advances that there is a possibility that Moses supervised the collection of the books ascribed to him since Numbers refers to certain leaders who assisted him in many ways (chaps 1, 11). Mattingly also posits that the Book of Numbers significantly attests to itself as Moses' work.[169]

On the aspect of the dating of Numbers, Dennis T. Olson considers the literary formation of the book in modern studies. This discussion goes a long way to answer questions bothering the dating of the book and the composition of its sources. According to Olson, modern scholarship on Numbers began in the 18th century. Much of its focus was disposed to the history of the literary development of the book and the four other Pentateuchal Books. The commentary of G.B. Gray (1903) on Numbers brings this overarching concern to the fore, identifying the earlier and later strands of material within the book. The basis of Gray's discerning efforts was on the foundation of the DH[170] which this writer has considered already.

Gray argues that most parts of Numbers were made up of P source, notably Numbers 1-10 and 26-36. According to Gray, the P material of Numbers came into being after the event of the exile of Judah to Babylon in 586 B.C. More so, the argument follows that the P source in Numbers 10-25 is a mixture of the earlier J and E materials. Thus, the viewpoint of P largely subjugates the present shade of Numbers. By implication, the longing of the new generation of Jews in exile to return to Jerusalem has its parallel in the new generation of Numbers, desiring to have a community of worship and service at the border of the Promised Land.[171]

The assumption and position of Gray about the dating of the material of the Book of Numbers persistently generated much debate. Some of the more conservative among them (both Jewish and Christian) dated the document to Mosaic period as they argue for the historicity of much of the book. The period was either before the rise of monarchy or shortly before Judah's exile in Babylon. Other scholars followed the position of Gray to date the material to either the exilic or postexilic period.

Mattingly, and Danny McCain have similar viewpoints on the dating of the book. They are two of the scholars whose dating was to Mosaic period. First, Mattingly argues: "The geographical, cultural, and linguistic data related to Numbers fit either to an early or a late date (the 1400s or 1200s BC respectively) for the Exodus and conquest."[172] In other words, various stories and events within the book fall within the period of Exodus (1400s BC) and conquest (1200s BC). Archaeological

---

[168] Mattingly, 248.

[169] Ibid.

[170] Dennis T. Olson, *Dictionary of the Old Testament Pentateuch,* eds., T. Desmond Alexander and David W. Baker (Leicester: InterVarsity Press, 2003), 613.

[171] Ibid.

[172] Mattingly, 248.

evidence from Sinai, Negev, and various nations of the Transjordan (Edom, Moab, and Ammon) agrees with this historical background of the event of the conquest. The only challenge with the truthfulness of this history is the inability to identify the exact locations of many of the places mentioned in Israel's wilderness journey. Besides, problems also exist about various other sites mentioned in Numbers.

Second, McCain advances that the Book of Numbers was written probably towards the end of the period of the wilderness wanderings. McCain's position is by the record of the facts of the wanderings up to the end of the experience. Given this, Moses might write the book around 1405 BC.[173]

Nonetheless, one overarching element of note with this debate is that most scholars at least agree that the perspective of Priestly tradition dominated Numbers either before the exile or after. However, there is no consensus among Pentateuchal scholars about the nature and date of what Olson called "the pre-Priestly traditions" within the book which Gray regarded as the mixture of the earlier J and E traditions. Some of these scholars completely doubt the reality of an independent E source in the Book of Numbers. They strictly speak of J material or simply of the mixture of J and E materials whose dating scholars can also dispute. In all of these debates, the reality of Numbers being the product of a much longer history of literary formation and editing is established from its earliest stage when the material was in pieces to the final shade of the book.[174]

c. Literary Forms and Genre of Numbers

There are certain literary issues to be addressed in the Book of Numbers. They are the following; namely, the title, genre, sources, and text of the material. In agreement with some scholars, the English title of "Numbers" derives its name from "*Arithmoi*" and "*Numeri*" of the Greek and Latin translations of the OT respectively. The basis for this is on account of two registrations of the men of war that took place among the Israelites in their wilderness wandering. The first of these registrations occurred two years after the Exodus and was of the generation that had the experience of the event (Num.1). The second census, however, took place almost 40 years in the wilderness and was of the generation born into that experience (Num. 14:20-35; 26:64-65).

However, Jewish scholars named the book בְּמִדְבַּר ("in the Wilderness") in the Hebrew Bible. Just like other Books of the Pentateuch, the naming of the book is according to the Jewish tradition which considers a critical word or phrase within the first line of the text as the title. The title in the Hebrew Bible emphasises the importance of the wilderness wandering experience of the people which served as the bridge between their life in an advanced society of Egypt and that of the Promised Land. Given this, the experience of the people in the wilderness was to serve an essential purpose for them. It was to train them a life of trust in God and obedience to

---

[173] Danny McCain, *Notes on Old Testament Introduction*, Revised Edition (Bukuru: African Christian Textbooks (Acts), 2002), 79.
[174] Ibid.

their covenant with Yahweh as they move to possess their permanent inheritance among the nations.[175]

Similarly, Mattingly advances that the title "Numbers" has interest in statistics, precisely in the censuses taken in the wilderness (chaps 1-4, 26). The basis of this title is to establish the fact that the generation of the Israelites that left Egypt was not the same generation that entered the Promised Land. However, the title in the Hebrew Bible *"bᵉmidbar"* ("In the wilderness") is the fourth word of 1:1. Mattingly argues in favour of the Hebrew title that it is more appropriate since it portrays both the geographical setting and chronological framework of the book.[176]

Moreover, the writer of Numbers employed many literary genres. According to Olson, Numbers possesses the greatest variety of genres than any other Book of the Bible. According to Olson, citing J. Milgrom, Numbers has 14 different literary forms; namely, narrative (ch. 4:1-3), poetry (ch. 21:17-18), prophecy (ch. 24:3-9), victory song (ch. 21:27-30), prayer (ch.12:13), blessing (ch. 6:24-26), lampoon (ch. 22:22-35), diplomatic letter (ch. 20:14-19), civil law (ch. 27:1-11), cultic law (ch. 15:17-21), oracular decision (ch. 15:32-36), registration list (ch. 26:1-51), temple archive (ch. 7:10-88) and itinerary (ch. 33:1-49). Olson also argues that the present form of the book is an intricate but meaningful collection of these individual literary genres woven together into this present pattern. On this wide-range collection of genres, some scholars argue that they probably emerged from the beginning of the history of ancient Israel to the postexilic time.[177] More so, Mattingly advances that chapters 4-6 contains law, 10:11-14:44 contains a narrative, and 23-24 has poetry. The book also contains a detailed analysis of facts and figures. Accounts of census tallies are in chapters 1-4, and offerings in 7. Analysis of travel details is also in chapter 33.[178]

Furthermore, literary sources which the author of the Book of Numbers found handy are critical to this work. The Hebrew Bible identifies some of the ancient materials which Moses made use, especially in the Book of Numbers. Some of these sources were also believed to have been consulted by later scribes. Among them are the following; namely, *The Book of the Wars of the LORD* in chapter 21:14-15, *the "Song of the Well"* in 21:17-18, and *the "Song of Heshbon"* in 21:27-30. The prophetic lines of Balaam, a non-Israelite prophet, in chapters 23-24, and a line that appears to be a "booty record" in 31:32-47 are all part of the book. Similarly, a written chronicle seems to form chapter 33.[179]

Lastly, the Hebrew text of the book is argued to be well preserved. The premise of the argument of Mattingly is on a close affinity that exists between the Hebrew MT (AD 900s) of Numbers and that of the much earlier discovered text (150 BC-AD 125) in the Dead Sea Scrolls. However, a few sections of poetry, especially in

---

[175] Olson, 611.

[176] Mattingly, 248.

[177] Olson, 614.

[178] Mattingly, 248.

[179] Ibid.

chapters 21-24, are difficult to interpret. Differences also exist between the MT, corresponding portions in the Septuagint, and the Samaritan Pentateuch. Nonetheless, these differences are argued to be deliberate variations of interpretation.[180]

d. Historical Situations and Central Themes of Numbers

The historical setting of the Book of Numbers is pertinent to this work. This need is by the writer's conviction that a proper understanding of this will enhance the exegetical interpretation of the chosen text. After the exodus experience, the children of Israel left for Mount Sinai where they remained for one year before the LORD. Within this period, they received the law before they continued their journey into Transjordan and camped on the plains of Moab. The entire generation that left Egypt for the wilderness failed God's test and had to face His judgment except for Joshua and Caleb. Given this, they perished in the desert, and a new generation was prepared to possess Canaan. The Book of Numbers instructed this new generation to obey the LORD on the plain of Moab.[181]

The work of Flavius Josephus, a first-century Jewish historian, attests to Israelites' failures in the wilderness. Many of these failures took place within the timeframe of the events recorded in Numbers. The first of these happened almost immediately after Moses had conducted the people from their camping ground at Sinai as they attempted to move towards the plains of Moab. At a place called *Hazeroth*, the people began to blame Moses for their misfortunes because there was no water and meat to eat. Upon adequate provisions after that, God punished the people for their insolence, and many of them died. The place was, therefore, named after the event and called *Kibroth-hattaavah*, meaning *"The Graves of Lust."*[182]

Similarly, At Paran, close to the borders of the Canaanites, Moses sent 12 spies to explore the land of Canaan and to bring the report of its various potentials to the assembly. After touring the entire area, the city of Hamath to Mount Lebanon, and having obtained information about the nature of the land and of its people within 40 days, the spies had their return. The spies at the beginning presented good reports, so good to motivate the people to go to war. They afterwards terrified the assembly with many difficulties such as the inhabitants of the land. With these in mind, both the spies and the people concluded that it was impossible to possess the land. The entire assembly began to wail and made attempts to stone both Moses and Aaron. More so, they decided to return to Egypt. The act of faithlessness of the people caused that generation almost 40 years of wandering in the wilderness until the last person perished. This punishment was except Joshua and Caleb who distinguished themselves by faith in God.[183]

Thus, Numbers is the record of how God's people were prepared in the wilderness to walk with God. Again, generations that succeeded them were also ready

---

[180] Ibid.

[181] Mattingly, 246.

[182] William A.M. Whiston, trans. *The Works of Josephus*, Complete and Unabridged, New Updated Edition (Peabody: Hendrickson Publishers, Inc., 1987), 99.

[183] Ibid, 99-101.

to hear the story using the literary efforts of Moses and the efforts of the scribes and editors that succeeded Moses. These literary works became necessary so that the succeeding generations might learn from history to avoid the mistakes of their fore-bearers.[184]

The two censuses taken of men of military age are of great significance to Numbers (chaps 1-4, 26). According to Mattingly, these registrations profoundly measured the strength of the fighting men and the Levites' number. The first registration was at the beginning of the book while preparing to depart their camp at Sinai and the second was as they set to cross to Canaan, the totals of which depict two different generations. The first one represents the rebellious generation that received the law and perished in the wilderness while the second was that of the new generation that got to the Promised Land. The two totals had a close margin, suggesting that the new generation successfully replaced the earlier one.[185]

Scholars suggested specific themes for Numbers. According to McCain, "A Practical Application of God's Laws" is argued to be the central theme. The idea found relevance in the wilderness wanderings of the people as they lost faith in the LORD and Moses, their human leader. Nonetheless, the issue has its most profound and practical applications in various ways the people implemented God's laws in the wilderness. Given this, the Book of Numbers has two main emphases; namely: the two censuses or registrations of the people with various genealogies and the people's history during the 40 years of wilderness wanderings.[186]

Similarly, Olson argues that transition between the old generation of the Israelites who was at the centre of the Books of Exodus and Leviticus (chaps 1-25) and the new generation addressed at the plains of Moab by Moses (chaps 26-36) is the central theme of this book. Given this, people could understand the literary structure of Numbers in the light of the general context of the Pentateuch. More so, the fundamental pillars of this structure are the two registrations.[187]

The first half of the book, on the one hand, is introduced by the early registration (Num. 1) and recounts the ultimate death of the generation that experienced the Exodus. It begins with the record and organisation of the twelve tribes at Sinai as they prepared for their march to the Promised Land (chaps 1-10). The section of the rebellious acts of the people (chaps 11-12) immediately follows this section before the story of the spies (13-14) that comes up later. Most parts of the rest of this first half are also characterised by this rebellious attitude and plagues which came as punishment with deaths (chaps 16, 17, 20, 21, 25). The second half, on the other hand, is introduced by the second registration which shares certain features with the first; namely, the same wording of Yahweh's command (chaps 1:2-3; 26:2), a

[184] Mattingly, 246.
[185] Ibid, 247.
[186] McCain, 79.
[187] Olson, 612.

related order of all of the 12 tribes and the registration of the tribe of the Levitical priests which follows the order of the listing of the 12 tribes (chaps 3-4; 26:57-62).[188]

In the same vein, there is also a significant difference between these two registration lists. There was no one among the community of God's people in the first list counted in the second list except for Joshua and Caleb, the two faithful spies (chaps 26:63-65; cf. 14:26-35). Besides, the second half of the Book of Numbers is equally different from the first in theme and tone. It is characterised by "life and hope" of the new generation instead of "rebellion and death" that marked the old one. Again, the narrative about the new generation began at the entry point of Canaan in the plains of Moab (ch 26:3) unlike that of the old age group that took place in the midst of the wilderness.[189]

Again, after the second registration in chapter 26, the second half of the book is marked by certain additional events which Oslo called "*inclusio*" in chapters 27 and 36. They are about legal dispute regarding family land inheritance brought to Moses and some other leaders of the people. In chapter 27, it was brought by the daughters of Zelophehad while the second one in chapter 36 was by the family head of their clan (Gilead son of Makir, the son of Manasseh). These matters were resolved using what Oslo called "mediation of competing legal principles and values, setting a positive and hopeful tone for the entire second half of the book." In addition to this, there is no record of the death of any among God's people in the second half.[190] More so, the people had a history of victory over the Midianites in their first military engagement (ch.31). Specific crises which were capable of turning to rebellion were also successfully handled (chaps 27:1-11; 31:14-15; 32:1-42). Lastly, the writer also set many laws for future life in the Promised Land (chaps 27; 34-36).[191]

e. Structural Flow of the Book of Numbers

According to Olson, the content and outline of the present form of Numbers are divided into two main themes as presented below:

1. The Death of the Old Wilderness Generation (Num. 1-25)

> i. Obedient Beginnings: Preparation for Israel's March in the Wilderness (Num.1-10)
>
> ii. An Abrupt Slide into Rebellion: The Death of the First Wilderness Generation Begins (Num. 11-20)
>
> iii. The Final End of the First Generation: Signs and Hope in the Midst of Death (Num. 21-25).

2. The Rise of a New Generation on the Edge of the Promised Land (Num. 26-36)

---

[188] Ibid.

[189] Ibid.

[190] Ibid, 612-613.

[191] Ibid, 613.

i. The Second Census, the Daughters of Zelophehad, the Succession of Leadership and Laws for the New Generation's Life in the Promised Land (Num. 26-30)

ii. A Military Victory and Words of Warning and Encouragement from a Generation Past (Num. 31-33)

iii. Law as Promise: Divine Commands in Anticipation of Residence in the Promised Land (Num. 34-36).[192]

2. Text and Translation of Numbers 35:9-34

Verse 9 וַיְדַבֵּר יְהוָה אֶל־מֹשֶׁה לֵּאמֹר:

Verse 9: Then Yahweh commanded Moses saying,

Verse 10 דַּבֵּר אֶל־בְּנֵי יִשְׂרָאֵל וְאָמַרְתָּ אֲלֵהֶם כִּי אַתֶּם עֹבְרִים אֶת־הַיַּרְדֵּן אַרְצָה כְּנָעַן:

Verse 10: "Command the children of Israel and say to them: 'when you pass from the Jordan to the land of Canaan,

Verse 11 וְהִקְרִיתֶם לָכֶם עָרִים עָרֵי מִקְלָט תִּהְיֶינָה לָכֶם וְנָס שָׁמָּה רֹצֵחַ מַכֵּה־נֶפֶשׁ בִּשְׁגָגָה:

Verse 11: you will ordain for yourselves towns which will become cities of refuge for you; any manslayer who has smitten a person in error may flee there.

Verse 12 וְהָיוּ לָכֶם הֶעָרִים לְמִקְלָט מִגֹּאֵל וְלֹא יָמוּת הָרֹצֵחַ עַד־עָמְדוֹ לִפְנֵי הָעֵדָה לַמִּשְׁפָּט:

Verse 12: They will be a refuge from the redeemer of blood, and he will not execute the killer as far as he stays in any of the cities until he appears before the assembly for judgment.

Verse 13 וְהֶעָרִים אֲשֶׁר תִּתֵּנוּ שֵׁשׁ־עָרֵי מִקְלָט תִּהְיֶינָה לָכֶם:

Verse 13: And the towns which you will give will be for you six cities of refuge.

Verse 14 אֵת שְׁלֹשׁ הֶעָרִים תִּתְּנוּ מֵעֵבֶר לַיַּרְדֵּן וְאֵת שְׁלֹשׁ הֶעָרִים תִּתְּנוּ בְּאֶרֶץ כְּנָעַן עָרֵי מִקְלָט תִּהְיֶינָה:

Verse 14: You will give three of these towns on this side of the Jordan and three in the territory of Canaan as cities of refuge.

Verse 15 לִבְנֵי יִשְׂרָאֵל וְלַגֵּר וְלַתּוֹשָׁב בְּתוֹכָם תִּהְיֶינָה שֵׁשׁ־הֶעָרִים הָאֵלֶּה לְמִקְלָט לָנוּס שָׁמָּה כָּל־מַכֵּה־נֶפֶשׁ בִּשְׁגָגָה:

---

[192] Ibid, 614.

Verse 15: These six cities will be for refuge for the children of Israel, the sojourner and the alien living among them; anyone that smites a person unintentionally may flee there.

Verse 16 וְאִם־בִּכְלִי בַרְזֶל ׀ הִכָּהוּ וַיָּמֹת רֹצֵחַ הוּא מוֹת יוּמַת הָרֹצֵחַ:

Verse 16: 'If a man smites another man with an iron object and the person dies, he is a murderer; the murderer shall be made to die.

Verse 17 וְאִם בְּאֶבֶן יָד אֲשֶׁר־יָמוּת בָּהּ הִכָּהוּ וַיָּמֹת רֹצֵחַ הוּא מוֹת יוּמַת הָרֹצֵחַ:

Verse 17: And if a man has a stone in his hand which could kill and he smites another man so that he dies, the man is a murderer; the murderer shall be made to die.

Verse 18 אוֹ בִּכְלִי עֵץ־יָד אֲשֶׁר־יָמוּת בּוֹ הִכָּהוּ וַיָּמֹת רֹצֵחַ הוּא מוֹת יוּמַת הָרֹצֵחַ:

Verse 18: Or if a man has a wooden object in his hand and smites another person with it so that the person dies; he is a murderer, and the murderer shall be made to die.

Verse 19 גֹּאֵל הַדָּם הוּא יָמִית אֶת־הָרֹצֵחַ בְּפִגְעוֹ־בוֹ הוּא יְמִיתֶנּוּ:

Verse 19: The redeemer of blood shall put this murderer to death as he meets him, he shall put him to death.

Verse 20 וְאִם־בְּשִׂנְאָה יֶהְדָּפֶנּוּ אוֹ־הִשְׁלִיךְ עָלָיו בִּצְדִיָּה וַיָּמֹת:

Verse 20: And if any man with hatred thrusts another person or throws something upon him intentionally and the person dies

Verse 21 אוֹ בְאֵיבָה הִכָּהוּ בְיָדוֹ וַיָּמֹת מוֹת־יוּמַת הַמַּכֶּה רֹצֵחַ הוּא גֹּאֵל הַדָּם יָמִית אֶת־הָרֹצֵחַ בְּפִגְעוֹ־בוֹ:

Verse 21: or if in hostility he smites another person with his hand so that he dies, he is a murderer; the redeemer of blood will put the murderer to death when he meets him.'

Verse 22 וְאִם־בְּפֶתַע בְּלֹא־אֵיבָה הֲדָפוֹ אוֹ־הִשְׁלִיךְ עָלָיו כָּל־כְּלִי בְּלֹא צְדִיָּה:

Verse 22: '"But if without enmity someone suddenly thrusts another person or throws an object upon him unintentionally

Verse 23 אוֹ בְכָל־אֶבֶן אֲשֶׁר־יָמוּת בָּהּ בְּלֹא רְאוֹת וַיַּפֵּל עָלָיו וַיָּמֹת וְהוּא לֹא־אוֹיֵב לוֹ וְלֹא מְבַקֵּשׁ רָעָתוֹ:

Verse 23: or without seeing him, causes a heavy stone to fall on him so that he dies without being his enemy and seeking evil against him.

Verse 24 וְשָׁפְטוּ הָעֵדָה בֵּין הַמַּכֶּה וּבֵין גֹּאֵל הַדָּם עַל הַמִּשְׁפָּטִים הָאֵלֶּה:

Verse 24: The assembly will judge between the accused person and the redeemer of blood according to these ordinances promulgated.

Verse 25 וְהִצִּ֣ילוּ הָעֵדָ֗ה אֶת־הָרֹצֵ֙חַ֙ מִיַּד֙ גֹּאֵ֣ל הַדָּ֔ם וְהֵשִׁ֤יבוּ אֹתוֹ֙ הָ֣עֵדָ֔ה
אֶל־עִ֤יר מִקְלָטוֹ֙ אֲשֶׁר־נָ֣ס שָׁ֔מָּה וְיָ֣שַׁב בָּ֔הּ עַד־מוֹת֙ הַכֹּהֵ֣ן הַגָּדֹ֔ל אֲשֶׁר־מָשַׁ֥ח
אֹתוֹ֖ בְּשֶׁ֥מֶן הַקֹּֽדֶשׁ:

Verse 25: The assembly shall make the one convicted of manslaughter escape from
the redeemer of blood by sending him back to the city of refuge where he had fled,
and he shall remain there until the death of the high priest anointed with the holy
oil.'"

Verse 26 וְאִם־יָצֹ֥א יֵצֵ֖א הָרֹצֵ֑חַ אֶת־גְּבוּל֙ עִ֣יר מִקְלָטוֹ֔ אֲשֶׁ֥ר יָנ֖וּס שָֽׁמָּה:

Verse 26: 'But if the one convicted of manslaughter goes out of the territory of the
city of refuge where he had fled

Verse 27 וּמָצָ֤א אֹתוֹ֙ גֹּאֵ֣ל הַדָּ֔ם מִח֕וּץ לִגְב֖וּל עִ֣יר מִקְלָט֑וֹ וְרָצַ֞ח גֹּאֵ֤ל הַדָּם֙
אֶת־הָ֣רֹצֵ֔חַ אֵ֥ין ל֖וֹ דָּֽם:

Verse 27: and the redeemer of blood finds him outside the border of the city of refuge;
the redeemer of blood may kill him without being guilty of murder

Verse 28 כִּ֣י בְעִ֤יר מִקְלָטוֹ֙ יֵשֵׁ֔ב עַד־מ֖וֹת הַכֹּהֵ֣ן הַגָּדֹ֑ל וְאַחֲרֵ֥י מוֹת֙ הַכֹּהֵ֣ן
הַגָּדֹ֔ל יָשׁוּב֙ הָרֹצֵ֔חַ אֶל־אֶ֖רֶץ אֲחֻזָּתֽוֹ:

Verse 28: for he must remain within the city of his refuge until the death of the high
priest. But after the death of the high priest, the accused person may return to the land
of his possession.

Verse 29 וְהָי֨וּ אֵ֧לֶּה לָכֶ֛ם לְחֻקַּ֥ת מִשְׁפָּ֖ט לְדֹרֹתֵיכֶ֑ם בְּכֹ֖ל מוֹשְׁבֹתֵיכֶֽם:

Verse 29: "'These will be a standard of judgment for you forever for all of your
generations in all of your dwelling-places.

Verse 30 כָּל־מַ֨כֵּה־נֶ֔פֶשׁ לְפִ֣י עֵדִ֔ים יִרְצַ֖ח אֶת־הָרֹצֵ֑חַ וְעֵ֣ד אֶחָ֔ד לֹא־יַעֲנֶ֥ה
בְנֶ֖פֶשׁ לָמֽוּת:

Verse 30: Anyone who smites a person to death shall die as a murderer but only by
the testimony of witnesses; no one is to die upon the testimony of only one witness.

Verse 31 וְלֹא־תִקְח֥וּ כֹ֙פֶר֙ לְנֶ֣פֶשׁ רֹצֵ֔חַ אֲשֶׁר־ה֥וּא רָשָׁ֖ע לָמ֑וּת כִּי־מ֖וֹת יוּמָֽת:

Verse 31: You must not collect a ransom for the life of a murderer who is guilty for he
is to die; he must be put to death.

Verse 32 וְלֹא־תִקְח֣וּ כֹ֔פֶר לָנ֖וּס אֶל־עִ֣יר מִקְלָט֑וֹ לָשׁוּב֙ לָשֶׁ֣בֶת בָּאָ֔רֶץ
עַד־מ֖וֹת הַכֹּהֵֽן:

Verse 32: You shall not collect ransom for anyone who has fled to the city of his
refuge to bring him back; he must remain within the territory until the death of the
high priest.

וְלֹא־תַחֲנִיפוּ אֶת־הָאָרֶץ אֲשֶׁר אַתֶּם בָּהּ כִּי הַדָּם הוּא יַחֲנִיף Verse 33
אֶת־הָאָרֶץ וְלָאָרֶץ לֹא־יְכֻפַּר לַדָּם אֲשֶׁר שֻׁפַּךְ־בָּהּ כִּי־אִם בְּדַם שֹׁפְכוֹ:

Verse 33: You must not pollute the land where you are living for blood pollutes the land. Atonement cannot be made for the land on which blood has been poured except by the blood of the person who poured it."'

וְלֹא תְטַמֵּא אֶת־הָאָרֶץ אֲשֶׁר אַתֶּם יֹשְׁבִים בָּהּ אֲשֶׁר אֲנִי שֹׁכֵן Verse 34
בְּתוֹכָהּ כִּי אֲנִי יְהוָה שֹׁכֵן בְּתוֹךְ בְּנֵי יִשְׂרָאֵל: פ

Verse 34: Do not defile the land on which you are living for I Yahweh live in the midst of the children of Israel."

3. Textual Analysis of the Chosen Text

Given textual corruption characterising not only biblical texts but almost all texts of the ancient literature as a result of errors inherent in copying and recopying for transmission, it becomes necessary to consider Critical Apparatus for proper investigation of Numbers 35:9-34. This step also becomes imperative considering uncertainties that surround the survival of the OT books in such a hostile land whose people are described by Bruce K. Waltke as, "The object of plunderers in their early history and of captors in their later history. That no other writings, such as the Book of Yashar or the Diaries of the Kings, survive from this period shows the determination of the scribes to preserve the OT books."[193] The step helps in no small measure to obtain a text close to the original which is non-existent.

Verse 10:

1. Instead of אַרְצָה (a land) that appears in the Masoretic Text (MT), Samaritan Hebrew Pentateuch (*secundum* A. von Gall, *Der hebraische Pentateuch der Samaritaner* 1914 – 1918)[194] has אל ארץ which implies *to a land*.[195] This rendition projects the idea of this verse better as used in the location of the chosen text placed under the appendices. In order words, the writer prefers Samaritan Hebrew Pentateuch to MT despite that MT is better in the order of significance for textual criticism according to William R. Scott.[196] The writer made this choice on account of the principle of intelligibility of the reading as suggested by Waltke.[197]

---

[193] Bruce K. Waltke, "The Textual Criticism of the Old Testament," in *Biblical Criticism: Historical, Literary and Textual.* eds., R.K. Harrison, B.K. Waltke, D. Guthrie, and G.D. Fee (Grand Rapids, Michigan: Zondervan Publishing House, 1978), 48-49.

[194] A. Schenker, A. Alt, O. Eißfeldt, P. Kahle ediderat, R. kittel, adjuvantibus H. Bardtke, W. Baumgartner et al. eds., "Numbers 35:9-34," *Biblia Herbraica Stuttgartensia* (BHS) (Nordlingen: Deutsche Forschungsgemeinschaft, 1997), XLVII.

[195] Ibid, 280.

[196] William R. Scott, *A Simplified Guide to BHS: Critical Apparatus, Masora, Accents, Unusual Letters & Other Markings,* Third Edition (Richland Hills: Bibal Press, 1995), 22.

[197] Waltke, 78.

65

Verse 11:

1. רֹצֵחַ meaning *a murderer* is an uncertain entry, and the writer is expected to delete it. This command is due to the presence of a "question mark and deletion" sign placed before it in the CA. The absence of this entry does not alter the meaning as וְנָס *(and he will flee)* already implies the subject of the verb "flee." The variant reading הר in *Pentateuchi textus* Hebraeo-Samaritanus, suggesting a particular mountain on the border of Edom (Num. 20:22),[198] is thus unfit based on the nuance of the text before and after this verse.

2. מַכֵּה־נֶפֶשׁ[b] (he causing to smite a person) has a variant reading of כָּל־מַ (the whole of he causing to smite). A few Manuscripts (Mss) of the Septuagint (LXX) contain this variant rendition. MT rendition is preferred because it is older than the variant reading of the LXX[199] and the version is more intelligible as advanced by Waltke.[200]

Verse 12:

1. There is every need to probably insert הַדָּם (the blood) after גֹּאֵל (a redeemer). The need becomes very evident when this situation is compared with what obtains from verse 19 following. This writer sees the need for this and hence, the basis for his interpretation of this verse.

2. Instead of יָמוּת some ancient manuscripts have יוּמָת which when compared with verse 17[201] with the addition of מוֹת connotes the idea of violent death as a capital punishment for the murderer.[202] This connotation is alien to the concept developed in this verse since capital punishment is to be carried out by a human authority which is the state while the redeemer of blood is the executioner in this verse. However, the idea of execution is implied here since the killing is a punishment for a crime committed by the murderer.

Verse 17:

Samaritan Hebrew Pentateuch (*secundum* A. von Gall, *Der hebraische Pentateuch der Samaritaner* 1914 – 1918) has יָמוּת (he will die) instead of יוּמָת (he will be caused to die) of the MT. The rendition of MT is preferred when compared with the internal evidence of verses 16 and 18 as advanced by Ellis R. Brotzman,[203] the nuances immediately preceding and following it respectively which depict the idea of causative action in the active voice of hiphil imperfect 3ms.

---

[198] BDB, 246.
[199] Waltke, 55.
[200] Ibid, 78.
[201] Schenker, 280.
[202] BDB, 559.
[203] Ellis R. Brotzman, *Old Testament Textual Criticism: A Practical Introduction*, forwarded, Bruce K. Waltke (Grand Rapids, Michigan: Baker Book House Company, 1994), 124.

Verse 18:

Instead of אוֹ (or), a few ancient manuscripts of the Samaritan Hebrew Pentateuch, The Syrian version of the OT, and The Vulgate have וְאִם (and if). The writer preferred the variant reading on account of its appearance in the preceding verse.

Verse 19:

Some of the Mss of an Oriental reading have כְ (like, as)[204] as the Qere (Q) of בְּ־פִגְעוֹ בוֹ (literally translated as: "in to meet him by him"). The writer prefers Q (pronounced) form on account of the principle of best reading as כְּפִגְעוֹ־בוֹ (as to meet him by him) conveys the idea of "as he meets him."[205]

Verse 22:

Samaritan Hebrew Pentateuch has הֲדִי (which depicts one of David's heroes in 2 Sam. 23:30)[206] as against הֲדָפוֹ (he thrust him). The rendition of the Samaritan Hebrew Pentateuch is against the nuance of this verse. Hence, the writer prefers MT reading to the variant one on account of the principle of best reading.[207]

Verse 23:

CA raises an issue on: בְּכָל־אֶבֶן (by the whole of a stone of). The prefixed בְּ preposition (in, at, by, with) may be unnecessary as the Hebrew construct word is to be read כָּל (all or the whole of) instead of בְּכָל. This writer goes by this in the interpretation of the verse since the idea of the instrument by which the death or killing takes place is already implied in אֶבֶן (stone). The idea of the size of the instrument remains, which כָּל depicts that the stone is heavy enough as to lead to such a death.

Verse 25:

The Samaritan Hebrew Pentateuch has הַמַּכֶּה (the one blowing, sounding, slaughtering) as against אֶת־הָרֹצֵחַ (the murderer) in MT of the BHS. מַכָּה (blow, sound, slaughter, wound) is from the root word נכה (nkd) employed almost 500 times. According to Marvin R. Wilson, one infers that OT was familiar with bloodshed and warfare owing to the commonality of this Hebrew root word.[208] Similarly, נָכָה is from the same root word meaning "he smote, struck, hit, beat, stayed, killed."[209] On this basis, this writer, therefore, goes for the rendition of the Samaritan Pentateuch of the OT because the projected nuance indicates someone already discharged of premeditated murder by the

---

[204] Ellis, 374.
[205] Brotzman, 129.
[206] BDB, 213.
[207] Brotzman, 129.
[208] Marvin R. Wilson, "מַכָּה" in *Theological Wordbook of the Old Testament*, eds., R. Laird Harris, Gleason L. Archer, and Bruce K. Waltke (Chicago: Moody Publishers, 1980), 577.
[209] Ibid.

assembly. It is because of this that the assembly had to protect him from the redeemer of blood by sending him back to the city of refuge. Thus, he is no longer "the accused of murder" but "the one guilty of manslaughter." To this writer, sending him back to the city of refuge where he had fled is enough punishment for manslaughter. It was the imprisonment or jail term of the time whose period used to be determined by the longevity of the period of the service of the serving high priest.

Verse 29:

The Syria version of the OT reads עוֹלָם (±ôl'm) (forever, ever, everlasting, evermore, perpetual, old, ancient, world)[210] as against מִשְׁפָּט (judgment). This writer goes for the idea of The Syria version even though MT is superior in term of value or order of significance. This decision is on the basis that the idea which לְחֻקַּת מִשְׁפָּט (statute of judgment) implies is repetitious. It is repetition because of לְחֻקַּת which connotes the idea of a system of law or rule already implied in מִשְׁפָּט and vice versa. Hence, the reading that has עוֹלָם (±ôl'm) following לְחֻקַּת may be more appropriate.

Verse 32:

1. The first issue raised is the proposition of the reading לָנֻס against that of לָנוּס. לָנֻס is לְ preposition meaning "*to, towards, until, at, in, of, about, into, in (regard to), concerning, according to, by, in relation to, in the direction of, for, because of*" prefixed to definite article "*the*" prefixed to verb hiphil perfect 3ms qere from נוּס meaning "he fled, escaped, slipped away;" hence, *for the he caused to escape*. This situation does not affect this translation. The interpretation of this verse may not even consider this proposition for the fact that it is the assembly that supposes to be the causation of the escape by receiving a ransom, not the man convicted of manslaughter himself which לָנֻס suggests.

2. The manuscripts of the following versions of the OT scriptures: the Samaritan Hebrew Pentateuch, the Septuagint (LXX), and the Syrian version of the OT have the addition of an adjective הַגָּדֹל (great) to the reading of verse 32. Therefore, bringing this adjective to qualify the noun הַכֹּהֵן (the priest) it follows; the idea of the great or high priest comes to the fore. Since the idea of "the high (great) priest" has been running through the reading since, specifically in verses 25 and 28, this writer is in support of the addition going by the principle of internal evidence.[211]

Verse 33:

CA suggests that there is an insertion of יֹשְׁבִים (you remaining or living) to the reading of verse 33 in a few manuscripts; namely, The Samaritan Hebrew Pentateuch, The Septuagint, The Syrian version of the OT, and The Vulgate. This insertion occurs immediately after אַתֶּם (you) bringing the idea of "where you are living" to the fore. The

---

[210] BDB, 763.
[211] Brotzman,, 124.

68

writer supported this based on the significance of these Mss.[212] Thus, אַתֶּם serves as an emphasis on the subject of the verb as it also happens in verse 34.[213]

Verse 34:

1. CA suggests that the Hebrew word תִטַמֵּא is to be located and read as *verb piel imperfect 2mp* (you [plural] will become grossly unclean) instead of *verb piel imperfect 2ms* (you [singular] will become grossly polluted) that MT renders it. This suggestion is on account of the readings of a few manuscripts; namely, The Samaritan Hebrew Pentateuch; The Septuagint; The Syrian version of the OT; The Targum according to A. Sperber, The Bible in Aramaic, vol. I-III 1959 – 1962; and Targum Pseudo-Jonathae according to M. Ginsburger, Pseudo-Jonathae 1903. The writer agreed with the suggestion of the CA on two bases; namely, the significance of the Mss and intelligible reading for the entire people of Yahweh are implied in this instruction.

4. Lexical Analyses of the Passage

In this section, the writer investigates the sanctity of human life lexically in the light of certain Hebrew words in Numbers 35:9-34 and other cognate vocabularies outside the text. The underpinning basis for this step is to bring to the fore various nuances that connote the idea of killing in the Hebrew worldview. Gaining this understanding fosters a better interpretation of the chosen text and appreciation of the Hebrew grammar. This action also affords the contemporary readers of the Hebrew Bible better revelation of the Hebrew and Jewish societies concerning the frequency of times that cases of murder were either committed or mentioned in their Scripture.

The OT biblical text is composed of certain Hebrew words with a connotation of "killing." In this light, Walter C. Kaiser, Peter H. Davids, F.F. Bruce, and Manfred T. Brauch emphatically posit that these words are seven in number. The scholars completely ignored analysis of any of these words other than רָצַח.[214] However, upon investigation, this writer came to the understanding that these words are 11 in number, three of which appear within the chosen text. According to Lawrence O. Richards, all these vocabularies bring to the fore the dreadful nature of sin, cutting short the hope of all people to realise the divine intention for humankind just as Cain crushed Abel's body and with his blood spilt on the earth.[215]

The words that appear within the chosen text which this writer considers in this lexical analyses section are רָצַח, נָכָה, and מוּת. These words are in noun and verbal forms. In addition to these, the writer also considered lexical analyses of the following cognate words: שָׁחַט, קָטַל, כָּרַת, טָבַח, חָלָל, זָבַח, הָרַג, and שָׁמַד

---

[212] Ibid, 124-125.
[213] Schenker, 281.
[214] Walter C. Kaiser, Jr. Peter H. Davids, F.F. Bruce & Manfred T. Brauch, *Hard Sayings of the Bible* (Downers Grove, Illinois: InterVarsity Press, 1996), 121.
[215] Lawrence O. Richards, *New International Encyclopedia of Bible Words* (Grand Rapids, Michigan: Zondervan, 1991), 448.

i. וְרָצַח = וְ vav consecutive *and* prefixed to verb qal perfect 3ms from רָצַח meaning *he murdered* or *slew* (both with intent and without intent); hence, *"And he will murder."*

This word appears mostly in noun within the text, and its first verbal appearance is in verse 27. According to F. Brown, S. Driver, and C. Briggs, its lexical meanings are mainly two; namely, 'to murder,' and 'to slay.' This verb has cognate Aramaic meanings such as 'to break,' 'bruise,' and 'crush.' Whenever this verb connotes the idea of premeditation, וְרָצַח נֶפֶשׁ, therefore, translates, "When a man murders his neighbour" (Deut. 22:26). While coming with the nuance of accidence, יִרְצַח אֶת־רֵעֵהוּ translate, "He or one who unintentionally slays his friend" (Deut. 4:42). In the same vein, when the redeemer of blood commits the slaying, גֹּאֵל הַדָּם וְרָצַח implies "And the redeemer of blood may slay him" (Num. 35:27).[216]

More so, W.E. Vine, Merrill F. Unger and William White, Jr. translate the verb as "to kill, murder, slay." Its occurrence in the Hebrew Bible is 40 times with its highest frequency in the Pentateuch. The verb is used predominantly in modern Hebrew and scholars exclusively interpret it as "to murder." The Septuagint translates it as *'phoneuein'* ("to murder, kill, put to death"). The verb occurs primarily in the legal document of the OT concerning God's law, giving special consideration to regulations on life. It also covers provisions for dealings and sanctions for the murderer.[217]

The first occurrence of this verb is in the sixth commandment. It comes with the idea of intentional killing, and scholars thereby translate Exodus 20:13 as: "Do not murder." The provision for sanction or penalty for the murderer, after the assembly might have conducted a necessary trial, is to put the same person to death (Num. 35:30). The OT distinguishes between premeditated murder and unintentional killing. This practice is evident in the provision for cities of refuge where a manslayer who killed unintentionally may run to (Num. 35; Deut. 19; Josh. 20; 21). Thus, the OT does not only recognise the principle of the sanctity of life but prioritises it. The same testament does the same as the principle of retribution. Also, the word appears in Arabic, meaning "to bruise, crush."[218]

Furthermore, the position of William White regarding the rendering of this verb is that it is purely Hebrew with no apparent cognate term in any of the neighbouring tongues. Its roots have 38 appearances in the OT, 14 of which appear in Numbers 35 with its initial use in the *Decalogue* (Exod.20:13). In other words, the root appears in the Mosaic Law, seeming to have a precise and particular connotation

---

[216] F. Brown, S. Driver, and C. Briggs, *The Brown-Driver-Briggs Hebrew and English Lexicon: With an Appendix containing the Biblical Aramaic* (Peabody, Massachusetts: Hendrickson Publishers, 1906), 953.

[217] W.E. Vine, Merrill F. Unger and William White, Jr., *Vine's Complete Expository Dictionary of Old and New Testament Words*, eds., Merrill F. Unger and William White, Electronic Version, 1940, 208.

[218] Ibid, 209.

of premeditated murder instead of the general rendition of "killing" by KJV. This idea is not the situation as its many appearances in Number 35 are about the organisation of six cities of refuge for those who killed by accidence. The case is pronounced in verse 11 which states that the metropolises are for those charged with unpremeditated killings. Thus, רָצַח applies to both premeditated murder and unpremeditated manslaughter.

Also, the root word brings to the fore "killing for revenge" (Num. 35:27, 30) and "assassination" (2 Kings 6:32). The connotation is in this way because scholars specifically use the root word for the killing of a man by another man in the entire OT corpus except Proverbs 22:13. Nonetheless, the context of Proverbs is primarily about "the enormity and horror of the deed." White views the general connotation of this verb as "man's crime against man and God's censure of it which is uppermost."[219]

According to Richards, this verb is the only word in the Hebrew language uniquely employed for killing without any similar concept. It is so exceptional that scholars have to explore the word for the development of human thoughts and convictions. Apart from the connotations of manslaughter and premeditated murder, Richards also advances that the verb could imply assassination (2 Kings 6:32) and killing for revenge (Num. 35:27, 30). However, it does not connote killing in warfare. Specifically, scholars use the verb in two contexts, namely, the Ten Commandment (Exod. 20:13; Deut. 5:17) and Numbers 35.[220] According to Richards, the setting of Numbers 35 is a judicial one where Yahweh laid down a standard for the nation of Israel on how to deal with murder upon their occupation in the Promised Land. In this passage alone, the word has its appearances 18 times out of 47 appearances in the OT.

Kaiser, Davids, Bruce, and Brauch, writing on the context of the sixth commandment, posit that this verb is the only Hebrew word which specifically depicts first-degree murder out of seven that generally imply killing. Although an objection has been raised to the number of verbs in Hebrew with this general connotation, the writer agrees with the scholars regarding the idea of first-degree murder. They also posit that רָצַח exclusively comes with the concept of deliberateness and premeditation to death (Psa. 94:6; Prov. 22:13; Isa. 1:21; Jer. 7:9; Hos. 4:2; 6:9). Scholars never employ this verb for killing animals for food (Gen 9:3), self-defence (Ex 22:2), accidental killings (Deut 19:5) or manslaughter (Num. 35:16, 25).[221]

Moreover, Kaiser et al. agree with Richards in term of the 47 appearances of the verb in the OT. Also, the verb refers to the killing of human beings alone, not to animals. Scholars do not use it for killing people in warfare. The scholars are also of the view that the verb is the only Hebrew word with the exclusive connotation of murder-attachment, "It refers to intentional, violent murder (Psa. 94:6; Prov. 22:13;

[219] William White, "רָצַח" in *Theological Wordbook of the Old Testament*, eds., R. Laird Harris, Gleason L. Archer, and Bruce K. Waltke (Chicago: Moody Publishers, 1980), 860.
[220] Richards, *New International Encyclopedia*, 449.
[221] Kaiser, Davids and Bruce, 121.

Isa. 1:21; Jer. 7:9; Hos. 4:2; 6:9). In each instance, the act was conceived in mind first, and the murderer chose the victim deliberately."[222]

Murder is a severe crime in God's sight. It is on this note that the offense is so unique in Numbers 35:31 as a capital offence. No ransom is for the life of the murderer, but the people had to enforce the death penalty. The situations of manslaughter and premeditated murder are both high because human life is so sacred and valuable to God that its termination causes guilt upon the land, demanding for some atonement. The atonement comes in the form of capital punishment for such first-degree murder because God respects His image in every human being. Failure to implement this divine mandate is tantamount to attacking the sanctity and dignity of all humanity.[223]

Given these analyses, people cannot ignore the importance of רָצַח and its uniqueness in bringing the idea of killing to the fore. The reality of this situation remains despite the conflicting figures given by some of the scholars consulted regarding the number of times the verb occurs in the Hebrew Bible.

On the one hand, people apply the verb for the termination of the lives of human beings. The application shows the exceptionality and matchlessness of this verb among the various 11 words considered in the study. It expresses the seriousness of shedding human blood before Yahweh for He made man in His image. On the other hand, premeditated murder is highly offensive to Yahweh. This reality is evident in the exclusive use of the verb specifically within two contexts, of which it does not appear in less than 14 times within the context of Numbers 35:9-34 alone. This situation is profound as the writer of the Pentateuch uses the verb about Yahweh in both settings. Yahweh hates shedding human blood for it is an abuse of the right of the victims and a gross violation of their lives' sacredness.

Finally, it is the position of this writer that רָצַח is applied to both premeditated murder and accidental manslaughter. This reality is not only evident in the analyses of the various scholars' views expressed; it is also glaring in the location exercise of the chosen text. Although one other verb is used specifically for accidental manslaughter by the author or editor of the biblical document in this context, רָצַח is not exclusively used for premeditated murder. For instance, the verb is used for the one guilty of manslaughter on two occasions in verses 25 and 27 and called הָרֹצֵחַ־ אֶת (the one guilty of manslaughter). רָצַח is the same Hebrew word employed for any murderer after he or she might have been tried and convicted in verses 16, 17, 18, 19, and 21.

This reality remains unchanged even when one considers the other verb employed for the one guilty of manslaughter. This rare instance is specifically in verse 15 of the context of the chosen text where the writer or editor of Numbers employs נָכָה (to smite) for the case of manslaughter. In this specific instance, the one guilty

---

[222] Ibid, 121.
[223] Ibid, 122.

of manslaughter is called כָּל־מַכֵּה־נֶפֶשׁ (all of the ones causing to smite a person).
More so, the verb has exclusive use for the termination of human lives. In the Hebrew
Bible, on no account does it apply to the killing of animals.

ii. מַכֵּה־נֶפֶשׁ verb hiphil participle masculine singular construct from נָכָה meaning
he smote, struck, beat, killed unintentionally, slew, exterminated, destroyed in
construct relationship to noun common feminine singular absolute from נֶפֶשׁ meaning
soul, living being, life, self, person, desire, appetite, emotion, and passion; hence, *"He
causing to smite a person."*

    The first appearance of the verbal form of the Hebrew verb נָכָה is in verse
11. The verb means 'to smite (strike)' by a weapon in war (2 Sam. 11:15), 'to smite
deadly' with the intention of killing (1Sam.17:35), and 'to smite,' 'attack' and
'destroy' a group of people (Gen. 32:9-12). It could be used of God, smiting with a
plague or disease such as blindness (Gen.19:11).[224]
    Wilson also advances that the word means 'to smite,' 'strike,' 'hit,' 'beat,'
'slay,' and 'kill.'[225] Its root is used almost 500 times in the Hebrew Bible as employed
for both man (Psa.3:7; Lam. 3:30) and animal (Num. 22:23, 25, 27). The root also
implies being smitten in conscience just like it happened to David when he cut off
Saul's skirt (1 Sam. 22:34). Again, it has the connotation of beating someone just as
Nehemiah did to some Jews for marrying foreign women (Neh.13:25). In most
biblical passages, the verb connotes slaying, killing and striking dead with the specific
meaning of committing intentional (2 Sam. 2:23) or unintentional murder (Deut.
19:4). The theological significance of this verb is God being the subject of the verb
most often. He smites people with blindness (2 Kings 6:18) and plagues (Deut. 28:22,
27-28, 35). He executes judgment due to man in payment for his sin (1 Kings 14:15).
Similarly, death and nature are under His control (Ps.105:33).[226] Richard's analysis of
this verb is in agreement with that of Wilson.[227]
    Given all this, the verb has the connotation of both intentional and
unintentional murder. It is also not discriminatory as the editor of the Pentateuchal
Books used it for the killing of both human beings and animals. Most of the time, the
verb is employed in the Hebrew Bible about Yahweh, depicting His justice in
judgment, faithfulness, and sovereignty.

iii. וַיָּמָת = וְ vav consecutive *and* prefixed to verb qal imperfect 3ms from מוּת
meaning *he died*; hence, *"And he died."*
    The first appearance of the verbal form of מוּת is in verse 16. This Hebrew
verb essentially implies 'to die' either naturally or by other causes. Some of these

---

[224] BDB, 646.
[225] Marvin R. Wilson, "נָכָה" *Theological Wordbook of the Old Testament*, Ed. R. Laird
Harris, Gleason L. Archer, and Bruce K. Waltke (Chicago: Moody Publishers, 1980), 577.
[226] Ibid, 578.
[227] Richards, *New International Encyclopedia*, 448.

could be of man (Gen. 25:8; 36:33-39; 2 Sam. 10:1), and of animals (Lev. 11:39) like cattle (Gen. 33:13), fish (Exod. 7:18), frogs (Exod. 8:9), lion (Eccl. 9:4), worm (Isa. 66:24), or a tree (Job 14:8). Death can be a penalty by a human authority as capital punishment (Gen. 42:20; Exod. 10:28; 21:14; Gen. 44:9; Jos 2:14; Num. 35:12, 30). Death can also take the form of assassination. The editor also employed it in narratives (Gen. 26:11; Exod. 19:12; Judg. 21:5). Death could be inflicted by God (Gen. 3:3; 20:3, 19; 28:35; Exod. 11:5; 12:36; Num. 35: 14:35; Josh. 10:11). Similarly, it could be the death or peril of a nation by divine judgment. Examples of this situation are; namely, Moab (Amos 2:2) and Ephraim (Hos. 13:1; Ezek. 18:31). One could also die prematurely, a consequence of the neglect of wise moral practice (Pro. 5:23; 10:21; 15:10; 19:16; 23:13).[228]

According to Elmer B. Smick, מות means 'to die, kill, and have one executed.' It has the connotation of death either by natural causes or violent means, the latter of which may be a penalty for a crime committed or otherwise. One other thing to be noted with this verb is that it is not limited to the death of human beings which is abundantly employed in this regard.

In Ezekiel, the notion that God has no pleasure in the death of any man is obvious but for them to live (18:32). The standard teaching of the OT for instructional purpose, as presented in Genesis 3:3, is that death is the consequence of man's rebellion against God's instruction. Therefore, the corruption of the human body and the resultant suffering and pain following the Fall of man are visible indicators of death. With all this, the biblical editor presents death as the consequence and punishment of sin which is "an ultimate separation from God." In this sense, the Hebrew philosophy views all human beings as, "ᵇᵉnê mᵊwet" which means "sons or children of death."[229]

Biblical scholars universally employ this root word within the context of the Semitic region for 'dying' and 'death.' The Canaanites used it to depict, "The name of the god of death and the netherworld, Mot."[230] It is occasionally used symbolically, an example of which was employed by Job when referring to the demise of wisdom in chapter 12:2.[231] Similarly, in Ugaritic culture, the god Mot was very prominent, ruling the netherworld, a land of slime and filth. As a result of fighting Baal, the god of fertility, El the leader of the pantheon hated Mot. Baal is frequently mentioned in the OT because the Israelites embraced him as the Canaanite god of fertility and rain, among others. Baal's cult became very popular to the entire inhabitants of the region of the Mediterranean, unlike Mot.[232]

Given the prominence of Baal over Mot, OT emphasises life, not death. As a result, the longevity of life is believed to be a great blessing (Prov. 3:2). By this

---

[228] BDB, 560.

[229] Elmer B. Smick, "מות" in Theological Wordbook of the Old Testament, eds. R. Laird Harris, Gleason L. Archer, and Bruce K. Waltke (Chicago: Moody Publishers, 1980), 497.

[230] Ibid.

[231] Ibid, 496.

[232] Ibid.

perception, there came up the teaching of the OT on capital punishment for intentional murder. Relating to this is God's order to execute those committed to abominable practices so that the Israelites may not learn their traditions, an example of which is a human sacrifice to demons.[233]

From this preceding, this Hebrew word primarily implies 'to die,' or 'to kill.' It is employed not only for human beings but for other things alike. As analysed, it is an effect of sin and a general term that brings the idea of killing to the fore within the context of the Semitic people, whether intentional or unintentional.

iv. הָרַג = Verb *qal* perfect 3ms from הָרַג meaning *he destroyed, killed, murdered, and slew;* hence, *"He destroyed."*

This Hebrew word translates as follows: 'to destroy,' 'kill,' 'murder,' or 'slay.' According to BDB, the verb has certain cognate meanings in the Aramaic language; namely, 'to fall into war,' 'conflict,' 'disorder, and 'slaughter.' In *Qal* pf.3ms, OT writers use the verb for killing or slaying human beings with the connotation of a hard kind of violence.[234] The ruthless killing of the Jews is an example, masterminded by Haman their enemy (Esther 3:13 and 7:4). The slaughter of the enemy of the Jews for the dual purposes of defence and revenge in Esther 8:11 is another. One other instance is the great slaughter of the Midianites after the battle (Num. 31:7-8, 17). It is also used of God executing judgment by slaying the offenders severely (Gen. 20:4; Exod. 4:23).[235]

According to Vine, Unger, and White, Jr., this word, in its verbal and noun forms, is a common term in modern Hebrew; depicting the idea of 'killing,' or 'slaughter.' Its verb occurs 170 times in the Hebrew Bible to connote termination of the life of both animals and human beings. Fundamentally, הָרַג scarcely suggests intentional killing or murder. Generally, biblical writers used it for the killing of animals and the ruthless violence of humankind against one's fellow being.[236]

Moreover, the verb is infrequently used of "judicial killing" by a human at the command of God (Exod. 32:27; Num. 25:5). It is used of the killing of animals (Num. 22:29) such as lions and serpents (2 Kings 17:25; Job 20:16). The verb also carries the nuances of destruction and ruin (Job 5:2; Prov. 7:26).[237] Similarly, Vine et al. are also in support of the idea that the verb often implies wholesale slaughter in and after the battle (Num. 31:7-8; Josh. 8:24; 2 Sam10:18) and that the writers scarcely used it for the killing of a man at God's instance. Generally, the verb means violent "killing" and destruction.[238]

Some of the ideas of Harold G. Stigers is slightly different from those of Vine et al. הָרַג is a Hebrew verb used 172 times in the entire OT corpus with a usual

---

[233] Ibid.
[234] BDB, 247.
[235] Ibid.
[236] Vine, Unger, and White, Jr., 208.
[237] BDB, 247.
[238] Vine, Unger, and White, Jr., 208.

rendition of 'to slay.' Its root connotes the ideas of "murder and judicial execution" and the killing of beasts with its first use in the crime of Cain (Gen. 4:8). Again, the verb was used in the judicial order of executing those who murdered Ishbosheth (2 Sam. 4:11-12). The legal execution connotation of הָרַג is on the basis that failure to atone for the blood of the victim by shedding the blood of the murderer implies that the people consented to the same crime. The consent would break God's covenant with them. It is also a denial of God's image in the life of the victim. One exemption to judicial killing is the killing of a housebreaker by the owner of the house. This exemption is on the ground that the robber would not stop at anything to achieve his intention.[239]

Biblical laws have certain parallels on the issue of murder in the literature of Mesopotamia. Atonement for the loss of the life of a man could be through payment of a fine. Imposition of the death penalty was only in exceptional cases. הָרַג is rarely used for the killing of animals but usually for that of men. Biblical writers also used the verb for the gruesome slaughter in war and conspiracy. However, it is never used for the "killing of sacrificial animals" and very rarely for the "killing of animals for food." Generally, the verb has the connotation of the gruesome killing of men whether there is justification or not.[240]

According to Richards, this verb connotes the idea of "a fact of life." The expression is because of the idea of the brutal killing of a human being by another it depicts. In addition to two instances cited by Stigers, the verb is also used in some other biblical occasions such as the killing of an Egyptian taskmaster by Moses (Exod. 2:14), of the entire members of a priestly family by King Saul (1 Sam. 22:21), and of the prophets of Baal at Elijah's request (1 Kings 19:1). All these are in addition to the killing of the Jews' enemies by the Jews in the day of Queen Esther (Esther 9:6, 10, 12). The same word is employed in the killing of Yahweh's prophets by Jezebel (1 Kings 18:13) and of the killing of all of the firstborn of the Egyptians while Pharaoh was holding on to his pride against God's command (Exod. 13:15). Richards agrees with Stigers by asserting that the verb is used for both justified and unjustified killings and of the judgments of God.[241] The theological implication of הָרַג is the divine call for accountability as God makes each man a participant in "the principle of social responsibility."[242]

Some scholars perceive this call to be essential to the idea of capital punishment for some reasons. First, capital punishment is by affirming God's image in man through the placement of the equivalent value on it. Second, it is on the basis that God Himself has set a penalty for murdering and mandated the society to effect it whenever the need arises. Third, failure on the part of the community to carry it out

---

[239] Harold G. Stigers, "הָרַג" *Theological Wordbook of the Old Testament*, eds., R. Laird Harris, Gleason L. Archer, and Bruce K. Waltke (Chicago: Moody Publishers, 1980), 222.

[240] Ibid.

[241] Richards, *New International Encyclopedia*, 448.

[242] Ibid, 449.

means an endorsement of such an awful act and a decline of the human worth within the particular context or society.[243]

From this, this writer can deduce that הָרַג basically means 'to destroy' or 'ruin.' It is a large scale killing with the connotation of overwhelming brutality. It is used not only for the gruesome killing of human beings but for the massive killing of animals also. Again, it is a fact that the vocabulary is used both for justified and unjustified forms of killing. Similarly, the Bible employs the verb for God's judgment as a means to demand accountability from man. In the case of the judicial order of execution which brings the idea of capital punishment to the fore, payment of a fine is alien to the Hebrew worldview. The life of the offender had to go for that of the victim before the people could meet the condition for the atonement of the land. Finally, הָרַג does not suggest a distinction between premeditated murder and accidental killing or killing in error.

v. זָבַח = Verb *qal* perfect 3ms from זָבַח meaning *he slaughtered* and *sacrificed;* hence, "*He slaughtered.*"

זָבַח basically means 'to slaughter for sacrifice.' It has certain other nuances in *Qal perfect* apart from this general connotation. The first is the sacrifice of animals (I Kings 8:62; Num. 22:40) and humankind (Ezek. 16:20; Hos. 13:2).[244] In the absolute state, the verb is used of deity (Lev. 17:7; Deut. 32:17) and other gods with the nuance of prostitution (Exod. 34:15). Many of the sacrifices of this kind are, however, about the LORD [Exod. 3:18 (JE); Lev. 17:5 (H); 19:5 (H); 22:29 (H)]. Similarly, the word also has a general connotation of 'sacrifice for eating' (1 Sam. 28:24; Ezek. 34:3; 2 Chron. 18:2). It is also employed for 'slaughter in divine judgment' (1 Kings 13:2; 2 Kings 23:20; Ezek. 39:17-19). In *Piel perfect*, the verb implies an abundance of sacrifices such as the type King Solomon offered to Yahweh (1 Kings 8:5; 2 Chron. 5:6) and that of King Hezekiah (2 Chron. 30:22). It is also used of sacrifices made to other gods (2 Chron. 28:23) or sacrifice made in unauthorised places (1 Kings 3:2-3).[245]

Similarly, Herbert Wolf agrees with BDB in term of the general connotation of זָבַח that the verb is used mainly for the killing of animal sacrifices. It appears in *Qal* stem mostly except for 19 times in *Piel* with the idea of sacrifices to idols in forbidden areas like high places (2 Kings 12:3; Hos.11:2). Similarly, the *Piel* of this verb implies lawful sacrifices of King Solomon (1 Kings 8:5; 2 Chron. 5:6) or that of King Hezekiah (2 Chron. 30:22-27).[246]

In this case, the biblical writer used זָבַח for killing for cultic purposes. It could be a sacrifice of animals to Yahweh. It could also be that of human beings to

---

[243] Ibid.

[244] BDB, 256.

[245] Ibid, 256-57.

[246] Herbert Wolf, "זָבַח" in *Theological Wordbook of the Old Testament*, eds., R. Laird Harris, Gleason L. Archer, and Bruce K. Waltke (Chicago: Moody Publishers, 1980), 233.

idols, a detestable sacrifice to God and foreign to the term of the covenant which Yahweh delivered to His people. Thus, the usage of זֶבַח is not discriminatory; it is used both for lawful sacrifices and forbidden types of human beings to the gods and for animal sacrifices in forbidden places.

vi. חָלַל = Verb *qal* perfect 3ms from חָלַל meaning *he bored*, and *pierced*; hence, "He *bored*."

The general meaning of this verb is "to bore or pierce." The people and situations pierced the heart of the psalmist within him (לִבִּי חָלַל בְּקִרְבִּי) in Psalm 109:22. This case implies that David's heart was wounded. This action can be carried out by the sword (Ezek. 32:26). In Isaiah 53:5, the suffering servant was pierced because of the people's transgressions.[247] The situation here figuratively suggests the brutal killing of the suffering servant.

Similarly, Donald J. Wiseman posits that this root basically means "to wound (fatally), bore through, and pierce." It occurs not less than 96 times altogether with its derivatives. חָלַל itself is employed eight different times in the OT especially in poetry. It usually carries the connotation of fatality in the wounding of individuals. However, the use of this verb is not limited to human beings as the verb refers to the escaping serpent, the expression that has its parallel is the action of the Lord in "smiting Rahab to death" (Isa. 51:9; Job 26:13).[248]

By implication, חָלַל essentially means to wound to the point of death. More so, biblical writers used the word for both humankind and animals. In this writer's view, חָלַל is one of the Hebrew verbs with the idea of killing for certain reasons. The verb brings the idea of "to kill" to the fore because of the agency by which the action is usually carried out. Sometimes, the action is performed using the sword or other dangerous weapons. Similarly, the connotation of "to bore" or "pierce" carries the nuance of killing for the blood of the victim is shed on the ground most of the time. Again, the writer observes that the possibility of nurturing an intention to take the life of the object of the verb or the victim by the subject of the verb is evident.

vii. טָבַח = Verb *qal* perfect 3ms from טָבַח meaning *he slaughtered, butchered,* and *slew;* hence, "*He slaughtered.*"

The general connotation of this verb is "to slaughter, butcher, slay." Specifically, it brings the idea of slaughtering animals for food (Exod. 21:37). A figure of this is the idea of "Wisdom's preparing her table" (Prov. 9:2), and a poetic instance is that of "to slay, kill ruthlessly" especially in judgment (Ezek. 21:15).[249] Also, Ralph H. Alexander asserts that this word has a basic meaning of deliberate

---

[247] BDB, 319.

[248] Donald J. Wiseman, "חָלַל " *Theological Wordbook of the Old Testament,* Ed. R. Laird Harris, Gleason L. Archer, and Bruce K. Waltke (Chicago: Moody Publishers, 1980), 288.

[249] BDB, 370.

butchering of animals for food. Its root is mainly used to portray the idea of God's judgment, especially against Israel and Babylon. Similarly, Ralph H. Alexander advances that the special use of מָבַח is in Proverbs 9:2.[250] Therefore, מָבַח is used for the killing of both human beings and animals.

viii. כָּרַת = Verb *qal* perfect 3ms from כָּרַת meaning *he cut off, cut down, rooted out, eliminated, removed, excommunicated,* and *destroyed;* hence, *"He cut off."*

כָּרַת comes with the idea of cutting off or cutting down. It could be cutting off of things (Lev. 22:24; Num.13:23) such as trees (Deut. 19:5; Isa. 37:24) or persons (Jer. 11:19; 50:16). It also implies hewing timber (Isa. 14:8) and cutting or making a covenant (Jer. 34:18).[251] According to Earl S. Kalland, כָּרַת implies cutting off a part of one's body such as the head or hand. The word also connotes cutting down of trees and idols. Again, it implies cutting out, eliminating, killing, and cutting or making a covenant.[252] Ellis's view is similar to that of BDB and Kalland.[253]

Furthermore, the word has related words in the Akkadian verb called *karātu* which means "to cut off" and the verbal adjective named *Kartu* which implies "to cut up." Again, the verbal equivalence of this verb in Tigre implies "to bring to an end." In addition to the ideas of "to cut off" (Exod.5:20; 1 Sam.5:4) and "to cut down" (1 Kings 5:20; Isa. 14:8), the verb also has allegorical meaning of "to root out, eliminate, remove, excommunicate or destroy violently either by man or nature." Nonetheless, the most significant use of this word is to cut or make a covenant (Gen. 15:18).[254]

By implication, biblical writers used the verb for both human beings and material objects like trees. It depicts the idea of cutting off or cutting down which metaphorically connotes the sense of killing or elimination of persons or material things. It also describes the design of cutting of covenant.

ix. קָטַל = Verb *qal* perfect 3ms from קָטַל meaning *"he slew* and *killed;* hence, *"He slew."*

Brown et al. posit that the Hebrew word means "to slay' (Job 13:15; Psa. 139:19).[255] Leonard J. Coppes[256] and William L. Holladay[257] are also in support of this idea. According to Ellis, the verb also has the connotation of 'to kill.' [258]

---

[250] Ralph H. Alexander, "מָבַח " in *Theological Wordbook of the Old Testament,* eds., R. Laird Harris, Gleason L. Archer, and Bruce K. Waltke (Chicago: Moody Publishers, 1980), 341.

[251] BDB, 503.

[252] Earl S. Kalland, "כָּרַת " in *Theological Wordbook of the Old Testament,* eds., R. Laird Harris, Gleason L. Archer, and Bruce K. Waltke (Chicago: Moody Publishers, 1980), 456.

[253] Ellis, 375.

[254] Kalland, 457.

[255] BDB, 881.

[256] Leonard J. Coppes, " קָטַל " in *Theological Wordbook of the Old Testament,* eds., R. Laird Harris, Gleason L. Archer, and Bruce K. Waltke (Chicago: Moody Publishers, 1980), 795.

[257] William L. Holladay, *A Concise Hebrew and Aramaic Lexicon of the Old Testament: Based upon the Lexical Work of Ludwig Koehler and Walter Baumgartner* (Leiden: Brill, 2000), 317.

x. שָׁחַט = Verb *qal* perfect 3ms from שָׁחַט meaning "*he slaughtered, slew, and killed;*" hence, "*He slaughtered.*"

This Hebrew verb generally translates as "to slaughter."[259] According to BDB, it could be the slaughter of an animal for food (1 Sam. 14:32, 34) or that of persons (1 Kings 18:40). According to Vine, Unger and White, Jr., the word has its occurrence not less than 80 times in the Hebrew Bible with its first appearance in Genesis 22:10: "And Abraham ... took the knife to slay his son." שָׁחַט is believed to be a common word in both ancient and modern Hebrew as well as in ancient Ugaritic. By implication, the word also can be interpreted as "to slay." The interpretation becomes necessary because "slaying" is the most frequent use of the word about sacrifice as it appears 51 times.

The verb applies to the killing of both human beings and animals. The expressions "slaying" and "killing" of people (Judg. 12:6; 1 Kings 18:40; 2 Kings 10:7, 14) are applicable to human life on one hand while that of 'slaughtering' is for animals for food (I Sam. 14:32, 34; Isa. 22:13). Similarly, the expression of the verb as "slaying" by the biblical writer of the Book of Numbers 14:16 is about God.[260]

Moreover, the emphasis of this verb is beating the victim for sacrifice.[261] According to Victor P. Hamilton, the Hebrew word appears 84 times in the OT, all of which are in *qal* stem with the exceptions of the *Niphal* in Leviticus 6:25 and Numbers 11:22. שָׁחַט primarily implies "to kill," especially for ritual purposes. It also applies to the killing of human beings in a few instances. However, it may also be used for the killing of animals in a non-sacrificial way (Gen. 37:31). The use of this word in the OT has five exceptions, where it implies "'beaten/hammered out' gold" (I Kings 10:16, 17; 2 Chron. 9:15, 16). שָׁחַט is only presented in Jeremiah 9:8 symbolically, using the tongue as the lethal weapon. There is only one occurrence in two contexts where the Pentateuchal writer employed this verb about the killing of a man. In other words, שָׁחַט is used explicitly for ritual purposes, the occurrence of whose root finds its usage most in the book of Leviticus 35 times.

The Greek equivalent root for this Hebrew verb in the LXX is *sphazœ*. John the beloved who wrote the biblical Book of Revelation employed the equivalent root four times, depicting Christ as the "'slain' lamb" (Rev. 5:6, 9, 12; 13:8) whose root also appears in Psalm 44:22.[262] Richards also shares the idea of slaughtering with Hamilton in his translation.[263] On this basis, this writer views the basic renderings of this verb to be "to slaughter, slay, kill." שָׁחַט is employed for the slaughtering, slaying or killing of both human beings and animals. These renderings are unlike רָצַח which

---

[258] Ellis, 379.

[259] BDB, 1006.

[260] Vine, Unger & White, Jr., 207.

[261] Alexander, 341.

[262] Victor P. Hamilton, "שָׁחַט" in *Theological Wordbook of the Old Testament*, eds., R. Laird Harris, Gleason L. Archer, and Bruce K. Waltke (Chicago: Moody Publishers, 1980), 915.

[263] Richards, *New International Encyclopedia*, 448.

specifically relate to the killing of human beings in both deliberate and unintentional capacities.

xi. שָׁמַד = Verb *qal* perfect 3ms from שָׁמַד meaning *he exterminateed, destroyed, and annihilated;* hence, *"He exterminated."*

This verb connotes the idea of "to be exterminated or destroyed" in its *Niphal* stem (Isa.48:19). It also implies "to be annihilated or exterminated" (2 Sam. 21:5) when relating to human beings either as the subject or object of the verb.[264] Holladay agrees with BDB by translating שָׁמַד in *Niphal* as "be exterminated" referring to persons (Gen. 34:30) and names (Isa. 48:19). It is also translated as "be made useless" of a plan (Jer. 48:8) and high places (Hos. 10:8).[265] By implication, שָׁמַד is used for both humankind and animals with the connotation of killing with utter destruction.

From all this, the analyses have brought to the foreground two important disclosures about the OT people. On the one hand, the quantum of the Hebrew vocabularies analysed in this lexical analysis is enough reason to declare that killing was a common phenomenon among the covenant people of Israel. This idea takes various derivatives like murdering, slaying, slaughtering, destroying, boring, and piercing, among others of this kind. It came in the form of a crime many times while it had divine approval sometimes in the case of judicial killing after necessary trials.

On the other hand, out of these 11 Hebrew verbs, רָצַח has greater intensity. The claim is evident in its exclusive use for the killing of human beings or shedding of human blood alone either with or without presentiment to commit a crime. The rest of the verbs can relate to both human and animal, but this particular one does not. Again, the contexts where biblical writers employ the verb in the Hebrew Bible are not many. This situation is unique, unlike others. Besides, everywhere the verb appears within the few contexts, it is about God. Both the context of Exodus and Numbers 35:9-34 are prohibitions from Yahweh against killing or indiscriminate termination of human life. Similarly, none of the other verbs connotes the idea of premeditated murder other than רָצַח.

Therefore, the choice of the context of Numbers 35:9-34 for this study on the concept of the sanctity of human life is needful. This writer made this claim because of the higher number of times רָצַח appears in the chosen text than in the other context of the Hebrew Bible. Again, the setting is on the imperative because murder is a crime not only directly against the victim but also directly against the Creator, the Giver of life.

5. Structural Analysis of the Chosen Text

The outline for the syntactical analysis of the chosen text has its foundation on the following: the general understanding of the growth and development of the Pentateuch as discussed, and the authorship and dating of the Book of Numbers

---

[264] BDB, 1029.
[265] Holladay, 375.

analysed. Similarly, the following are a guide: analyses of the various Hebrew words related to the sanctity of human life, the location of the passage conducted (as an appendix), and the textual analysis of the chosen text carried out with the aid of CA.

Thus, the working outline for the syntactical analysis of Numbers 35:9-34 follows this pattern:

I. Law concerning Cities of Refuge (35:9-15)
II. Law concerning Premeditated Murder and Blood Revenge (35:16-21)
III. Law concerning Accidental Manslaughter and Cities of Refuge (35:22-28)
IV. Law Concerning Bloodshed and Atonement (35:29-34)

6. Syntactical Analysis of Numbers 35:9-34

The concern of this section considers the syntax and grammar of the chosen text following the outline stated above. This writer discusses the interrelatedness among the various components of the passage; namely, verbs, nouns, phrases, clauses, and sentences. The writer also examines the function of each of these language elements to bring out the meaning of the passage grammatically. The understanding of the world of the author of the Book of Numbers, literary and genre, and textual analysis of the chosen text also reflect on this analysis.

While the new generation of Israel was on the plains of Moab by the Jordan River, Yahweh gave the people all the contents of Numbers 34-36 through Moses as instructions to follow upon their occupation of the Promised Land in all of their generations (35:1, 29; 36:13). Oslo regards this as: "Law as Promise: Divine Commands in Anticipation of Residence in the Promised Land" (Num. 34-36). The law concerning cities of refuge is prominent among these regulations (35:9-15). In this law, the people were instructed to appoint six cities of refuge in the land. Richards regards this provision a unique feature in the general legal system of the OT.[266] According to Warren W. Wiersbe, three of these cities were to be on the east of the Jordan while the rest three were to be on the west within the territory of the land of Canaan.[267] Certain definitive elements are of note in this law.

Verse 9 וַיְדַבֵּר יְהוָה אֶל־מֹשֶׁה לֵּאמֹר:

Verse 9: Then Yahweh commanded Moses saying,

The vav consecutive וְ prefixed to the verb דבר in וַיְדַבֵּר performs two main functions in this verse. It inverses the action of the verb דבר from being imperfect ("Then he will speak") to a perfect verb ("Then he spoke").[268] The verb has completed its action already. In line with this, the preceding pericope (Num. 35:1-8) is also linked together with the pericope of the chosen text for this study (Num. 35:9-

[266] Lawrence O. Richards, "Expectation: Numbers 26-36 - Cities of Refuge," *The Teacher's Commentary*. Electronic Database (Wheaton, Illinois: Victor Books [A Division of Scripture Press Publications Inc.], 1987), par. 1.
[267] Warren W. Wiersbe, "The Cities of the Land (35)," *The Bible Exposition Commentary/Pentateuch*, Electronic Database (Colorado Springs: Cook Communications Ministries, 2001), par. 2.
[268] Ellis, 162-65.

34). This action is done using the same vav consecutive. The preceding pericope concerns Yahweh's instruction to Moses to command the Israelites to appoint 48 towns for the Levites to live in with all the pasturelands that surround the towns (35:1-8). The people must appoint six of these towns as "cities of refuge" where whoever killed someone may run to (verse 6).

At this juncture, Yahweh wanted to expand or build on what He had said earlier in the preceding pericope. This situation is another indication of the coordinating role of this prefixed vav וֹ. Also, what Yahweh was about to say was on the imperative, demanding the obedience of His covenant people. The imperativeness is evident in the action of the verb whose subject is Yahweh as evident in the clause: וַיְדַבֵּר יְהוָה אֶל־מֹשֶׁה (Then Yahweh commanded Moses). The verb וַיְדַבֵּר is in *piel* imperfect. Thus, its action is intensive, and one major way of expressing the intensification is to render the verb as a language of command or order from Yahweh to Moses. This mindset is the basis of Matthew Henry's analysis of the chosen text.[269] In addition to this, the personality of the subject of the verb (Yahweh) ideally makes whatever that comes from Him to Moses explicitly an order.

Verse 10 דַּבֵּר אֶל־בְּנֵי יִשְׂרָאֵל וְאָמַרְתָּ אֲלֵהֶם כִּי אַתֶּם עֹבְרִים אֶת־הַיַּרְדֵּן אַרְצָה כְּנָעַן:

Verse 10: "Command the children of Israel and say to them: 'when you pass from the Jordan to the land of Canaan,

The same sense of imperativeness continues in verse 10 with the phrase: דַּבֵּר אֶל־בְּנֵי יִשְׂרָאֵל (Command the children of Israel). In this phrase, the *piel* imperative of the verb דַּבֵּר also combines the attribute of intensification to its original sense of order. Again, the children of Israel אֶל־בְּנֵי יִשְׂרָאֵל who were the covenant people of Yahweh were the recipients of the command that was expected to be given by Moses. More so, אֶת־הַיַּרְדֵּן (the Jordan) is the direct object of the sentence, indicating the location of the people where Yahweh was speaking to them. The participle plural absolute עֹבְרִים (passing from one side to the other) is indirectly in construct relationship to אֶת־הַיַּרְדֵּן (the Jordan). In other words, the command was given at the Jordan (on the plain of Moab) while the content of the instruction was expected to be carried out by the people after they might have crossed to the other side of the Jordan called אַרְצָה כְּנָעַן (the land of Canaan).

Therefore, the command has two elements with an implication. The first element was on the part of Moses to listen to what Yahweh commanded him to do while the other was for the people of Israel to obey the order. The implication of this is that if Moses failed to instruct the people and the people also failed to adhere strictly to the instruction given by Moses, there would be a great consequence.

---

[269] Matthew Henry, "Num. 35:9-35 – The Cities of Refuge. (B.C. 1452.)," *Matthew Henry's Commentary on the Whole Bible*, Electronic Database (Biblesoft, Inc., 2006), par. 2.

Verse11 וְהִקְרִיתֶם לָכֶם עָרִים עָרֵי מִקְלָט תִּהְיֶינָה לָכֶם וְנָס שָׁמָּה רֹצֵחַ
מַכֵּה־נֶפֶשׁ בִּשְׁגָגָה:

Verse 11: you will ordain for yourselves towns which will become cities of refuge for you; any manslayer who has smitten a person in error may flee there.

The content of Yahweh's instruction to Moses which the Israelites were to obey is the basis of verse 11 following. First, the verb וְהִקְרִיתֶם in *hiphil* stem which indicates a causative action in an active voice implies *"and you will cause to ordain."* The object of the verb is the combination of two nouns which stand in construct relationship to each other מִקְלָט (refuge) עָרֵי (cities of) meaning עָרֵי מִקְלָט ("cities of refuge"). Thus, the people were to take the step of ordaining the cities volitionally, not by accident.

The cities were to be within the land allocated to the tribe of Levi. According to John F. Walvoord, Roy B. Zuck, Kenneth L. Barker, Eugene H. Merrill, and Stanley T. Toussaint, Yahweh apportioned 48 towns to the tribe of Levi. Out of these, the Israelites were to make six of them as cities of refuge to which those who committed "accidental homicide" could flee. Yahweh expected His people to fairly assign the Levitical tribal portion from the remaining tribal parts of Israel.[270] Additionally, Warren W. Wiersbe advances that the scattering of the Levites by Yahweh, among the rest of the Israelite tribes, was for a vital reason. Yahweh apportioned this so that the Levites could serve their people in the things of God. One significant aspect of service of this kind is the teaching of God's law (Josh.21). Hence, the Levites were the teachers of the Law of which the aspect of the cities of refuge was prominent.[271]

Similarly, further explanation was made to express the purpose that the cities were to serve. The goal is the next provision of the order which takes certain forms in ancient Israel. First, the towns were for those who killed unintentionally. This understanding is evident in the subordinate clause of verse 11: מַכֵּה־נֶפֶשׁ בִּשְׁגָגָה וְנָס שָׁמָּה רֹצֵחַ (Any manslayer who has smitten a person in error may flee there). The subordinate clause of verse 15 also makes the same expression: נֶפֶשׁ־בִּשְׁגָגָה לָנוּס שָׁמָּה כָּל־מַכֵּה ("Anyone that smites a person unintentionally may flee there"). The repetition is for emphasis.

Two action words are essential to consider in this provision. מַכֵּה־נֶפֶשׁ (*"He causing to smite a person*) expresses the first action word. It is the verbal participle of נָכָה ("he smote or killed") in the *hiphil* stem ("he causing to smite or kill") and in construct relationship to נֶפֶשׁ (a person or soul). Thus, the cities of refuge are for those whose actions caused the death of their fellow human beings. Nonetheless, the

[270] John F. Walvoord, Roy B. Zuck, Kenneth L. Barker, Eugene H. Merrill and Stanley D. Toussaint, eds., *Bible Knowledge Commentary/Old Testament*. Electronic Database (Colorado Springs: Cook Communications Ministries, 2000), par. 1.

[271] Wiersbe, par. 1.

prepositional phrase בִּשְׁגָגָה (in error) qualifies the kind of killers for which Yahweh designated the cities; these killers are those who committed the crime unpremeditatedly.

C.F. Keil and F. Delitzsch regard מַכֵּה־נֶפֶשׁ as, "unpremeditated manslayer." Addition of the prepositional phrase בִּשְׁגָגָה (in a sin of error) justifies this connotation. This provision was in fulfilment of Yahweh's promise to His people that He would provide a place where those who killed unintentionally would flee (Exod. 21:13). The provision is expanded in Deuteronomy 19:1-13.[272]

The other word is the verb וְנָס which implies ("and he may flee or escape"). This verb נוּס is in *qal* perfect 3ms prefixed by *vav* consecutive which further brings the purpose of the cities to the foreground. The cities were to harbour or protect those who killed in error if they could take a conscious step of fleeing to any of the cities nearest to them. Given this, the cities are for those who killed unintentionally (called "unpremeditated manslayer" by this writer).

Moreover, Tokunboh Adeyemo advances that the location of the cities of refuge within the territory of the 48 towns given to the Levites by inheritance (Num.35:1-8) presupposes that the Levites were in charge of the enforcement of the law in the land. In other words, they were to protect the sanctity of the judicial life of the people. According to Adeyemo, these cities had the exclusive function of providing refuge for the Israelites and strangers (Num. 35:13-15). They were for those accused of murder which legislatively carried death sentence as punishment. Execution of this capital punishment was given to two entities (Num. 35:16-21). The redeemer of blood is one, a close relation to the victim by blood. He has the right to demand blood revenge which this writer calls an act of seeking for redress. The redeemer of blood has to request this redress from the assembly which acted among the people like today's court of law. More so, the provision was to cover human errors since some killings could be unintentional and people could also be accused falsely (Num. 35:11-12). Therefore, the cities of refuge were to serve as custody for the accused until they appear before the assembly for trial.[273]

Verse 12 וְהָיוּ לָכֶם הֶעָרִים לְמִקְלָט מִגֹּאֵל וְלֹא יָמוּת הָרֹצֵחַ עַד־עָמְדוֹ לִפְנֵי הָעֵדָה לַמִּשְׁפָּט:

Verse 12: They will be a refuge from the redeemer of blood for you, and he will not execute the killer as far as he stays in any of the cities until he appears before the assembly for judgment.

The second part of the purpose of the cities of refuge is ultimate. The provision of the towns in the law was for the preservation of human lives. The reality

---

[272] C.F. Keil and F. Delitzsch, "Numbers 35:9-11," *Commentary on the Old Testament*, Electronic Database, Trans. James Martin (Peabody: Hendrickson Publishers, Inc., 1996), par. 1.

[273] Tokunboh Adeyemo, ed., "Numbers 35:9-34 Cities of Refuge," *Africa Bible Commentary (ABC Commentary); A One-Volume Commentary written by 70 African Scholars* (Nairobi: WordAlive Publishers, 2006), 208.

is evident in verses 12 to15. The qal participial form of the verb גָּאַל ("he redeemed or delivered") מִגֹּאֵל prefixed by מִן preposition ("from" or "out of") implying "from a redeemer" brings another undertone to the nature of the purpose of the cities of refuge. According to CA, as expressed and analysed in the textual analysis of verse 12, the author or editor of the Book of Numbers had "the redeemer of blood" in mind. The verb qal infinitive construct עַד־עָמְדוֹ from עָמַד ("he stood or stayed") has to be considered to bring the idea to the fore. This verb is in construct relationship to עַד ("as far as, while, or during") and with the initial vav consecutive it implies, "As far as he stays or remains." The subject of this verb is הָרֹצֵחַ verb qal participle singular absolute prefixed by definite article meaning "the killer." Thus, as far as the one who killed in error stayed or remained in the city of his or her refuge, the redeemer of blood would not execute the person.

This writer translated גֹּאֵל הַדָּם as a "Redeemer of blood" against "Avenger of blood" which is the most popular translation among many of the scholars consulted such as Robert Jamieson, Andrew Robert Fausset, and David Brown.[274] The basis for this uniqueness is because גֹּאֵל was a popular extant concept in ancient Israel translated as "Kinsman-Redeemer." The kinsman-redeemer had specific roles to play to his deceased kinsman in ancient Israel. To further this tradition, therefore, the writer had to take to this interpretation as employed in this paper.

The function of the negative particle וְלֹא ("not") prefixed by vav consecutive ("and") meaning "and not" in the statutory responsibility of the redeemer of blood is great here. The redeemer of blood will not be able to take vengeance over the killer with the condition that the killer stayed in the city of his or her refuge. This expression is also evident in the main clause: וְהָיוּ לָכֶם הֶעָרִים לְמִקְלָט מִגֹּאֵל ("And the cities will be a refuge from the redeemer of blood for you) coupled with the subordinate clause: וְלֹא יָמוּת הָרֹצֵחַ עַד־עָמְדוֹ ("And as far as the killer stays").

In this regard, John Marsh presents staying in the city of refuge as a right to seek for asylum by a manslayer which the scholar regarded as a common institution in human history. According to Marsh, the custom began from Greco-Roman period and continued down the Middle Ages. In the OT times, the asylum was not offered to just any killer but only to those who killed accidentally. Whenever the assembly granted the right, it continues until the killer stands before the assembly for judgment.[275] This situation is expressed thus: הָרֹצֵחַ עַד־עָמְדוֹ לִפְנֵי הָעֵדָה לַמִּשְׁפָּט (Until he [the manslayer] appears before the assembly for judgment). הָרֹצֵחַ is rendered

---

[274] Robert Jamieson, Andrew Robert Fausset, and David Brown, "Num. 35:11," *Jamieson, Fausset, and Brown Commentary*, Electronic Database (Grand Rapids, Michigan: William B. Eerdmans Publishing Company, 2006), par. 1.

[275] John Marsh and Albert George Butzer, "Exegesis of Numbers 35:9-34," *in The Interpreter's Bible*, eds., George Arthur Buttrick, Walter Russell Bowie, Paul Scherer, John Knox, Samuel Terrien, and Nolan B. Harmon (Nashville: Abingdon Press, 1953), 303.

"manslayer" by this writer, instead of "murderer," because the accused remains not guilty of murder until the trial proves otherwise.

Furthermore, one more thing is of note in this verse and the rest of the chosen text. The verb רָצַח is employed for one who killed in error as stated in its lexical analysis. Scholars also use the same verb for those who killed intentionally but not for the killing of any other things like animals. The fact shows the uniqueness of this Hebrew word not only in this passage but in the entire Hebrew Scripture. Therefore, the cities were for the ultimate purpose of preserving the life of the manslayer from the redeemer of blood pending the time the former would stand a trial before the assembly.

Verse 13 וְהֶעָרִים אֲשֶׁר תִּתֵּנוּ שֵׁשׁ־עָרֵי מִקְלָט תִּהְיֶינָה לָכֶם:

Verse 13: And the towns which you will give will be for you six cities of refuge.

Verse 13 adds another dimension or colouration to this command. It explicitly states the number of cities. The expression of the noun שֵׁשׁ־עָרֵי ("six cities of ") standing in construct relationship to מִקְלָט ("refuge") connotes that these cities must be six in number. Given the lexical analysis of מִקְלָט, the cities of refuge were six for easy accessibility and proximity to the killers from any part of the land.

Each of these cities is unique in meaning. They are all a type of Christ Jesus, the Ultimate Redeemer whose blood would redeem all sinners who care to run to Him for safety from sin and the imminent judgment of God. According to R.S. Eaton, בֶּצֶר (Bezer) was a plain country belonging to the Reubenites. It connotes the idea of "a stronghold, or fortified place." This name pointed any sinner (manslayer in this case) towards Christ Jesus as their refuge and defence from their enemy (redeemer of blood also in this context). A refuge of this kind is God's provision for sin, a common problem to humankind. Second, רָאמֹת (Ramoth) was of the Gadites in Gilead which implies "high, or exalted." The city was a type of Christ as the walls raised around any sinner that runs to Him (manslayer in this case) for safety. Third, גּוֹלָן (Golan) was a town in Bashan of the Manassites and implies "joy, or revelation." The joy of this kind is argued to be the reality that happens to the mind of whoever had escaped the wages of sin in Christ Jesus.[276]

Fourth, קֶדֶשׁ (Kedesh) was in Galilee of Mount Naphtali with a unique meaning of "holy or set apart." Kedesh is the name that symbolises all the cities of refuge for no redeemer of blood dared to enter any in search of the one accused of manslaughter since they were holy. This symbolism found fulfilment in Christ Jesus whom the scholar regards as "a sanctified defence to His people." Fifth, שְׁכֶם (Shechem) was located in Mount Ephraim and it implies "a shoulder, expressive of power and readiness to bear burdens, and used about magisterial and regal authority."

---

[276] R.S. Eaton, "Num. 35:9-34 (The Cities of Refuge)," *The Biblical Illustrator: Old Testament Volumes*, Electronic Database, ed., Joseph S. Exell (Ages Software, Inc. and Biblesoft, Inc., 2006), par. 1.

Eaton regards this as a prophetic declaration that found fulfilled in the Messiah in Isaiah 9:6, "The government shall be upon His shoulder." The last of these cities is חֶבְרוֹן (Hebron) located in the mountain of Judah with a unique connotation of "fellowship, or association." The name was equally a type of the Messiah because those who run to Him for protection remain in communion with Him. Their fellowship is with the Father and the Son at all times. They will also enjoy continual fellowship with all the saints.[277]

Verse 14 אֵת ׀ שְׁלֹשׁ הֶעָרִים תִּתְּנוּ מֵעֵבֶר לַיַּרְדֵּן וְאֵת שְׁלֹשׁ הֶעָרִים תִּתְּנוּ בְּאֶרֶץ כְּנָעַן עָרֵי מִקְלָט תִּהְיֶינָה:

Verse 14: You will give three of these towns on this side of the Jordan and three in the territory of Canaan as cities of refuge.

Verse 14 further brings to the foreground Yahweh's design to bring about the ultimate purpose of the provision of these cities of refuge. These six cities were to be in two regions. Yahweh expected the children of Israel, who were the subject of the verb qal imperfect 2mp תִּתְּנוּ ("you will give"), to carry out the order while the object of the verb is אֵת ׀ שְׁלֹשׁ (numeral cardinal feminine singular construct from שָׁלֹשׁ meaning ["three of"]) as indicated by the direct object marker. אֵת ׀ שְׁלֹשׁ is in construct relationship to הֶעָרִים ("the cities") meaning, "Three of the cities." Thus, אֵת ׀ שְׁלֹשׁ הֶעָרִים "three of the cities" were to be at either side of the land since Yahweh had informed the division of the 12 tribes into two; some were at the eastern side of the Jordan while the rest were to the west in the land of Canaan. This addition to the colouration is to bring about Yahweh's ultimate purpose of preserving human lives using easy accessibility to the cities.

To this end, the Israelites had to centrally locate these six cities to the entire community of ancient Israel. The Israelites were instructed to divide the land into three. They should appoint the city at the centre of each of the three portions for this purpose. Moses himself selected the three on the other side of Canaan. The rationale behind their centrality was easy accessibility from every part of the land to each of these cities. The convenience would afford the manslayer easy passage to the nearest town before the redeemer of blood could catch up with him or her.[278]

Furthermore, the people selected all of these cities from the towns belonging to the Levites and priests. This selection was for two main purposes. First, the Levites and priests were in charge of "administration of justice." Second, the cities were so selected because they were more of Yahweh's property than the remaining parts of the land. In other words, whoever sought for protection in any of these places was

---

[277] Ibid.
[278] Keil & Delitzsch, "Num. 35:11," par. 1.

under God's special grace which served as an antidote to any possible revenge from the redeemer of blood, a common culture in human history.[279]

לִבְנֵי יִשְׂרָאֵל וְלַגֵּר וְלַתּוֹשָׁב בְּתוֹכָם תִּהְיֶינָה שֵׁשׁ־הֶעָרִים הָאֵלֶּה Verse 15
לְמִקְלָט לָנוּס שָׁמָּה כָּל־מַכֵּה־נֶפֶשׁ בִּשְׁגָגָה:

Verse 15: These six cities will be for refuge for the children of Israel, the sojourner, and the alien living among them; anyone that smites a person unintentionally may flee there.

Another colouration added to this ultimate purpose is that the law was not only for the covenant children of Yahweh. As it is for לִבְנֵי יִשְׂרָאֵל ("for the children of Israel), it was also for וְלַגֵּר ("and for the sojourner"), and וְלַתּוֹשָׁב ("and for the alien") living among them. The repetition of Yahweh in the main clause: לְמִקְלָט תִּהְיֶינָה שֵׁשׁ־הֶעָרִים הָאֵלֶּה (These six cities will be for refuge), as also stated in verse 11, is for emphasis and to establish how Yahweh was so keen to the sanctity of human life.

וְאִם־בִּכְלִי בַרְזֶל | הִכָּהוּ וַיָּמֹת רֹצֵחַ הוּא מוֹת יוּמַת הָרֹצֵחַ: Verse 16

Verse 16: 'If a man smites another man with an iron object and the person dies, he is a murderer; the murderer shall be made to die.

The next provision in the law guiding the establishment of the cities of refuge is the aspect that controls premeditated murder and the action of the redeemer of blood whose duty was to act as an executioner of the judgment on behalf of the family and the state. This second section of Yahweh's provision clearly shows the difference between premeditated murder and accidental manslaughter. The writer views this provision as a way to strengthen the ultimate purpose why Yahweh organised the cities of refuge for ancient Israel. It was to forestall possible errors inherent in the task of identifying those who killed intentionally from those who slew by accidence so that each could receive the deserved punishment.

The first thing to consider in verse 16 is the employment of three out of the 11 Hebrew verbs whose lexical analyses show that they carry the general connotation of killing. The first of them is נָכָה ("he smote") appearing in הִכָּהוּ hiphil perfect 3ms suffixed with the pronominal 3ms meaning "he caused to smite him." The second one is מוּת ("he died") appearing in וַיָּמֹת qal imperfect 3ms ("he will die") prefixed by vav consecutive meaning "and he died." Lastly, רָצַח is expressed in verb qal participle masculine singular absolute form meaning "a murderer." However, the same רָצַח has a stronger intensity and carries the idea of murder and manslaughter as will be seen later.

There are general rules that show differences between murder and manslaughter in this provision. Some verses of the chosen text express this difference

---

[279] Ibid, 2.

with the use of certain agency or instruments in the process of committing the act of killing. Whoever killed with any of these objects have committed premeditated murder. The first of these is with the instruments of בְּרְזֶל "an iron" just as appeared in the conditional phrase: וְאִם־בִּכְלִי בַרְזֶל (And if with an iron object v. 16).

Verse 17 וְאִם בְּאֶבֶן יָד אֲשֶׁר־יָמוּת בָּהּ הִכָּהוּ וַיָּמֹת רֹצֵחַ הוּא מוֹת יוּמַת הָרֹצֵחַ:

Verse 17: And if a man has a stone in his hand which could kill and he smites another man so that he dies, the man is a murderer; the murderer shall be made to die.

The next agency is the object of בְּאֶבֶן "with a stone" as expressed in the conditional clause: וְאִם בְּאֶבֶן יָד (And if a man has a stone in his hand v.17).

Verse 18 אוֹ בִּכְלִי עֵץ־יָד אֲשֶׁר־יָמוּת בּוֹ הִכָּהוּ וַיָּמֹת רֹצֵחַ הוּא מוֹת יוּמַת הָרֹצֵחַ:

Verse 18: Or if a man has a wooden object in his hand and smites another person with it so that the person dies; he is a murderer, and the murderer shall be made to die.

The last of these instruments is עֵץ־יָד "wood in hand," with this expression in verse 18: אוֹ בִּכְלִי עֵץ־יָד (or if a man has a wooden object in his hand). Whoever kills with any of these objects have murdered for the use of these objects has a link with premonition to kill. According to Marsh and Butzer, an intention to kill has a direct connection with the use of all these objects, and all murderers must die.[280]

Verse 19 גֹּאֵל הַדָּם הוּא יָמִית אֶת־הָרֹצֵחַ בְּפִגְעוֹ־בוֹ הוּא יְמִיתֶנּוּ:

Verse 19: The redeemer of blood shall put this murderer to death as he meets him, he shall put him to death.

In addition to the various colourations to this law, another one of vital importance is the provision for the executioner of the judgment delivered. Since there was no police system in ancient Israel, the law demands the redeemer of blood, the nearest kinsman-redeemer to the victim of the murder, to act in this capacity. The reality is expressed in the main clause of the verse: יָמִית אֶת־הָרֹצֵחַ בְּפִגְעוֹ־בוֹ גֹּאֵל הַדָּם הוּא ("The redeemer of blood shall put this murderer to death as he meets him"). It shows that the culture of ancient Israel was that of a community as everyone was to live for others. According to Jamieson, Fausset, and Brown, the task of avenging the death of one's deceased kinsman by the redeemer of blood was an established practice before the time of Moses. However, the tradition was with many cases of abuse.[281] Thus, this law with necessary guidelines becomes necessary to avoid any of these abuses.

---

[280] Marsh and Butzer, 303
[281] Jamieson, Fausset, and Brown, "Num. 35:11," par. 1.

Moreover, the identity of the redeemer of blood in ancient Israel was attached to his functions. Marsh and Butzer posit that this person had to take the life of the convicted murderer for the life of the kinsman victim. He also played the functions of collecting debts and contracting a levirate marriage. Again, the person served as a redeemer of "kinsman slave."[282] The redeemer of blood was the family relation to the victim, having the responsibility of restoring the integrity of the family once violated by shedding the blood of his kinsman. He also had the mandate of restoring family landed property once separated from the family (Lev. 25:25ff). This situation was called "the right of inheritance" (Num.27:8ff). More so, the mandate of redeeming the enslaved member of the family from slavery was also given him (Lev. 25:47ff). Keil and Delitzsch tag this "redeeming from bondage" (Lev. 25:49).[283]

According to Richards, since there was no system of police in ancient Israel, the redeemer of blood was to execute the divine mandate. Similarly, provision of the cities of refuge was to protect any person who killed in error from the hand of the redeemer of blood. This system protected the innocent and secured ancient Israel from unnecessary bloodshed that pervaded many ancient societies.[284] Yahweh occasioned the provision of the redeemer of blood for lack of "general and secure administration of justice" demanding the punishments of the murderer as a family responsibility.[285]

Verse 20 וְאִם־בְּשִׂנְאָה יֶהְדָּפֶנּוּ אוֹ־הִשְׁלִיךְ עָלָיו בִּצְדִיָּה וַיָּמֹת׃

Verse 20: And if any man with hatred thrusts another person or throws something upon him intentionally and the person dies

Yahweh provided another agency to identify a murder case in this verse. In this case, it is the agency of previous hatred in the mind of the murderer to the deceased person. The conditional phrase, וְאִם־בְּשִׂנְאָה ("And if any man with hatred") vividly expresses this provision.

By implication, death associated with the use of the weapons automatically releases the murderer from the city of protection. The person would be handed over to the redeemer of blood who would put the murderer to death. Second, death associated with previous disgust or premeditation is liable to murder for the act is associated with intention to kill.[286] Again, the assembly would establish the act of intentionality or premeditation when the victim is dead by stabbing or lying in wait, or when enmity is involved. The killer is guilty of murder and shall die at the hands of the redeemer of blood.[287] Verse 21, גֹּאֵל הַדָּם יָמִית אֶת־הָרֹצֵחַ בְּפִגְעוֹ־בוֹ ("The redeemer of blood will put the murderer to death when he meets him") also establishes the verdict.

Verse 21 אוֹ בְאֵיבָה הִכָּהוּ בְיָדוֹ וַיָּמֹת מוֹת־יוּמַת הַמַּכֶּה רֹצֵחַ הוּא גֹּאֵל

---

[282] Marsh and Butzer, 304.
[283] Keil and Delitzsch, "Num. 35:12-15," par. 3.
[284] Richards, Bible Reader's Companion, 114.
[285] R. Winterbotham, "Num. 35:9-34 – The Cities of Refuge," The Pulpit Commentary, Electronic Database. ed., H.D.M. Spence and Joseph S. Exell (Biblesoft, Inc., 2006), par. 2..
[286] Marsh & Butzer, 304-305.
[287] Ibid.

הַדָּם יָמִית אֶת־הָרֹצֵחַ בְּפִגְעוֹ־בוֹ:

Verse 21: or if in hostility he smites another person with his hand so that he dies, he is a murderer; the redeemer of blood will put the murderer to death when he meets him.'

Another agency through which the assembly would convict any killer of murder is בְּאֵיבָה ("in enmity"). The subordinate clause: וַיָּמֹת בְּיָדוֹ הִכָּהוּ אוֹ בְאֵיבָה "or if in enmity he smites another person with his hand so that he dies" expresses this. The agency of enmity is what Walvoord, Zuck, Barker, Merrill, and Toussaint regard as "evidence of hostility toward the victim," a stable condition to establish a proof of premeditation against the killer.[288]

According to Adeyemo, Yahweh categorically differentiated between premeditated murder and unintentional manslaughter using certain criteria to avoid possible errors. It was an intentional murder when a person died as a result of any of the following means; being struck with an iron, a stone or a wooden weapon that is capable of killing. It was also murder when a person died by a tool thrown with the motive of causing harm. Lastly, it was intentional murder when a person died using punching or pushing in an unfriendly manner.[289] The idea of Walvoord, Zuck, Barker, Merrill, and Toussaint is similar to that of Adeyemo.[290]

Verse 22 וְאִם־בְּפֶתַע בְּלֹא־אֵיבָה הֲדָפוֹ אוֹ־הִשְׁלִיךְ עָלָיו כָּל־כְּלִי בְּלֹא צְדִיָּה:
Verse 22: "But if without hostility someone suddenly thrusts another person or throws an object upon him unintentionally

The third section of this law is a provision guiding the aspect of accidental manslaughter. Just as the law concerning premeditated murder. This provision monitors the process of the establishment of cases of manslaughter in the land.

The criteria for cases of manslaughter are the direct opposite of what happens in murder cases. In the case of accidental manslaughter, for one to be discharged of murder and be convicted of manslaughter instead the agency of presentiment must be proved to be absent. The conditional clause, וְאִם־בְּפֶתַע בְּלֹא־אֵיבָה הֲדָפוֹ ("But if without enmity someone suddenly thrusts another person") or in עָלָיו כָל־כְּלִי אוֹ־הִשְׁלִיךְ (or throws an object upon him") expresses this reality. The assembly must establish the two actions by the condition of lack of intentionality as expressed in the prepositional phrasal expression: בְּלֹא צְדִיָּה ("without malice aforethought").

Verse 23 אוֹ בְכָל־אֶבֶן אֲשֶׁר־יָמוּת בָּהּ בְּלֹא רְאוֹת וַיַּפֵּל עָלָיו וַיָּמֹת וְהוּא לֹא־אוֹיֵב לוֹ וְלֹא מְבַקֵּשׁ רָעָתוֹ:
Verse 23: or without seeing him, causes a heavy stone to fall on him so that he dies without being his enemy and seeking evil against him.

[288] Walvoord, Zuck, Barker, Merrill, and Toussaint, "Num. 35:16-21," par. 1.
[289] Adeyemo, 208.
[290] Walvoord, Zuck, Barker, Merrill, and Toussaint, "Num. 35:16-21," par.1.

Verse 23 continues with the criteria required for proving the lack of agency or premonition case that began in the previous verse. The proof is a necessity for the discharge and acquittal of the killer. The use of the phrasal expressions, בְּלֹא רְאוֹת

אוֹ ... ("or without seeing him") and וְהוּא לֹא־אוֹיֵב לוֹ וְלֹא מְבַקֵּשׁ רָעָתוֹ ("without being his enemy and seeking evil against him") express this.

According to Marsh and Butzer, if the victim is dead without any acts of premeditation or by accident, the killer is only guilty of manslaughter and shall be protected from the redeemer of blood by keeping the person in the city of refuge. The person shall remain there until the death of the high priest. Marsh and Butzer advance that the title "high priest" reflects P source which normally employed the term in place of "'priest.'" They are of the view that the situation is in association with the Persian period.[291] More so, Adeyemo advances that death is accidental when a person was struck by a tool without aiming at killing the person or causing harm (35:22-24).[292] Nonetheless, the question remains: how will this notion be determined in this case? Adeyemo advances that this is the task given the assembly to perform.

Verse 24 וְשָׁפְטוּ הָעֵדָה בֵּין הַמַּכֶּה וּבֵין גֹּאֵל הַדָּם עַל הַמִּשְׁפָּטִים הָאֵלֶּה:
Verse 24: The assembly will judge between the accused person and the redeemer of blood according to these ordinances promulgated.

The next provision of this law is that of the duty of הָעֵדָה "the assembly." Two verbs are very key in the understanding of the duty. On the one hand, the first of these verbs appears in verse 24: וְשָׁפְטוּ in qal perfect stem 3cp from שָׁפַט ("he judged") prefixed by vav consecutive; hence "And they will judge." By implication, an assembly is a group of people with the responsibility of judging cases of this kind between two categories of people; namely, הַמַּכֶּה "the one causing to smite" (the accused person who smote to death) and גֹּאֵל הַדָּם "the redeemer of blood." One thing also guides the assembly in the process of going about their duty; they will have to judge "according to these ordinances promulgated" as evident in הָאֵלֶּה עַל הַמִּשְׁפָּטִים.

According to Keil and Delitzsch, the manslayer that fled from the redeemer of blood will have to stand at the entrance of the gates of the city before the elders to state the reasons why he fled. It is the responsibility of these elders to receive and assign him a place to dwell within the city. In other words, they have to protect the accused from the redeemer of blood until he stood before the assembly for a trial. Also, the elders had to investigate the case of the accused person before they would grant such protection. They would not hand the person over to the redeemer of blood until a trial which comes upon a petition from the redeemer of blood to the assembly.

---

[291] Marsh and Butzer, 304-305.
[292] Adeyemo, 208.

The identity of the assembly is of two-fold; it was either the congregation to whom the murderer belonged or the people among whom the crime was committed. By law, the assembly had the mandate of inquiring the case and deciding whether the act was intentional or unintentional.[293] These elders had the mandate to fetch for anyone guilty of murder that fled to the city of refuge described as a "free city." They had to hand the murderer over to the redeemer of blood (Deut.19:11-12).[294]

Verse 25 וְהִצִּילוּ הָעֵדָה אֶת־הָרֹצֵחַ מִיַּד גֹּאֵל הַדָּם וְהֵשִׁיבוּ אֹתוֹ הָעֵדָה אֶל־עִיר מִקְלָטוֹ אֲשֶׁר־נָס שָׁמָּה וְיָשַׁב בָּהּ עַד־מוֹת הַכֹּהֵן הַגָּדֹל אֲשֶׁר־מָשַׁח אֹתוֹ בְּשֶׁמֶן הַקֹּדֶשׁ:

Verse 25: The assembly shall make the one convicted of manslaughter escape from the redeemer of blood by sending him back to the city of refuge where he had fled, and he shall remain there until the death of the high priest anointed with the holy oil.'"

The second verb that brings the duty of the assembly to the for is in verse 25: וְהִצִּילוּ hiphil perfect 3mp from נָצִיר ("he rescued or saved") prefixed by vav consecutive meaning "And they will cause to escape." The assembly is the subject of this verb. By implication, the assembly will cause the one guilty of manslaughter to escape from the hand of the redeemer of blood as expressed in this clause: גֹּאֵל הַדָּם

וְהִצִּילוּ הָעֵדָה אֶת־הָרֹצֵחַ מִיַּד "The assembly shall make the one convicted of manslaughter escape from the redeemer of blood." The assembly does this by sending the person back to the city of refuge where he had fled at the initial stage. However, this person would have to remain in the city until the death of הַכֹּהֵן הַגָּדֹל "the great priest." By implication, this person will be deprived of his freedom and access to his possession all through the period of the asylum in the city until the death of the anointed high priest. This situation is similar to the modern-day imprisonment or jail term whose period is undetermined - life-imprisonment.

According to Richards, the system of justice of the OT did not deeply rely on imprisonment as much as restitution as a punitive measure against criminals. This situation is evident in the limitation of the number of reported cases of imprisonment in the Hebrew Bible. Instances of this are cases under foreign rule (Gen. 39:20-22; 40:3,5,14; 42:16,19; Judg. 16:21,25; 2 Kings 17:4; 25:27,29; Jer. 52:11,31,33; Ezek. 19:9) and under some of the Jewish rulers whose reigns were directly under foreign powers. A few cases of imprisonment at this time in Israel and Judah took the forms of house arrest or restriction to one's room or city and could also be in a pit.[295] Nonetheless, the provisional aspect of this law that required the death of the murderer and restriction of the one guilty of manslaughter to the city of refuge became necessary because of the value that Yahweh attaches to human blood.

---

[293] Keil and Delitzsch, "Numbers 35:9-11," par. 4.
[294] Ibid, par. 1.
[295] Richards, *The Teacher's Commentary*, "Cities of Refuge (Num. 35)," pars. 2-3.

וְאִם־יָצֹא יֵצֵא הָרֹצֵחַ אֶת־גְּבוּל עִיר מִקְלָטוֹ אֲשֶׁר יָנוּס שָׁמָּה: Verse 26

Verse 26: 'But if the one convicted of manslaughter goes out of the territory of the city of his refuge where he fled

The need for the one guilty of manslaughter to stay within the city of refuge to avoid being killed by the redeemer of blood is on the imperative. This fact is the emphasis of verses 26-28. The verses place a premium on the provisional aspect of the law in verse 25 that the assembly had it as a duty to protect the person guilty of this case by sending the one to the city of refuge. However, if the guilty man failed to remain there as expressed by the conditional clause of verse 26: גְּבוּל עִיר מִקְלָטוֹ

וְאִם־יָצֹא יֵצֵא הָרֹצֵחַ אֶת ('But if the one convicted of manslaughter goes out of the territory of the city of his refuge), he would face the consequence of death. The doubling of the verb יֵצֵא qal imperfect 3ms ("he will come out") is the emphasis placed on the danger of the volitional action of the subject of the verb (the one convicted of manslaughter). וְאִם־יָצֹא יֵצֵא roughly means, "But if he comes out of he will come out of." According to Keil and Delitzsch, the exiled person would be restricted to the free city of refuge and be deprived of accessibility to the person's "hereditary possession" throughout.[296]

וּמָצָא אֹתוֹ גֹּאֵל הַדָּם מִחוּץ לִגְבוּל עִיר מִקְלָטוֹ וְרָצַח גֹּאֵל הַדָּם Verse 27
אֶת־הָרֹצֵחַ אֵין לוֹ דָּם:

Verse 27: and the redeemer of blood finds him outside the border of the city of refuge; the redeemer of blood may kill him without being guilty of murder

The next conditional clause to this volitional danger is contingent on the action of the redeemer of blood as the subject of the verb וּמָצָא ("and he will find him). גֹּאֵל הַדָּם ("the redeemer of blood") is the subject of the verb whose action in this verse has a tremendous effect on the object of the verb (the one guilty of manslaughter) represented by the pronoun אֹתוֹ "him." The object of the verb is safe as long as he wilfully stayed within the territory of the city of refuge. However, the danger lies in the expression: מִחוּץ noun common masculine singular absolute from חוּץ ("outside") prefixed by מִן preposition ("out of") roughly translated "out of outside." Verse 27 further defines this location in לִגְבוּל עִיר מִקְלָטוֹ "to (the) border of the city of (the) refuge."

Thus, if the guilty man goes out of the city of refuge, the person has trespassed by the exercise of the volitional will of his or her mind to move out of the divine protection consciously. Thereby, the person is liable to be killed by the redeemer of blood. The people should not regard this killing as murder or manslaughter but a reward for the disobedience of the sinful man. In this case, the redeemer of blood only

---

[296] Keil and Delitzsch, "Num. 35:26-28," par. 1.

acted on behalf of the society to execute the judgment. Thus, the sin of disobedience has not only made the sinful person forfeited his or her sanctity but has equally sent the person to the grave over an avoidable action performed.

Verse 28 כִּי בְעִיר מִקְלָטוֹ יֵשֵׁב עַד־מוֹת הַכֹּהֵן הַגָּדֹל וְאַחֲרֵי מוֹת הַכֹּהֵן הַגָּדֹל יָשׁוּב הָרֹצֵחַ אֶל־אֶרֶץ אֲחֻזָּתוֹ:

Verse 28: for he must remain within the city of his refuge until the death of the high priest. But after the death of the high priest, the accused person may return to the land of his possession.

The content of verse 28 explains the reason why the sinful may is subject to a death of this kind. In this case, the sinful man died for not fulfilling the condition attached to his safety by remaining within the city of the refuge until the death of the high priest, after which the person may return to the land of his possession. One should consider the expression אֶל־אֶרֶץ אֲחֻזָּתוֹ "to the land of his possession." This need becomes necessary because one major thing the guilty person would miss all the time he would remain in the custody of the Levites in the city of refuge was the heritage of his tribal land and people.

Although the restriction of the one who killed without any premeditation to the city of refuge is a punishment, Keil and Delitzsch object to this as banishment. The objection is on account of the fact that the restriction was an act of God's mercy for the person's deliverance from imminent revenge that could terminate the life of the concerned individual. This reason indeed stands against all that the idea of banishment connotes as the cities are places of escape from death.[297] This grace takes another better form apart from the initial flight. The death of the anointed high priest, which has the potency to discharge the life of the person entirely from the danger, is another reflection of God's grace. Death of this kind is referred to as expiatory death by many Rabbis as well as many of the fathers and former commentators.[298]

Verse 29 וְהָיוּ אֵלֶּה לָכֶם לְחֻקַּת מִשְׁפָּט לְדֹרֹתֵיכֶם בְּכֹל מוֹשְׁבֹתֵיכֶם:

Verse 29: These will be a standard of judgment for you forever for all of your generations in all of your dwelling-places.

The same verse begins a discourse about the horror of killing which covers verses 29-32. The horror of killing, either premeditated murder or manslaughter, is always great in the sight of Yahweh. Certain provisions within this section make this fact plain.

Verse 29 marks the beginning of the fourth section of this law. The demonstrative pronoun אֵלֶּה ("these") is referring to all of the provisions of the Law regarding the cities of refuge as contained in this chosen text, especially verses 9-28. The same pronoun is functioning as the subject of the verb וְהָיוּ qal perfect 3cp

---

[297] Ibid, par. 2.
[298] Ibid.

"They became" prefixed by vav consecutive "and" meaning, "And they will be." Thus, these provisions were expected to be a standard of judgment for His people who are the object of the verb as represented by the preposition לְ ("for") with pronominal suffix 2mp כֶם ("you") meaning "for you." The noun common feminine singular חֻקָּה ("a statue") prefixed with the preposition לְ ("for") meaning "for a statute" stands in construct relationship to noun common masculine singular absolute ("a judgment"). Hence, the literal translation of this expression can be "for a statute of judgment" which this writer expresses as "for a standard of judgment."

Given this analysis, the first provision that brings the horror of killing to the fore is Yahweh's instruction to His covenant people. The Israelites had to follow this law as a standard of judgment forever in all of their generations. This provision is evident in the main clause, וְהָיוּ אֵלֶּה לָכֶם לְחֻקַּת מִשְׁפָּט לְדֹרֹתֵיכֶם בְּכֹל ("And these will be a standard of judgment for you forever for all of your generations").

Verse 30 כָּל־מַכֵּה־נֶפֶשׁ לְפִי עֵדִים יִרְצַח אֶת־הָרֹצֵחַ וְעֵד אֶחָד לֹא־יַעֲנֶה בְנֶפֶשׁ לָמוּת:

Verse 30: Anyone who smites a person to death shall die as a murderer but only by the testimony of witnesses; no one is to be put to death upon the testimony of only one witness.

Verse 30 is the second provision. Yahweh designed premeditated killing always to attract capital punishment in ancient Israel. However, before the assembly could convict anyone of murder and the redeemer of blood put him to death, it must be at the instance of witnesses. This situation is the emphasis of עֵדִים noun common masculine plural absolute from עֵד meaning *witness; hence "witnesses."* No murderer must die by the testimony of a single witness, וְעֵד אֶחָד לֹא־יַעֲנֶה בְנֶפֶשׁ לָמוּת (And no one is to be put to death upon the testimony of only one witness). In this regard, Walvoord, Zuck, Barker, Merrill, and Toussaint advance that it was theologically imperative for the redeemer of blood to take revenge upon the murderer so that the land could regain its sanctity and the people could always have Yahweh in their midst.[299] Nonetheless, this should be after the assembly had convicted the murderer upon the testimony of not less than two witnesses.

Verse 31 וְלֹא־תִקְחוּ כֹפֶר לְנֶפֶשׁ רֹצֵחַ אֲשֶׁר־הוּא רָשָׁע לָמוּת כִּי־מוֹת יוּמָת:

Verse 31: You must not collect a ransom for the life of a murderer who is guilty for he is to die; he must be put to death.

The third provision is in verse 31 which forbids payment of כֹפֶר "a ransom" לְנֶפֶשׁ רֹצֵחַ אֲשֶׁר־הוּא רָשָׁע "for the life of a murderer who is guilty." This provision of the law brings to the foreground that human life is worth more than anything else like money. The value which Yahweh attaches to the being of any

---

[299] Walvoord, Zuck, Barker, Merrill, and Toussaint, "Num. 35:30-34," par. 1.

humans is priceless, and this is because of the sacredness of humankind as a result of His image in them. In this regard, Adam Clarke expresses the insufficiency of any other form of atonement such as payment of ransom to atone for the life of the murderer but by the shedding of the blood of the same culprit on the ground.[300]

Verse 32 וְלֹא־תִקְחוּ כֹפֶר לָנוּס אֶל־עִיר מִקְלָטוֹ לָשׁוּב לָשֶׁבֶת בָּאָרֶץ
עַד־מוֹת הַכֹּהֵן:

Verse 32: You shall not collect ransom for anyone who has fled to the city of his refuge to bring him back; he must remain within the territory until the death of the high priest.

This third provision is not limited to a case of murder in verse 31 but is also expected to come to play in the case of accidental manslaughter in verse 32. This reality is evident in the main clause: תִקְחוּ כֹפֶר לָנוּס אֶל־עִיר מִקְלָטוֹ לָשׁוּב וְלֹא ("And you shall not collect ransom for anyone who has fled to the city of his refuge to bring him back"). The emphasis of this provision lies in the verb לָשׁוּב "to bring him back." This emphasis indicates the purpose of the payment of ransom in the case of manslaughter. Although no intention is attached to the imbursement of a ransom in the case of murder in verse 31, the implication is that when payment of this kind takes place, it will pervert justice by preventing the murderer from being executed. Thus, no one is allowed to escape the mandatory penalty for the crime committed.

According to Richards, Yahweh's command prohibiting payment of ransom for murder was against some ancient cultural practices which encouraged payment of this kind to the deceased family so that the murderer could avoid facing necessary punishment. However, the murderer must surely die in the OT. The basis of this injunction was the fact that God made man in His image and likeness. This basis depicts the unique value of all human lives. Imposition of capital punishment is to uphold this value. Any society that carries out this imposition shows due respect to the sacredness of human life.[301]

Verse 33 וְלֹא־תַחֲנִיפוּ אֶת־הָאָרֶץ אֲשֶׁר אַתֶּם בָּהּ כִּי הַדָּם הוּא יַחֲנִיף
אֶת־הָאָרֶץ וְלָאָרֶץ לֹא־יְכֻפַּר לַדָּם אֲשֶׁר שֻׁפַּךְ־בָּהּ כִּי־אִם בְּדַם שֹׁפְכוֹ:

Verse 33: You must not pollute the land where you are living for blood pollutes the land. Atonement cannot be made for the land on which blood has been poured except by the blood of the person who poured it.

The last two verses of this section fundamentally explain why murder is such a great crime and why Yahweh assigned an appropriate penalty to it without any option of fine. This simple reason is that blood pollutes the land. Therefore, the atonement

---

[300] Adam Clarke, Numbers 35:31," *Adam Clarke's Commentary*, Electronic Database (Biblesoft, Inc., 2005), par. 1.

[301] Lawrence O. Richards, *Bible Reader's Companion* (Colorado Springs: Cook Communications Ministries, 2004), 114.

provision that is explained in verses 33 and 34 is a necessity. The emphatic particle לֹא negative (meaning "not") makes this evident. It is in construct relationship to verb hiphil imperfect 2mp from חָנֵף meaning "he polluted or profaned;" hence, "and you will not cause to pollute." The object of the sentence is אֶת־הָאָרֶץ ("the land") which is qualified by the adjectival clause of place: אֲשֶׁר שֹׁפֵּדְ־בָּה ("where you are living"). After this, Yahweh gave the reason for this order as evident in the subordinate clause, כִּי הַדָּם הוּא יַחֲנִיף אֶת־הָאָרֶץ ("for blood pollutes the land"). The highest pollution from the perspective of Yahweh is the shedding of the blood of human life. It desecrates the land where the crime is committed. This reality also emphasises the worth of human life in the sight of God.

Furthermore, given the imminent blood pollution envisaged by the foreknowledge of Yahweh, a provision was made for the cleansing of the land. This provision brings the issue of atonement to the fore as evident in the employment of יְכֻפַּר verb imperfect 3ms from כָּפַר meaning ("he/it covered over, atoned") prefixed by the particle negative; hence "It (the land) will not be atoned." In verse 33, the only way by which the people could atone for the land is by shedding the blood of the murderer. This reality is the emphasis of the subordinate clause, אִם־בְּדַם שֹׁפְכוֹ כִּי (except by the blood of the person who poured it" v. 33).

Clarke advances two main reasons for the necessity of the shedding of the blood of the murderer on the ground. First, God is the author of life, and He alone has the exclusive right to terminate it. Second, since life is the only time to prepare for eternity and the salvation of the human soul also depends on it, therefore, it is of a tremendous blessing to the humanity to experience the fullest of one's span of life.[302]

Verse 34 וְלֹא תְטַמֵּא אֶת־הָאָרֶץ אֲשֶׁר אַתֶּם יֹשְׁבִים בָּה אֲשֶׁר אֲנִי שֹׁכֵן בְּתוֹכָהּ כִּי אֲנִי יְהוָה שֹׁכֵן בְּתוֹךְ בְּנֵי יִשְׂרָאֵל: פ

Verse 34: Do not defile the land on which you are living for I Yahweh live in the midst of the children of Israel.

Verse 34 is emphatic on the prohibition of blood pollution in ancient Israel. This ban is evident in the main clause תְטַמֵּא אֶת־הָאָרֶץ אֲשֶׁר אַתֶּם יֹשְׁבִים בָּה וְלֹא "Do not defile the land on which you are living." The need to adhere strictly to the divine instruction is contingent on two reasons. First, although the greatness of the cost of the atonement does not appear in verse 34, it is evident in the preceding verses especially in verse 33. The life of the person who willfully caused the blood pollution will have to go for it. Second, Yahweh's presence in the midst of His people is the other reason. This reason is the basis of the prepositional clause, בְּתוֹךְ בְּנֵי יִשְׂרָאֵל אֲשֶׁר אֲנִי שֹׁכֵן בְּתוֹכָהּ כִּי אֲנִי יְהוָה שֹׁכֵן "for I Yahweh live in the midst of the children of Israel." According to Walvoord, Zuck, Barker, Merrill, and Toussaint

---

[302] Clarke, "Num. 35:33," par. 2.

blood pollution was capable of separating God from His polluted people. Thus, blood revenge was a necessity.[303] The inevitability of the presence of Yahweh in the midst of His covenant people is well communicated in the Hebrew Bible and adequately known to the people. Therefore, the primary priority of the people of ancient Israel was to secure this presence for necessary and adequate protection from external dangers and their prosperity.

7. Inferences of Sanctity of Human Life in Numbers 35:9-34

As a reminder, the thesis of this study is that a comparative understanding of Numbers 35:9-34 and *Yorùbá* worldview of the sanctity of human life can be a veritable tool for identifying and correcting deviant practices among the modern-day *Yorùbá* people. It is the view of this writer, therefore, that adequate understanding of the chosen text is possible only after the writer has established the thrust of Numbers 35:9-34. In this section, efforts are made to ensure this by drawing necessary inferences of the sanctity of human life as analysed in the chosen text. This task follows two steps; the writer provides a summary of the exegesis written, and draws necessary exegetical deductions from the passage.

a. Summary of Exegesis of Numbers 35:9-34

In Numbers 35:9-34, certain instructions were handed down to the new generation of Israel while they were on the plain of Moab by the Jordan as they prepared to cross to the Promised Land. According to this writer, these instructions are of four divisions. First, the law concerning cities of refuge where any manslayer who killed by accident could flee is of vital importance to this study (vv.9-10). Given His holiness and foreknowledge, Yahweh backed up this provision with instructions which His people must obey in all of their generations to achieve its purpose continually. The writer or editor of the Book of Numbers regards these instructions as the law governing the cities of refuge. More so, various cases of abuse occasioned the law on the ground to the existing culture of seeking for the right of asylum in the ancient societies. Certain things are worthy of note in this law.

The law was an order from Yahweh to His covenant people of ancient Israel. Moses was the intermediary between Yahweh and the people. He was also the agency through whom Yahweh gave and delivered the contents of the law to His people. The people must obey the law in all of their generations and any failure on their part would be of significant consequences. More so, the cities were exclusively for unpremeditated manslayer (vv. 11, 15). Once the assembly established a case of murder, the murderer would be handed over to the redeemer of blood to kill. However, if the manslayer is guilty of unpremeditated manslaughter, the person would be protected from the redeemer of blood by sending the one back to the city of protection where one had fled. Moreover, the towns had some aspects in common (v. 11); namely, they were all at the centre of the entire community of God's people, the

---

[303] Walvoord, Zuck, Barker, Merrill, and Toussaint, par. 1.

roads to these cities were to be kept free of obstacles, they were all located within the territory of the tribal inheritance of the Levites and priests, and on hills.

Furthermore, each of the six cities of refuge was unique in meaning and served as the type of the Messiah. On the east of the Jordan, there were three of these cities; namely, Bezer (a stronghold or fortified place), Ramoth (high or exalted), and Golan (joy or revelation). The locations of the rest three of the cities were on the west of the Jordan in the land of Canaan; namely, Kedesh (holy or set apart), Shechem (shoulder) and Hebron (fellowship or association). Finally, the ultimate purpose of the provision of the law concerning cities of refuge was to preserve human life (vv. 12-15). This provision shows the worth which Yahweh accorded human life since all humanity is in His image and likeness. Yahweh expected each person to have the same value irrespective of their social status, race, gender, and colour. By this, He categorically declared that the law was not only for the children of Israel but also for both the sojourners and aliens among them (v.15).

Second, the next division of these instructions was the law governing premeditated murder and blood revenge (vv. 16-21). On the one hand, this law contains some specific general rules by which the assembly could convict a person of premeditated murder. Whoever killed with the use of any of the lethal objects made of iron (v. 16), stone (v.17) and wood (v.18) was liable to be convicted of murder. This fact is because there was an association between the uses of such weapons with the intention to kill in ancient Israel. Again, death associated with evidence of previous disgust or hatred is liable to murder for they both are in association with plan to kill (v.20). One way to establish the two acts of previous disgust or hatred was when the death occurred by stabbing or lying in wait or when enmity was involved.

On the other hand, there was a great need for the redeemer of blood in ancient Israel. This need is because there was nothing like the modern police system at the time except for an army. It was the redeemer of blood that performed this role on behalf of the society. According to the exegesis of the chosen text, the writer identified the redeemer of blood as the family relation to the victim who had some roles to perform on behalf of the family and society. On this list is the task of restoring the integrity of the family which the killer once violated by shedding the blood of his kinsman. Another one is recapturing family landed property once separated from the family (Lev. 25:25ff). Also, the task of redeeming the enslaved member of the family from slavery (Lev. 25:47ff) was vital to the family. He also had to collect debts and contract levirate marriage. Thus, the redeemer of blood was to execute the divine mandate.

Third, the writer considered the law concerning accidental manslaughter and the city of refuge (vv. 22-28) next. In this law, the writer identified some general rules for unintentional homicide (vv.22, 23). In the first instance, death is accidental when the victim was struck by a tool without aiming at killing the person or causing harm (vv. 22-24). The non-intentionality behind this killing was part of the duties of the assembly who would judge by the given instructions. Similarly, if the assembly of God's people discharged a person from murder, the person had to be protected from the redeemer of blood by sending the culprit back to the city of refuge. This killer had to remain there until the death of the serving high priest.

Furthermore, the identity and duties of the assembly were also considered (vv. 24-25). The assembly was made up of the elders of the city of the murderer or where the killing took place. The elders had some duties to perform concerning the killing of any person. They had to fetch for anyone guilty that fled to a city of refuge for trial upon petition from the redeemer of blood. Also, they had to hand over the murderer to the redeemer of blood while protecting the one innocent of murder by sending the person back to the city of refuge. Again, they judged the case between the redeemer of blood and the manslayer.

Moreover, the writer established the need for the one guilty of manslaughter to stay within the city of one's refuge in the explanation of the chosen text (vv. 25-28). The guilty one had to be protected by the assembly. The person also had to remain within the territories of the city of one's protection until the death of the serving high priest. The restriction was necessary because should one left the town, the redeemer of blood would kill the person without being guilty of murder when they both meet.

Fourth, the law concerning bloodshed and atonement (vv. 29-34) is the last of the divisions. In the analysis, premeditated murder was argued to always be of great concern and consequence before Yahweh. To this fact, the writer elucidated this fact with some scriptural expressions within the pericope of the chosen text. The assembly must never collect a ransom for the life of the murderer (v.31). Instead, the redeemer of blood must put the person to death.

Similarly, no ransom must be taken from those guilty of manslaughter as to bring them back from their cities of refuge to their places of inheritance (v. 32). Another expression is that shedding of innocent blood defiles the land before Yahweh (v. 33). The only possible way of removing pollution from the land was by the atonement. The people must carry out this provision either by shedding the blood of the murderer (v. 33) or sending the one guilty of manslaughter back to the city of his or her refuge in anticipation of the death of the anointed high priest who was a type of the Messiah. It was the death of this serving high priest that could atone for the bloodshed as a result of manslaughter while it was the blood of the murderer alone that could atone for the land in the case of murder. Lastly, atonement became necessary because Yahweh dwelt in the midst of His people (v. 34).

Thus, since human lives are very dear to Yahweh owing to the presence of His image and likeness in them, Yahweh issued an order which would bring about the establishment of six cities of refuge exclusively for those who killed accidentally. This order contained certain provisions guiding the right of asylum within the towns so that the elders of the land could protect the sanctity of the entire community of God's covenant people. Ultimately, Yahweh provided for these elements of the law to identify those guilty of manslaughter from murderers so that each could receive an appropriate punishment. They were also put in place to avoid various extant abuses which marked the cultural right of asylum seeking in ancient societies like Greece.

The truth of the matter is that human blood brings about the highest form of land pollution anytime someone sheds it, and there would be a need for atonement.

In ancient Israel, if pollution of this kind was as a result of premeditated murder, the atonement must as a matter of necessity be made by spilling or shedding the blood of the murderer on the ground by the redeemer of blood without any option of payment of ransom. This type of killing is judicial and legitimate without leading to any further desecration on the land. In other words, the redeemer of blood is only executing the divine order on behalf of the state and family of the deceased. However, if the pollution were not intentional in cases of manslaughter, the killer would be restricted to a city of refuge for as long as the anointed high priest would live. This is primarily a reflection of God's grace upon the killer, not essentially a punishment. Nonetheless, the death of the high priest would perform two things; liberating the restricted person from the city of refuge and atoning for the land so that the people could ensure Yahweh's presence in their midst.

b. Exegetical Deductions of Numbers 35:9-34

The need to draw necessary deductions from the exegesis of Numbers 35:9-34 is on the imperative to this study. The necessity is to ensure an essential understanding of the worth of human life in the chosen text by today's readers, especially the contemporary *Yorùbá* people. The first deduction is on the love of God for His covenant people. The divine command in the text is altogether an essential expression of God's love and care for the lives of His covenant people in ancient Israel. Yahweh expected His people to obey the law for it was to preserve the sacredness of the life of individuals and that of the generality of their community.

Moreover, the ordination of cities of refuge in ancient Israel was to protect the worth or sacredness of the lives of the people. Persons guilty of manslaughter had to be sent back to the person's city of refuge to protect the individual from imminent attack and death by the redeemer of blood. W. Roberts described the picture of the man guilty of manslaughter before the city of his refuge as a parallel to the case of every sinner before the cross. The scholar also illustrated the situation of the killer in the city of refuge as a type of security that every sinner enjoys while remaining under the sanctuary of the cross.[304] More so, this provision was on account of the value Yahweh attached not only to the lives of His covenant people of Israel but to all human beings. This provision is evident in Yahweh's instruction that the regulations were not only for the Israelites but also for the aliens and sojourners living among them (v. 15).

Similarly, violations of the sanctity of human life were real in the OT despite the given sound biblical system of justice. This claim is on account of the very many appearances of various words analysed which connote the idea of killing in biblical accounts. The Hebrew verb רָצַח which has the particular connotation of murder-

---

[304] W. Roberts, "The Cities of Refuge (Num. 35:9-34)," *The Biblical Illustrator: Old Testament Volumes*, Electronic Database, Ed. Joseph S. Exell (Ages Software, Inc. and Biblesoft, Inc., 2006), par. 1.

attachment with either premeditation or lack of intentionality to itself is an example to consider. It appears in not less than 38 times in the OT, most of which are in the Pentateuch, and 14 times particularly in the chosen text. When biblical students consider these figures with those of the remaining 10 words, the reality of the prevalence of killings of all types in ancient Israel is made evident. However, Yahweh hates bloodshed, and He is the greatest promoter of the sanctity of human life in human history.

Moreover, the basis of the biblical system of justice is the preservation of God's image in humankind. God's image in humans is the totality of God's treasures, investments and worth in them and God would do everything to protect His investment in humanity. This reality was the premise for the biblical system of justice as considered in the chosen text. One way by which one can hamper this system is through bribery and corruption. Yahweh guided against this by prohibiting collection of bribes to spare any murderer from facing capital punishment or person guilty of manslaughter to return to the place of comfort.

Likewise, the sanctity of human life is not racial, gender, social, economic, and cultural biased. Yahweh's law governing the administration of the cities of refuge was not limited to the children of Israel alone; the provision was also for the sojourners and aliens among them. More so, capital punishment is biblical. Yahweh gave this provision by the principle of retribution which is not limited to a particular time. It was a way of atoning for the land in the OT to preserve the covenant relationship between Yahweh and His people through holy living.

Furthermore, the redeemer of blood in ancient Israel was God's provision for the execution of the divine mandate on behalf of the family and society. The basis of this is the sacredness of human life, violation of which demands retribution. This situation is a reflection of the nature of God's system of justice. Again, the need for atonement is excellent at all times to preserve God's created order. There were precisely two ways by which the people did this in ancient Israel. The first way was by shedding the blood of the murderer. The writer regards this as an expression of God's grace and capital punishment. The second was through the death of the high priest, a type of Christ Jesus. In the OT, the passing away of the anointed great priest would automatically free whoever held hostage in various cities of refuge. The fulfilment of this is found in the NT when Christ Jesus died on the cross. He is the Great High Priest whose death has eternal effects in the lives of those who run to Him for safety from the wages of sin. Thus, capital punishment remains valid.

Lastly, the greatest form of land pollution is that of bloodshed. God is holy and sanctioned a system by which His people would remain holy in their covenant relationship with Him. The system was to run through the blood of animals in the OT. This system was perfected in the NT using the blood of Christ Jesus whose sacrifice was supreme and final. All this provision is aimed at preventing the land from pollution which happens whenever there is a shedding of human blood. However, each time the land is free of this impediment, God would dwell in the midst of His people, and the safety and comfort of their lives are always guaranteed.

CHAPTER FOUR

SANCTITY OF HUMAN LIFE IN *YORÙBÁ* WORLDVIEW

The value of the sanctity of human life seems to be fading away among *Yorùbá* people today. In the time past, it was traditionally part of the lives and practices of the people just like the Jews. For instance, in ATR, there is respect for human life, human relations, community, hospitality, family affinity, authority and elders, and spirituality. These are a few examples of the various ways by which respect for human life reflected among the people. All of these practices are similar to the legal requirements of the OT Law. Nonetheless, there seems to be a reversal of the belief and practice of this cultural heritage with the spate of incessant killings that pervade the land at this time. With this, the life of an average person appears to be at risk for its worth, sanctity and sacredness.

In this section, the writer's primary concern is to determine how much appreciation the people gave to the value of the sanctity of life among the *Yorùbá* going by their traditions and cultural practices. Thus, it becomes imperative to investigate certain aspects of the *Yorùbá* worldview; namely, the geographical context, philosophy, rituals, vocabulary, and socio-political relations of the people.

1. Geographical Context of the *Yorùbá*

The location of *Yorùbá* people in Nigeria is vital to this study. According to Samuel Johnson, the *Yorùbá* nation is located below the confluence of the Western part of the Niger River and above the junction of the Western tributary of the same, known as the "South of the Quorra." The nation has Dahomey to the West and Bight of Benin to the South between latitude 6° and 9° to the North and longitude 2° 30' and 6° 30' to the East.[305] In another sense, they occupy the Southwest part of Nigeria. Regarding population, they are the second largest tribe in Nigeria accounting for about 21-35% of the nation's population.[306]

However, whenever the people use *Yorùbá* as a term, it is all-encompassing. According to Oladejo, the word means the ethnic group within Nigeria that includes North-West Yorùbá, Central Yorùbá, and South-East *Yorùbá* and the dialects in the areas of south-western Nigeria are entirely different from those in Benin and Togo.[307] In another development, Oladejo also argues that *Yorùbá* people predominantly occupy South-Western part of Nigeria with some of them living in the Diaspora. They have certain things in common as an ethnic group, irrespective of their differences in

---

[305] Samuel Johnson, *The History of the Yorubas: From the Earliest Times to the Beginning of the British Protectorate*, ed., O. Johnson (Lagos: C.M.S. Bookshop, 1937), xix.

[306] Omobolaji Ololade Olarinmoye, "Yoruba Politics 1999 – 2003," *African Journal of Political Science and International Relations* Vol. 1 (2) (November 2007):020.

[307] Olusayo B. Oladejo, "Reciprocal Impacts of Yoruba Culture on the Yoruba Bible," *Ogbomoso Journal of Theology (OJOT)*, Vol. XVII No. 2 (2012): 115.

dialects. They have common culture adjudged to be rich which has survived to this time. Also, they have common origin traced to the ancient town of Ile-Ife and common progenitor called Oduduwa.[308]

While analysing the distinctive features of the *Yorùbá* language, Roger Blench argues that *Yorùbá* is both the language of the people and their ethnic name. People in the following states in Nigeria speak the language: most of the Kwara, Lagos, Osun, Oyo, Ogun, Ondo States, as well as in the western LGAs of Kogi State.[309] In the opinion of this writer, Blench's omission of the people of Ekiti State as part of the *Yorùbá*-speaking States in Nigeria is a great one. Also, some of the people in the Benin Republic, Togo, Cuba, and Brazil speak the language as a ritual language. The approximate number of those who speak the language, based on the 1952 UBS and 1984 estimates, is 5,100,000 and 15,000,000 respectively.[310] Nonetheless, the figure rose to an approximate number of 25 million people in 1990 as presented by Margaret Thompson Drewal, citing Rowland Abiodun.[311] The language has several dialects; namely, Afo, Akono, Amusigbo, Awori, Aworo, Bunu, Ẹgba, Ẹgbado, Ekiti, Gbedde, Igbomina, Ifaki, Ifẹ, Ifira, Igbena, Ijẹbu, Ijẹsa (Ijọsha), Ijọ Akpọi, Ijumu, Ikalẹ, Ila, Ilajẹ, Ọba, Ondo, Ọra, Owe, Ọwọ, Ọyọ, Ufe, and Yagba. According to Blench, "A partial and preliminary subgrouping is: Central, including Ìfẹ̀, Ìjẹ̀shà, Èkìtì; North West, including Ọ̀yọ́, Ẹ̀gbá, Ọ̀shùn; North East, including Yagba, Gbédé, Ìjùmú; South West, including Tsábẹ and Kétu (both spoken in Benin and adjacent border areas of Kwara and Ogun States); and South East, including Ondo, Ọwọ, Ijẹba, Ìkálẹ́, Ìlàjẹ̀ and Ìjọ̀–Àpọ̀i."[312]

Similarly, Oladejo advances that although *Yorùbá* has over fifteen dialects, the standard one is the written form which has its origin in the 1850s, the period Samuel Ajayi Crowther published a *Yorùbá* grammar. Crowther released this publication to translate the English Bible into Yorùbá, the exercise that finally came to fruition in 1884. It is this Yorùbá Bible that became the standard for the written *Yorùbá* and is widely adopted by the majority of *Yorùbá* dialects.[313] Nonetheless, the grouping of these dialects linguistically grouped into certain forms of languages which include and not limited to the following: Oyo, Ijebu, and Ekiti. The people have a pluralistic kind of religious life because three religions are predominant among the people — Christianity, Islam, and ATR.[314]

---

[308] Ibid, "Household Gods in Jewish Cosmology and the Challenges of Syncre-Fetish Practices among Yoruba Christians," *International Journal of Research in Humanities and Social Studies* Vol. 2, Issue 12 (December 2015): 59.

[309] Roger Blench, *An Atlas of Nigerian Languages,* 3rd Edition (Cambridge: Kay Williamson Educational Foundation, 2012), 91.

[310] Ibid.

[311] Margaret Thompson Drewal, *Yoruba Ritual: Performers, Play, Agency,* eds., Charles S. Bird, Ivan Karp, James Fernandez, Luc de Heusch, John Middleton, and Roy Willis (Indianapolis: Indiana University Press, 1992).

[312] Blench, 91.

[313] Oladejo, *Reciprocal Impacts,* 103.

[314] Olarinmoye, 020-021.

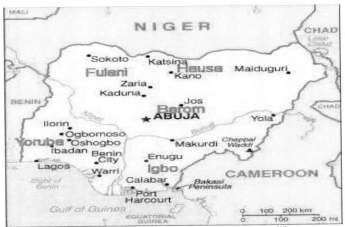

Figure 1: Map of Nigeria Showing Location of Yorubaland[315]

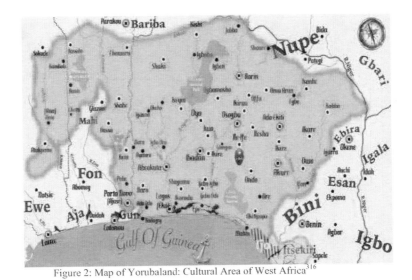

Figure 2: Map of Yorubaland: Cultural Area of West Africa[316]

[315]*http://www.google.com.ng/search?q=Map+of+Nigeria+Showing+Location+of+Yor%C3%B9b%C3%A1land+pdf* (accessed August 22, 2018).
[316] *Map of Yorubaland_Cultural_Area_of_West_Africa*<Accessed on Feb. 15, 2018>

2. Human Life in *Yorùbá* Philosophy

The writer investigated the philosophy of *Yorùbá* to determine how much appreciation is within the fabrics and practices of the people. Scholars express their philosophy in some ways; namely, their system of religious beliefs and practices, cosmology and cosmogony, metaphysics, and ethics. Essentially, *Yorùbá* were predominantly adherents of ATR in the time past. The presence of Islam and Christianity in the land was a later addition. According to Johnson, the people believe in the existence of the Supreme Being called *Olorun* (LORD of Heaven), the Maker of the universe. However, it is the opinion of this writer that *Olorun* as a disgination is an import from the Christian faith. The people also believe in the presence of many *Orisa* (deities) regarded as intermediaries between them and God.[317]

Certain other aspects of this belief system include: future state and "invocation of spirits" of the dead closed persons; and belief in a future judgment as expressed in this adage, "*Ohun gbogbo ti a se l'aiye, li a de idena Orun ka*" (Whatever we do on earth we shall present its account at the portals of heaven). The people also hold the doctrine of reincarnation in high esteem. They regard this idea as "transmigration of souls" which implies that the departed parents are reborn into the family line after sometimes. Hence, the idea behind some specific *Yorùbá* names is on this basis; namely, *Babatunde* (father has come again), and *Yetunde* (mother has come back).[318]

Moreover, the people express the origin of human life in *Yorùbá* metaphysics. *Ifa* Corpus, the "philosophy, knowledge, and acts of *Orunmila* while on earth" contains this expression.[319] *Orunmila* is believed to be one of the 401 divinities of Olodumare who is in charge of wisdom and knowledge of all things both in the material and invisible world of the spirits while *Ifa* corpus is his scriptures. According to Wande Abimbola, *Ifa* is given certain other names; namely, "*Afedefeyo*" ("master of the Oyo dialect as well as other languages"), "*Akerefinusogbon*" ("the small man with a mind full of wisdom"), and "*Obarisa*" ("king of the divinities"). His priests gave the divinity this last name as an expression of his prominent place among the divinities.[320] The myths that explain how *Yorùbá* divinities or deities made their way to the earth from heaven are diverse. Nonetheless, one thing is very certain; they all came to Ife Township in the modern State of Osun, Nigeria. In this regard, Abimbola advances, "Ife is therefore regarded not only as the cradle of the Yoruba people but also as the cradle of humanity."[321]

Each of these divinities was given a specific assignment to carry out by *Olodumare*, "the Yoruba High God." *Ifa* was to mould the earth by the profundity of his wisdom and vastness of his understanding, *Ogun* was to confront all problems relating to bravery and warfare using his mighty physical power with his courage and skills. Moreover, *Orisanla*, the divinity of creation, was to give adequate shape to human bodies as obtained today while *Esu*, the deity of trickster, was for the upkeep

---

[317] Johnson, 26.
[318] Ibid.
[319] Akintola, 12.
[320] Wande Abimbola, *Sixteen Great Poems of Ifa* (Niamey: UNESCO and Abimbola, 1975), 2.
[321] Ibid, 2-3.

of *ase* (divine authority and power). In other words, *Esu* divinity is the divine policeman in charge of the entire cosmos and keeper of the heavenly ability and control of the High God.[322]

Abimbola also advances that upon the arrival of the divinities at Ife, they all took positions; occupying different places of Yorubaland. *Esu* went to Ketu, *Ogun* to Saki, *Orisanla* to Ifon, and *Orunmila* (called *Ifa*) remained at Ife where he raised his eight children who later became prominent kings in Yorubaland. However, Orunmila was forced to return to *orun* (heaven) as a result of what is called "an unbearable insult" from his last son.[323]

According to Abimbola, Orunmila's return is the cause of the disorder in the world. Although his children made efforts in bringing him back, Orunmila refused. However, he gave each of them "the sacred sixteen palmnuts" instead to consult him at any time. These later became the most significant symbol of *Ifa* divination. Hence, *Ifa* became the *Yorùbá* divinity of three important aspects of human life; namely, wisdom, knowledge, and divination.[324] This writer observed that the aspect of divination is to gain a better understanding of situations, events or circumstances. The children of Orunmila took the sixteen palm nuts from *opa Ifa* (a special palm-tree under which they met their father in *orun*) regarded as "*ikin.*"[325] The *Ifa* priest keeps these nuts sacred and in the metallic or wooden "Ifa bowl" placed at a corner of the house. The priests regard this location as the *Ifa* shrine of the priest where they make prayers and sacrifices.[326] Some of the other paraphernalia of this divination, aside *Ikin*, are; namely, *Opele* ("the divining chain"), *Ibo* ("instruments for casting lots"), *Iyerosun* ("divination power"), *Iroke* ("carved wooden or Ivory object used to invoke *Ifa*"), and *Opon Ifa* ("the divining tray").[327]

It should be clear at this juncture that both *Olorun* and *Olodumare* (the Supreme Being) are the divine names of God in Yorubaland and the two are used interchangeably in this study. According to Akintola, all divinities were on the ground in heaven while *Olodumare* was making humankind. They gave Him a helping hand in supplying the clay with which He moulded humankind. They were equally with Him throughout the process. However, *Olodumare* alone gave life to man and man became a living soul in the end.[328]

The nature and worth of human life in *Yorùbá* metaphysics are of equal importance to this section. *Yorùbá* believe that man's existence and earth-life are temporary and one's biological birth does not mark the beginning of one's life. The creation of man has first taken place in heaven, after which every one prepares for one's short earth-life which requires a biological process. At the time of departure, there is the participation of some other divinities apart from *Olodumare*; examples of

---

[322] Ibid, *Ifa Divination Poetry*, trans., & ed. Wande Abimbola (New York: NOK Publishers Ltd, 1977), 1.
[323] Ibid, *Sixteen Great Poems of Ifa*, 3.
[324] Ibid, 4.
[325] Ibid, *Ifa Divination Poetry*, 4.
[326] Ibid, 4-5.
[327] Ibid, 5-9.
[328] Akintola, 54-55.

whom are: *Elenini* (Divinity in charge of Misfortune), the keeper of the Divine Altar in *Olodumare's* palace; *Eledaa* (the Guardian Angel of Man or "spirit-double"), and *Ori-Inu* ("man's spirit-personality"). *Olodumare* Himself gives the final order for departure.[329]

In these departure arrangements, the exercise of each man's free will comes first such that each person will show interest in earth-life. The effort of *Eledaa* to lead him to appear before *Olodumare* comes next. The third step is also directed by *Eledaa* who leads the man to kneel before the divine altar to approach *Olodumare*. In this place and posture, the individual personality departing to the world will present his desired wishes. The wish or wishes presented will later be the basis for the person's life purpose on earth. One of these wishes is the length of time that the person wants to spend on earth. All these wishes, called *kadara* or *ayanmo* (fate or destiny), are presented to God in the presence of *Elenini* who only is the divinity that keeps the Divine Altar. *Olodumare* endorses whatever wishes presented before Him using stamping down His *Ase* (divine sceptre of authority"). After this, the departing human being's *Eledaa* will trail him or her to get fully prepared to depart.[330]

Fulfilment of anybody's *kadara* or *ayanmo* on earth is not automatic. If the departing human being did well to *Elenini* by paying necessary "sacrificial homage" at the point of coming for earth-life, no impediment would trail his or her wishes. If not, *Elenini* will resist the individual from the beginning to the end.[331] Thus, the quality of human life on earth, according to *Ifa* Corpus, partly depends on the kind of wishes presented and sanctioned by *Olodumare*. Similarly, it also depends on whether or not the person paid necessary homage to *Elenini* before leaving for earth. These two factors eventually playoff in the kind of destiny one will have on earth – either *Ori-rere* ("good fortune/destiny") or *Ori-buruku* ("ill-luck, bad destiny"). A reflection of this reality appears in an *Ifa* poem titled, "Fortune Suspended in *Ahira* Sack" as extracted from *Ogundaghorogbe* Corpus.[332]

There is another form of resistance that human life may witness on earth in the process of fulfilling his or her destiny. The opposition is from *Esu* or *Elegbara* (the Divinity who resists human beings by dishing out a necessary punishment retributively for the sins committed in the world). *Esu* does this on God's behalf for he is an agent of *Olodumare*.[333]

Additionally, Ruth Finnegan regards *Eshu-Elegba* as "the messenger deity" and a god who specialises in causing mischief. Some hymns used in praising this deity can shed more light on his person, an example of which is:

When he is angry he hits a stone until it bleeds. When he is angry he sits on the skin of an ant. When he is angry he weeps tears of blood. Eshu, confuser of men. The owners of twenty slaves is sacrificing, So that Eshu

---

[329] Ibid, 67.
[330] Ibid, 67-68.
[331] Ibid, 68.
[332] Yemi Elebuibon, *Ifa: The Custodian of Destiny* (Bodija: Penthouse Publications (Nig.), 2004), 11.
[333] Akintola, 70

may not confuse him. The owner of thirty 'iwofa' [pawns] is sacrificing. So
that Eshu may not confuse him. Eshu confused the newly married wife.
When she stole the cowries from the sacred shrine of Oya 16
She said she had not realized That taking two hundred cowries was
stealing. Eshu confused the head of the queen— And she started to go
naked. Then Eshu beat her to make her cry. Eshu, do not confuse me!
Eshu, do not confuse the load on my head . . .17
Eshu slept in the house— But the house was too small for him. Eshu slept
on the verandah— But the verandah was too small for him.
Eshu slept in a nut— At last he could stretch himself.

Eshu walked through the groundnut farm. The tuft of his hair was just
visible. If it had not been for his huge size, He would not have been visible
at all. Having thrown a stone yesterday—he kills a bird today. Lying down,
his head hits the roof. Standing up he cannot look into the cooking pot.[334]

Thus, this writer can advance that *Esu*, in addition to *Elenini*, is also a significant
factor to consider in the fulfilment of human destiny according to *Yorùbá*
metaphysics. Therefore, this is why he has to be appeased by sacrifice so that one may
avoid trouble or hindrance.

Given all this, one's fate is both pre-determined before conception and after
delivery to earth-life. On this situation, Akintola advances:

> All these suggest, too, that the spirit or destiny, or fate, as ordained by
> *Olodumare* for each person coming to the world, is already determined prior
> to the moment of biological conception. Something mystical happens at the
> unknown moment of the fertilization of the female ovum by the male sperm. It
> is at this mystical moment that the fate of the nascent life is determined. Its
> fortune, its temperament, it (sic) biological genes which pre-determines its
> features, mood, character, idiosyncrasies, and genetic typing, giving it its
> entire human personality, or what the ancient Romans called 'genius', and
> what in the Book of Genesis 2:7, is characterized as the breath of life, the
> "sneezing of life" which animated the human clay mould and transforms him
> (man) mysteriously into a 'living being, with a personality and a self.'[335]

If the fate of humankind is so determined this way, the question then is where the
place of the subsequent exercise of the free will given to each human being is? Again,
on what basis shall the future judgment be if God has so fixed a person's life on earth
before coming for earth life when one is not conscious and knowledgeable enough to
decide on good wishes to present before *Olodumare*?

Furthermore, the writer has to consider the foundation of *Yorùbá* ethics.
According to *Ifa* Corpus, there is a body of rules which Olodumare gave to the
divinities after the creation of the earth with the instruction that they should make the
world habitable. These rules are for proper conducts on earth and regarded as a "code
of Natural Laws." The people derived the rules from the metaphysics of *Orunmila*
bothering the divine nature of God and creation narration of the universe. This code is

---

[334] Ruth Finnegan, *Oral Literature in Africa: World Oral Literature Series*, Volume 1
(Cambridge: Open Book, 2012), 173-74.
[335] Akintola, 71.

also regarded as the basis of all ethics; namely, to love *Olodumare* as the Supreme Being and to recognise Him as the "Father of the universe and Creator of All Things," and everyone should treat others the way one wants others to treat him or her. The people regard this as the "Golden Rule" in *Yorùbá* ethics.

An instance of the second aspect of this rule is that since no one wants to die, no one should kill anyone also.[336] Apart from the fact that this code serves as the basis of all ethics, it is also the foundation of all legal systems which includes the Ten Commandment of the OT called *Decalogue*. Akintola advances that the code is to govern the inter-personal relationship among the divinities and humanity.[337]

The concept of a good life or virtuous life in *Yorùbá* worldview is by *Yorùbá* ethics. According to Akintola,

> A virtuous life or good life is one which gives happiness and pleasure; and that happiness or pleasure can be substantiated only in terms of the individual's possession of prosperity (money, houses and landed property – in Yoruba, *owo ati oro, ile ati ile*), wives (*aya*), and all other good things of life – in Yoruba, *ire gbogbo, ile aye, alaafia* (good health), *aiku, bale oro* (longevity), *ati omo* (children).[338]

The basis of this belief system is that the concept of the good life in *Yorùbá* worldview is contingent on how much happiness and pleasure one possesses. The argument of this writer, therefore, is that this belief system possibly informs the unnecessary increase in the quest for some of these good things of life by the contemporary *Yorùbá* boys and girls, and men and women. Many of them also show utter contempt for the sacredness of human life by using human life for rituals to become rich overnight since almost everyone wants to be happy and live a pleasurable existence.

Moreover, the value of human life among the people can be understood when scholars consider the ways and manners by which the people worship the deities. According to Oladejo, citing T.F. Jemiriye, an emphasis is placed on "concreteness of the divine as it is available to man that it emphasises the ultimate." Given this, *Yorùbá* people view the *Orisa* as functional gods while Olodumare is the Ultimate Leader, the Supreme Being. In addition to this, *Yorùbá* are believed to have "four-tiered system" of spiritual beings; namely, Olodumare, the Supreme Being, occupies the top level, the *orisa*, in their hierarchy, come next to Him and the "deified ancestors" follow in rank, examples of whom are *Sango, Oya, Ogun,* and *Oranmiyan.*

At the lowest level of the rank are spirits associated with certain material parts of the universe such as the earth, the rivers, trees, and the mountains. These divinities occupy the fourth tier and are worshipped by traditional *Yorùbá* to obtain their favour at any given time. The people do this with the belief that the deities are intermediaries between God and humanity. Worship of this kind takes place using different sacrifices, depending on the taste of the god(s) and occasion that determines the

---

[336] Ibid, 98-99.
[337] Ibid, 99.
[338] Ibid, 100.

adoration. Oladejo termed religious belief of this kind "Henotheism."[339] By implication, human beings never come close to any of these four-tiered spirit beings in value and worth. This writer equally views this belief-system as a basis for the perceived low estimate of human life among the people.

Moreover, *Yorùbá* appreciation of human life is further understood when scholars consider the concept of beings. In their cosmology, the earliest creatures of *Olodumare* (also called *Eleda*, meaning Creator) are the *Irunmoles* (divinities). *Ejiogbe*, the most senior apostle to *Orunmila* among the gods that followed him to the world, brings this understanding to the fore.[340] The *Irunmoles* are 401 in number, and their creation predated the making of the universe. 201 of them are significant divinities while the remaining 200 are minor in rank.[341] Akintola advances that all of them lived in a place called "Divinosphere" which the people regard as the earliest and first place of residence for the spirits beings. Again, they were all endowed with a power to communicate or navigate between the celestial chamber of *Olodumare* (heaven) and earth. In other words, they are potent enough to know what takes place in the realms of the spirit and material. This situation is by additional visionary powers which gave them a direct communication link with *Olodumare* whom nobody can contact physically.[342]

In the *Yorùbá* pantheon of the deities, the 201 divinities are called higher and benevolent beings. In other words, they are often graciously and generously disposed to human beings. Among them are the following: *Orisa-nla, Orunmila, Olokun, Ogun, Sango, Osun, Oya*, and the 16 *Olodus* whom the people regard as *Orunmila's* disciples. However, the remaining 200 are lower and evil spirit beings. By implication, the dispositions of these beings are harmful to humankind. A few examples of them are; namely, *Iku* (Death), *Ofo* (Loss), *Arun* (Disease), *Egba* (Paralysis), *Ejo, Idena* (Obstacles), and *Elenini* (Misfortune). The people regard these divinities jointly as *Alajogun* or *Ese*.[343] On the deity of *Iku* (Death), Philip John Neimark advances that the people consider death as one of the *orisa* (servants) of *Olodumare* whose responsibility is to take people home at their preordained time, but sometimes in a careless manner.[344]

By the friendly nature of the benevolent deities about the plight of humankind, this writer argues that the possibility of consulting them to obtain a good life is high among the people. Since these spirits are disposed to human beings compassionately by nature, anybody can contact them for assistance whenever there is an impediment or delay to destiny fulfilment. Similarly, the need to appease their evil counterparts for a life of happiness and pleasure is equally great. Since the *Yorùbá* concept of the good life is all about possessing sure beauties of life on earth, whoever, therefore,

---

[339] Oladejo, *Household Gods*, 59.

[340] Akintola, 9.

[341] Ibid.

[342] Ibid, 49-50.

[343] Ibid, 52-53.

[344] Philip John Neimark, *The Way of the Orisa: Empowering Your Life through the Ancient African Religion of Ifa* (San Francisco: Harper Publishers, n.d), 43.

desires to have a life of fulfilment will have to appease any of these gods. This situation arises because the forces are often the hindrance. Examples of inhibitions caused by these deities are the following: untimely death, loss, sicknesses and diseases, troubles, obstacles, and misfortune. The demand for the sacrifice of human blood is a possibility in the course of appeasement because of the sacredness of life.

Furthermore, investigating the objects of worship that the people traditionally venerate is also essential to this study. One of them is *Orisala*, to whom the people ascribe creative powers. He is believed to be one chief divinity among God's co-workers. His role in the making of man is the task of giving definite shape to the human lump. This divinity is venerated by different townships with different designations; namely, *Orisa Oluofin* (at Iwofin), *Orisako* (at Oko), *Orisakire* (at Ikire), *Orisagiyan* (at Ejigbo), *Orisaeguin* (at Eguin), *Orisarowu* (at Owu) *Orisajaye* (at Ijaye) and *Obatala* (at Oba). Another one is *Ori* (head) that the people worship as the household god of destiny or fate. A common belief is that it is the will or decree of this god that attends one's way, either good fortune or ill type. Hence, propitiation is carried out by an average *Yorùbá* person to gain the goodwill of *Ori* to obtain great luck.[345] In this writer's view, there is every tendency for *Ori* to demand *Ebo kanka* (a big sacrifice) which most likely may involve human blood.

Esu who receives an extraordinary propitiation is another example. His worshippers offer specific offerings to avert his anger or evil. Some other objects of worship include but not limited to the following; namely, *Sopona* (Smallpox), *Ogun* (god of war, the blacksmiths' god), and *Egungun*.[346]

Equally, the concept of life and death and that of the afterlife are some other areas to examine. Oladejo, citing Osadolor Imasogie, argues that the *Yorùbá* explain life and death in term of commerce. They present this world as a marketplace or farm in their worldview.[347] More so, their concept of the afterlife is in association with the ancestors whom they regard as the living dead. Oladejo argues that when a person dies, he lives on hereafter and continues to play a significant role within the family life after death. It is by this underpinning factor that the people perform certain rites for the deceased over some time.[348]

According to Drewal, the actual *Ifehin oku-tile* (interment), one of these rites of passage, begins the funeral process of a deceased person. This celebration is followed by a seven-day event, the first day of which is called *ojo-isinku* ("funeral day of ritual"), the third day is called *itaoku* (a day of feasting), and the fourth day is *irenoku* (a day of playing on behalf of the deceased). This fourth day is usually a day of public celebration or play. The seventh day, which is the last day of this programme, is called *ijeku*; it is a day of celebration.

Ifehin oku-tile (interment) comprises of certain other ceremonies, including the following: *"Iweku"* ('washing the corpse'), *"Ikefunlowo"* ('rubbing chalk on the

---

[345] Johnson, 27.
[346] Ibid, 26-29.
[347] Olusayo B. Oladejo, *Life and Death in the Old Testament and Yoruba Worldview*, 51.
[348] Ibid, 197.

deceased's palms'), *"Ikosunlowo"* ('rubbing camwood on the palms'), *Idiku Ologbon* ('wrapping the corpse of the wise elder'), *"Iwegi"* ('washing the coffin'), *"Ifehinkutile"* ('laying the back of the deceased on the earth'), *"Ibokuu-yaju"* ('entertaining with the deceased'), and *"Ikanku"* ('sending away the spirit of the deceased').[349] More so, the people usually perform the following ceremonies on *ojo-isinku* ('the funeral day of rituals'): *"Owoetiweku"* ('collecting money for the deceased'), *"Ereisinku"* ('playing for the funeral'), *"Imoran Oku, Imu oran oku"* (taking the achievements of the deceased'), and *"Ikankuolowo"* ('invoking the soul of the deceased'). The third day called *"Itaoku"* was always a day of sacrifice at *"Igbo Oro"* ('sacrifice at the grove of Oro') at night, feasting and *Ila oku l'oun* ('opening the voice of the deceased'). The fourth day called *"Irenoku"* was usually reserved for elaborate feasting and parade through the town by the deceased children and friends with pomp and pageantry.[350] All this shows the worth that *Yorùbá* attached to human life in their traditional setting, especially when their relations embarked on a final journey home to join the ancestors.

Similarly, E. Bolaji Idowu advances that *Yorùbá* people highly regard the end of life on earth because whatever happens at this end is consequential. It dramatically determines how the deceased will continue their existence hereafter.[351] Again, Neimark argues that *aye* (the world) is viewed as a marketplace for everyone while *Ikole-Orun* (heaven) is the home. This belief system teaches that everyone visits the earth for a specific learning and growth experience. The moment this is achieved, one will have to return home in one's turn.[352]

3. Sanctity of Life and *Yorùbá* Rituals

Sanctity of human life among *Yorùbá* is better understood when scholars consider issues relating to rituals. The basis of this section is about the worship of the gods. The traditional *Yorùbá* people are of the view that certain powers are around them that are superior to humankind in all respects. These powers are environmental and have influences and control throughout nature, including human beings. Therefore, the people accord the spirits prime positions, veneration and worth better than what the people could give to any among their ranks. In most cases, these spirits largely determine achievement of a life of happiness and pleasure that forms the basis of the good human existence in *Yorùbá* ethics. Hence, the people have to worship the forces for the welfare, care, and security of their worshippers or devotees. Given this belief system, the worth of human life among the *Yorùbá* seems to be low. According to G.J. Afolabi Ojo, some of these powers are "prominent natural objects of natural (sic) environment, ancestors considered as connected with the natural environment, and

---

[349] Drewal, 39-41.

[350] Ibid, 41-43.

[351] E. Bolaji Idowu, *Olodumare: God in Yoruba Belief* (Ikeja: Longman Nigeria Plc, 1996), 201.

[352] Neimark, 45.

other phenomena, inexplicable to the minds of the Yoruba, which derive from the natural environment."[353]

Again, some of the environmental powers of veneration in *Yorùbá* religion have a connection with highlands and hills. These objects are believed to be the dwelling places of the gods. Examples of these sacred objects are essential to this study. *Yorùbá* people worship the hill *Orosun* and her consort *Olofin* at Idanre town of Ondo State in May and June respectively. They also worship *Olosunta* hill as the first *Orisa* in Ikere-Ekiti. The worship of *Ajo* and *Okelota* hills of Ado-Ekiti during the *"Etado"* festival is another. Many of the inhabitants of Efon Alaye and those of the nearby towns also venerate *Efon Alaye-Okemesi* ridge. *Olumo* rock, the "deity of Abeokuta," also gains veneration of many devotees long after its usefulness. Among others is *Okebadan*, worshipped in March, and one of the hills in Oke Iho.[354]

Similarly, these powers are in connection with rivers, lagoons, and the sea temples. An average traditional *Yorùbá* person worships river-spirit gods for many reasons, of which aversion of peril associated with crossing the rivers during the raining season is critical. Sometimes, some of the devotees give human offerings to the gods in the process of averting dangers. According to Ojo, worship of the river-gods is everywhere in Yorubaland. Some of these gods and goddesses of the biggest rivers are River *Ogun* flowing past Abeokuta, River *Osun* of Oshogbo, Ede and Iwo, *Oni* River of Efon-Alaye, and *Ogbese* of Ado-Ekiti. Another deity of river-spirit is *Oya* which is considered to be "the goddess of the River Niger." People of the northern part of the land worship the river. *Oloso* is another centre of veneration in the Lagos lagoon. Also in Lagos are the worship of the duo of *Olokun* (the owner of the sea) and his wife *Olokunsu* (the goddess of the bar).[355]

Moreover, these superior powers inhabit the thick and abundant vegetation of trees, and the people worship them. Examples of these big trees with over-towering effects over others in the rainforest zone are; namely, silked cotton tree (*Eriodentron orientale*), *Iroko* (Chlorophora excelsa), and the baobab (Andansonia digitata) in the deciduous and savanna zones. According to Yemi Elebuibon, *Iroko* tree, called African Teak Chlorofora Excelsa, gains awe of this kind by the people for inhabiting spirits that possess procreation power. This situation is evident in an *Ifa* poem titled, "Iroko Tree that Conspired" as contained in *Okanranrosun* Corpus.[356]

Some others of this kind but regarded as "less imposing trees" are the following; namely, *Akoko* tree (Newboldia laevis), *awusa* (Tetracarpiduium conophorum) and *ekika* (hog plum). *Yorùbá* people believe that *Abiku* "born to die in infancy" children have their dwelling places with the spirits in these shady forests.[357] Also, they are also of the belief that all trees that are of great benefits to humans equally harbour certain deities. These include the following trees: *ayan* (African

---

[353] G.J. Afolabi Ojo, *Yoruba Culture: A Geographical Analysis* (Warwick Lane, London: 1966), 158-159.

[354] Ibid, 161-162.

[355] Ibid, 162-166.

[356] Elebuibon, *Ifa: The Custodian of Destiny*, 3.

[357] Ojo, 166.

satinwood) inhabiting the *Yorùbá* god of drums, *omo* (Cordia millenii) and *asorin*. One other prominent tree that the writer has to mention is the "uncommon palm tree with seven trunks." The people of Aiyetoro-Ekiti in Ekiti State worshipped it annually. The market-trees are of equal importance.[358]

Furthermore, *Yorùbá* people regard certain animals in Yorubaland as embodiments of various deities. They, therefore, believe that they should worship them. An instance is the worship of monkeys by most of the mothers of twins for their belief that these animals inhabit dead twins. Similarly, vultures are regarded as the "reincarnated ancestors" and are, therefore, sacred. The people also worship the god in the python in places like Abeokuta. The same thing applies to crocodiles-spirits in places like Ibadan, Iwo, and Ede. Many of the wild animals are believed to possess certain powers that make them superior to man and worthy of human adoration. A prominent example of these animal-spirits is the chimpanzee whose veneration is famous among the hunters for possessing ability that defiles hunters' guns.[359]

Likewise, the earth or land gained the worship of the traditional *Yorùbá* people everywhere. According to Ojo, this was very prominent among the people of Oba, a small village in Akure. Again, the worship has also witnessed a transformation in the Ogboni cult which "sanctions the Earth as a spirit." Therefore, the people offer sacrifices to the land on the basis that "it is the giver of most things that are needed for human sustenance." Thus, members of this cult offer the first thing that comes from the land back to the Earth-spirit in the form of libations. This understanding is also the basis for ancestor worship or adoration.[360] Among other superior powers related to natural objects in the human environment is *Orisa-Oko* (the farm-god), safeguarding *Yorùbá* people from natural disasters associated with farming such as infertility of the soil, drought, and pests and crop diseases. Another one is *Ogun* (the deity of iron and war) of which Ire-Ekiti is the main centre of its worship while places like Ilesha, Ondo, Akure, Owo, Ado-Ekiti, Efon-Alaye, Otun, and Okemesi are others.

Ogun, "the ancient god of iron, warfare, and hunting," has become a deity of interest. How the people have kept the worship of this deity alive to expand beyond the shore of West Africa to other continents like Latin America, the Caribbean, and North America, and keep it flourishing like the Christian and Islamic faiths, have become a focus of many scholars in many fields. Some of these fields are anthropology, religious studies, art history, linguistics, history, folklore, sociology, and performance studies. According to Sandra T. Barnes, "As a consequence, more than 70 million African and New World peoples participate, in (sic) or are closely familiar with, religious systems that include *Ogun*, and the number is increasing rather than declining." To this end, *Ogun* has become one religion from African soil gaining

---

[358] Ibid, 167.
[359] Ibid, 168.
[360] Ibid.

117

comparison with some of the beliefs of the ancient Greek and Roman peoples or those of the present-day Hindus.[361]

Some ways by which one can identify the devotees of *Ogun* are by the wearing of iron emblems, displaying of flaming red eyes when in anger, and dancing with swords.[362] According to Elebuibon, it is a familiar saying that *Ogun* does not have his garments except palm fronds. The scholar analysed the underlining factor behind this situation in a poem titled, "The Market of Tolerance" as enshrined in *Iwori Were* Corpus.[363] More so, one thing of note that serves as the underlining factor that leads to the flourishing of this cult, according to Robert G. Armstrong, is its social appeal to people who are directly dealing with the use of modern technology rooted in iron. As a result of this reality, scholars regard *Ogun* as "the cult of revolution."[364] In addition to all this, both Barnes and Paula Girshick Ben-Amos posit that the cult of *Ogun* was the basis of the building and development of various empires along the Coast of Guinea in West Africa around 1400 and 1700,[365] of which the Kingdom of Benin, *Yorùbá* Kingdom of Oyo, and that of Dahomey were the dominant types.[366]

Thunder and Lightning are two natural events of worship associated with past *Yorùbá* heroes and ancestors. *Yorùbá* people do worship these heroes to gain more prominence. *Sango* or *Jakuta*, the fourth Alaafin of Oyo, is known as the "god of lightning and thunder" and Oyo is the home of the deity, although its worship spreads across Yorubaland to West African nations like Ghana, Togo, and Ivory Coast and among *Yorùbá* in Cuba and Bahia in Brazil.[367] Winds and gales, *Olojo* (the deity of the day), the moon-deity are some others. The people worship all these for different purposes such as fruitfulness, good fortune, and bountiful harvest.[368]

Almost all the gods in association with the environment have gained recognition among the people. This situation is so because the gods are believed to possess some specific powers and could render some assistance to the people. An example of the aid of this kind is solving environmental problems. Prominent among these deities with power over environmental hazards are; namely, ancestral cult, the

---

[361] Sandra T. Barnes, "Introduction: The Many Faces of Ogun," in *Africa's Ogun: Old World and New*, eds., Sandra T. Barnes, Charles S. Bird, Ivan Karp, Thomas O Beidelman, James Fernandez, Luc de Heusch, John Middleton, and Roy Willis (Indianapolis: Indiana University Press, 1989), 1.

[362] Ibid, 2.

[363] Elebuibon, *Ifa: The Custodian of Destiny*, 10.

[364] Robert G. Armstrong, "The Etymology of the Word 'Ogun'," in *Africa's Ogun: Old World and New*, eds., Sandra T. Barnes, Charles S. Bird, Ivan Karp, Thomas O Beidelman, James Fernandez, Luc de Heusch, John Middleton, and Roy Willis (Indianapolis: Indiana University Press, 1989), 29.

[365] Sandra T. Barnes & Paula Girshick Ben-Amos, "Ogun, the Empire Builder," in *Africa's Ogun: Old World and New*, eds., Sandra T. Barnes, Charles S. Bird, Ivan Karp, Thomas O Beidelman, James Fernandez, Luc de Heusch, John Middleton, and Roy Willis (Indianapolis: Indiana University Press, 1989), 39.

[366] Ibid, 42-48.

[367] Ojo, 168-172.

[368] Ibid, 172-175

gods of diseases, evil and divination, and *Olodumare*. However, there are specific other deities which have no relationship to any physical objects.[369]

Deities introduced as a result of sicknesses, diseases, and other life hazards are also of equal importance. The people established this system of belief as a result of problems like the prevalence of an epidemic, its toll on human life and its weakening effects on the survivors. Some of these deities are *Sopono* (smallpox), responsible for the infection of smallpox among the people when they do not adequately appease the god. The god of the twins is another for it is capable of protecting the twins from illnesses, keeping them together on earth or separating them upon the demise of one of them, and preventing the mother from experiencing the misfortune of having another set upon the death of the previous one. *Osanyin* ("the special consultant deity of medicinal and psychical cures"), the god-of-all-diseases in Ado-Ekiti; and *Olorosa* (the deity of houses) worshipped to check the excesses of witches and wizards are some others accorded recognition in this direction.[370]

Esu, the supreme power of evil, is a deity in charge of bad omens such as "illnesses, diseases, suffering, misfortunes, accidents, calamities and catastrophes." Yoruba believe that they could control *Esu* or, at least divert his evils to the enemies, and they could appease him to gain his favour. Therefore, the deity gained worship among the people.[371] *Orunmila* ("the oracular deity") is one prominent deity in Yorubaland with his oracular system called *Ifa*. People often consult *Orunmila* for various degrees of life-threatening situations or uncertainties which characterise man's present and future environmental challenges. The deity is regarded as the intermediary god and a spokesman for the rest of the gods and they thus consult him on almost every critical decision to be made. *Ifa* system is practised not only throughout the entire Yorubaland but also in Benin and Ibo lands in Nigeria and outside the Nigerian soil in Dahomey, Togo, and Ghana.[372]

Also, ancestor worship is of equal importance to this study. Geoffrey Parrinder argues that ancestor worship is deeply rooted generally in Africa, most especially in the sub-region. Parrinder made this claim in a study the scholar conducted on the beliefs and practices of certain people groups within West Africa sub-region, of which *Yorùbá* is one. In the analysis of this scholar, one practical way by which people practice this belief is libation. An average traditional African pours out a little wine on the ground for the ancestors before drinking. In some other instances, the people place a mouthful of food on the floor before eating. Again, at the evening meal, pots are not entirely emptied. Should any of the ancestors come on the visit, they must have something to eat. This belief is by African understanding of the fact that ancestors are the pious dead for they are part of the living. And so, they are regarded as the living dead, a belief that reflects Africa's nature of communal life.[373]

---

[369] Ibid, 175.
[370] Ibid, 177-178.
[371] Ibid, 179.
[372] Ibid, 180-181.
[373] Geoffrey Parrinder, *West African Religion: A Study of the Beliefs and Practices of Akan, Ewe, Yorùbá, Igbo and Kindred Peoples* (London: Epworth Press, 1978), 116.

Similarly, according to J. Omosade Awolalu, ancestors are believed to have specific exclusive functions to perform before God on behalf of the living within the family or community life. These functions include but not limited to the following: care and protection, discipline, and guidance of family affairs and traditions. Among Yorùbá, it is also a common belief that any offence against the culture and customs of the family or land is equally against the ancestors.[374]

Additionally, Joseph Healey and Donald Sybertz are of the view that in the Traditional African society, the concept of the ancestor is of great importance to the life of an average person, most especially in Yorubaland. The ancestors are believed not taking the place of "the Supreme God" in any way but are mediators between Him and the living as they are still part of the life of the family and that of the community. Again, an average African traditionalist holds the custom of sacrifice to ancestors in high esteem. The practice could be blood sacrifice (either of animals or humans) or of any material thing for propitiation so that members of the family may be free of any trouble.[375]

As a result of the high estimate given to the ancestors at the expense of the humans, there is a cult of the dead and that of the ancestor. There is a difference between these two. According to Awolalu, not all the dead obtain worship from the living in YTR except those who lived piously on earth and were justified by *Olodumare*. These ancestors will gain access to "*Orun-Rere*" (good heaven) and be permitted to reincarnate after final post-mortem judgment.[376]

Egungun (masquerade) worship is in connection with the concept of the ancestor in Yorubaland. While analysing this belief system, Awolalu argues that the spirits of the ancestors are believed to materialise in *Egungun*. It is a bodily representative of the spirit of a deceased person believed to return from the spirit world in an attempt to visit his or her children. As a result, the people regard *Egungun* as *Ara-Orun* (one who comes from heaven). However, *Yorùbá* people equally believe that not all families have *Egungun*, but every family has ancestors. Again, as part of this belief system, witches, wizards, and sorcerers, as well as charms, are believed to be powerless over anyone unless one's ancestors are sleeping or have neglected one.[377]

Furthermore, John S. Mbiti claims that it is part of *Yorùbá* belief that God created death for the specific purpose of recalling people to heaven at their specified time. In this sense, they perceive that passing away is a debt for all.[378] Mbiti also claims that when a man dies, the soul first becomes a ghost. It is after the family has erected a shrine at the final funeral ceremony that it becomes a spirit and travels to the

---

[374] J. Omosade Awolalu, *Yoruba Beliefs and Sacrificial Rites* (London: Longman Group Ltd, 1979), 61.

[375] Joseph Healey, and Donald Sybertz, *Towards an African Narrative Theology* (Nairobi: Pauline's Publications Africa, 2000), 211.

[376] Awolalu, 65.

[377] Ibid.

[378] John S. Mbiti, *Concepts of God in Africa* (Nairobi: Action Publishers, 2012), 426.

land of the departed ones.[379] While advancing the need for certain rites after death, Mbiti argues that the performances of these rites aim at "bringing the spirit of the deceased into the house" and giving the living the opportunity to have social intercourse with the deceased once more.[380] This situation, therefore, explains the reason why an average *Yorùbá* values funeral rite than the care of the living.

Moreover, according to Oladejo, scholars like Turaki advance the idea of personal gods among the Yorùbá. The people call these gods household and tribal deities. The designation is by a particular class of distinguished and unique people. Many of them are worshipped generationally within the family line as consultants, guides, guardians, and benefactors.[381]

Specifically, it is necessary for this writer to consider the practice of human sacrifice among the people. After analysing the *Yorùbá* worldview about human sacrifices to the gods, Oladejo posits that the entire life of humankind is both sacred and of great worth. The reason is that the gods often demand the best and the people present the same to them.[382]

Similarly, Adedayo Emmanuel Afe argues that human sacrifice is a common belief among the *Yorùbá* and the people regard the same as the highest form of sacrifice.[383] This is corroborated by Drewal as she wrote on the preponderance of this practice among the people of Ijebu-Ode, "An expression well-known even today about the insular nature of Ijebu society is 'Ijebu-Ode, a town forbidden to strangers; if a stranger enters it in the morning, he is sure to be made a sacrifice in the evening.' *Ijebu-Ode ajeji ko wo; bi ajeji ba wo laro, won a fi sebo lale.*"[384]

The needs for sacrifices of this kind are many and diverse. Maintenance of social order and justice is one of them. A vivid example of this among the Ikale, Ilaje, and Apoi is *Ayelala* - meaning "the world is terrible." *Ayelala* was a deity whose power and sphere of influence in the administration of justice among the afore-mentioned people was extensive. According to Ilaje traditions, *Ayelala* was a slave woman originally. The people used the woman for sacrifice over a matter of adultery committed by a man of low status with the wife of a high ranking chief. When this slave woman was about to be drowned, she exclaimed *Ayelala*. Right from that time, this has been revered and engaged in criminal and civil matters.[385]

4. Sacredness of Human Life in *Yorùbá* Vocabulary

The focus of this section is to investigate the value of human sanctity in the vocabulary of the *Yorùbá* people. In this regard, the writer will examine *Yorùbá* names and proverbs.

---

[379] Ibid, 425.

[380] Ibid, 162.

[381] Oladejo, *Household gods*, 59.

[382] Ibid, *Life and Death in the Old Testament and Yoruba Worldview*, 209.

[383] Adedayo Emmanuel Afe, "Taboos and the Maintenance of Social Order in the Old Ondo Province, South-western Nigeria," *African Research Review: An International Multidisciplinary Journal* Vol. 7 No. 1 (January 2013): 102.

[384] Drewal, 216.

[385] Afe, 102.

a. *Yorùbá* Names

The importance of names christening newborn children by the *Yorùbá* is vital to this study. According to Johnson, "Names are not given at random because of their euphony or merely because of a distinguished member of the family or the community was so named but of a set of purposes from circumstances connected with the child itself, or concerning the family fortunes at the time etc."[386] Hence, the name given to any child is an accurate reflection of the perception of the people about the child's worth, significance, and value to the family, community and the world at large. This reality might be part of the reasons why the people make consultations with the household god and sacrifices are offered in a traditional *Yorùbá* setting to gain a better understanding of the child's destiny before they give any name.[387] According to Drewal,

> Just as a funeral is a rite of separation for the community, but is also conceived as a new spiritual beginning for the individual, the first rituals performed for a newborn infant are incorporations into the material world. Like funerals, these rituals focus on the metaphysical journey between two realms. Whereas funerals are costly public displays in the form of sacred send-off parties, the entry of an infant into the world is a much more subdued, private affair marked by a brief, relatively simple ritual performed by a diviner for the parents to discover the quality of the child's coming. The parents passively and patiently await the diviner's interpretation. The action is more thoughtful and contemplative than physical, quiet rather than loud.[388]

In other words, *Yorùbá* people hold the birth of a new child into their community in high esteem. Usually, this is primarily on the basis that such an infant is on a journey from another realm to this world. The secondary reason is that the newborn child is either a grandfather or grandmother (ancestors) who came back to the family again with a new destiny.[389]

There are three sets of names from which a child may receive. A child may have at least one, but no child may have the three. The first of these three is the *Amutorunwa* (the name with which the child is born). Examples of names in this category are; namely, *Taiwo*, the name given to the first born of twins of either sex, is the short form of "*To-aiye-wo*" (have the first taste of the world) and *Kehinde* (One who lags at delivery) the second born. Some others are: *Idowu* (the child born after a set of twins), *Idogbe* (the male child born after *Idowu*), *Alaba* (the female child born after *Idowu*), Ojo or *Aina* (the child born with "cord twined around its neck") and *Ajayi* (the child born with its face downwards).[390]

Second, these are names called the *Abiso* ("the christening names"). The choice of names to be given in this category is also contingent on certain factors. If the name is to have reference directly to the child itself, some of these names are often

---

[386] Johnson, 81.
[387] Ibid, 79.
[388] Drewal, 51.
[389] Ibid.
[390] Johnson, 79-81.

chosen from: *Ayodele* ("Joy enters the home"), *Onipede* ("the consoler has come"), *Morenike* ("I have someone to pet"), *Omoteji* ("A child big enough for two"), and *Akinyele* ("A strong one befits the house"). When focus is directly on the family but indirectly on the child, the following names are a few examples: *Ogundalenu* ("Our home has been devastated by war"), *Ogunmola* ("The River Ogun took away our honour"), *Laniyonu* ("Honour is full of troubles"), and *Kurumi* ("Death has impoverished me"). When a child is princely born, names with the attachment of *Ade*, *Ola*, *Olu*, and *Oye* are given, such as *Adebiyi* ("The crown has begotten this"), *Adegbite* ("The crown demands for a throne"), and *Olubiyi* ("A chief has begotten this").

Again, some names have fetish attachment indicating the divinity that the people worship in the family line. An example is *Sangobunmi* ("Sango [the god of thunder and lightning] gave me this"). Also in this direction are the *Abiku's* (children that are born to die) names. Children in this category are believed to belong to "a fraternity of demons living in the woods, especially about and within large *Iroko* trees." While coming to earth, these children would have arranged the exact times they would return. Given the worth or value attached to the possession of children with good fortune, certain steps are taken to prevent the return of children in this category. They often tie charms on them, brand ugly marks on them, and give them certain names. They make all this effort to disfigure the children in such a way that their comrades in the fraternity would not accept them again and such children would finally come to stay with their parents. Examples of names usually given in this category are; namely, *Malomo* ("Do not go again"), *Kosoko* ("There is no hoe [to dig the grave with])," *Banjoko* ("Sit down [or stay] with me"), and *Oku* ("The dead").[391]

Lastly, the third category of names is the *Oriki* (the Cognomen, Attributive or Pet names). These names are given to express what the child is or what he or she is believed to be. These are few examples of male attributive names: *Ajamu* ("One who seizes after a fight"), *Ajani* ("One who possesses after a struggle"), *Akanbi* or *Akangbe* ("One conceived after a single touch"), and *Alabi* or *Alade* (One who comes after several female deliveries). Examples of female attributive names are *Amoke* (One "whom to know is to pet"), *Ayoka* ("One who causes joy all around"), and *Abebi* ("One born after a supplication").[392]

b. *Yorùbá* Proverbs

The linguistic expressions of the *Yorùbá* people are in connection with their language. These expressions reflect their belief system and practices. The concern of this section is to consider the worth placed on human life in some of the manners by which *Yorùbá* people express the language. These expressions often take the form of 'proverbs' which Ojo claims that it reveals abstract ideas using familiar things within the immediate surroundings like hills, rivers, animals, birds and domestic objects.[393]

---

[391] Ibid, 81-84.
[392] Ibid, 85.
[393] Ojo, 226.

The following are two of these proverbial saying as many more are presented in Table 2 below:

i. *Eniti yio je oyin inu apata ki nwo enu ake* ("He who would extract the honey embedded in a rock should take no notice of the wear and tear of the axe-blade used"): The meaning of this proverbial saying is that every great success or achievement in life comes with a price attached to it.[394] By implication, there is always a need to make some sacrifice for one to fulfil in life. In other words, there is nothing without a price-attachment.

ii. *Bi eiye ko ba ni feiye niron, oju orun to eiye fo laifara kanra*: This proverb translates thus, "If the birds do not seek a cause for a quarrel, the sky is wide enough for them to fly without any interference." The adage expresses the idea that nature is sufficient since there is no conflict in the rank of the birds despite their countless number.[395] In other words, *Yorùbá* people believe that God's provision is enough to take good care of all creations of which human beings are prime. Given this divine reality, life is not about competition but collaboration.

5. Worth of Life in *Yorùbá* Social Relations

In this section, the writer will have to consider some of the various war expeditions that have taken place in the history of the people. In earliest times, war expeditions were mainly to obtain spoils and keeping their hands busy. One can reasonably conclude that the worth placed on human life among the people was low when one is to consider the inherent dangers with such expeditions. The basis of most of these expeditions is the desires of the influential people of the time for wealth, position and power.[396] When one considers the various war expeditions towards the recovery of Ilorin from the Fulani, this situation becomes more vivid.

Ilorin, one of the important *Yorùbá* towns at these earliest times, was founded by *Laderin* whose great-grandchild called *Afonja* brought the city to its zenith. At the time of his rule as king, *Afonja* had become the *Kakanfo* of Yorubaland, but due to his high-handedness against his various chiefs and provincial *Bales* and his preference for the *Jamas* who were of Fulani origin, he died an ordinary man. History holds that *Afonja* died in the hands of his former confidants (the *Jamas*) headed by *Alimi*. The tragic loss of Ilorin to the Fulani was another awful consequence that attended *Afonja's* administrative carelessness.

Consequently, attempts to restore Ilorin to *Yorùbá* nation led to various war expeditions, some of which are; namely, the battle at *Ogele*, the *Mugbamugba* war, and the battle of *Pamo*.[397] These expeditions are entirely different from various others fought within the kingdom after *Yorùbá* had become disintegrated and disorganised. Some of them are the following: the Owu war, the *Lasinmi* war, the *Kanla* expedition,

---

[394] Ibid, 225.
[395] Ibid.
[396] Johnson, 131.
[397] Ibid, 197-205.

the *Gbogun* war, and the *Pole* war.[398] Again, various battles fought in the process of Ibadan becoming a *Yorùbá* town are later additions to the tragic ways that ravaged human lives on the altar of quests for fame, status and wealth. Prominent among these wars are; namely, the *Gbanamu* war and the *Erumu* war. Battles fought for consolidation and balance of power within Ibadan, Egba and Ijebu are equally part of the list, such as the *Ipetumodu* and *Owiwi* wars (A.D 1819), the *Oniyefun* war, the *Arakangba* or *Jabara* war, the *Onidese,* and *Oke Isero* war, and the *Iperu* war.[399] Various civil wars fought within the land are also to be considered.

Similarly, one can also comprehend appreciation for the sanctity of human life among the people when one examines and understands the manner of governance in Yorubaland through taboos. According to Odejobi Cecilia Omobola, specific cultic, religious, socio-economic and political prohibitions are instituted by the authorities within the *Yorùbá* society. The people regard these prohibitions as taboos and are to promote the sacredness of the lives of people in any given community. Breaking any of these social norms is always consequential. It brings certain misfortunes which are regarded as repercussions either directly to the dissident(s) or the concerned community. Asides, some taboos are universal. Among them are the following: murder, cannibalism, incest, swearing, using foul languages, cursing, and killing. Omobola grouped *Yorùbá* taboos into seven; namely, restrictions guiding against accident, those relating to religions, those relating to respect for elders, bans to ensure cleanliness, prohibitions for human values, those to avoid waste, and those on things challenging to explain.[400]

The setting of *Yorùbá* people, Africans in general, is communal. What belongs to one belongs to all most of the time and one's conduct can affect the entire life of the community either for good or bad. Given this, *Yorùbá* people in their wisdom set specific mechanisms to guide people's conducts and preserve the social order of the community. One of these mechanisms is the use of taboos, called *eewo* by the people. It forbids anything perceived to be evil or has resemblance with evil. According to Afe, the prohibition was one mechanism that *Yorùbá* people of the Old Ondo Province used to safeguard the traditions of the people against any form of infiltrations of indiscipline and criminality before the advent of the British to ensure peace and tranquillity in the society.

Practically, the people governed almost all aspects of their social life by taboos. This situation was to protect the social norms and values of the people. These taboos covered the following areas; namely, the relationship between the leaders and the led, political life, and socio-economic life of the people. The sexual life and family life of the society were not left out.[401] The authorities established them within the traditional religious settings as agents and keepers of the dictates of the gods and ancestors. In other words, this social mechanism varied in contents from one

---

[398] Ibid, 206-222.
[399] Ibid, 248-255.
[400] Odejobi Cecilia Omobola, "An Overview of Taboo and Superstition among the Yoruba of Southwest of Nigeria," *Mediterranean Journal of Social Sciences.* Vol. 2 No. 2 (May 2013): 222-23.
[401] Afe, 96.

community to the other during this period. Whenever anybody broke any of these taboos, it usually had adverse effects not only on the breachers but on the entire people in general. Similarly, certain blessings regularly attended whoever obeyed these social prohibitions. Examples of these blessings are the following; namely, joy, happiness, wealth and longevity of life. Taboos are different from superstitions and are held in high esteem by the *Yorùbá* people.[402] The writer examines some of these categories of restrictions.

a. Taboos relating to Chieftaincy

Some specific prohibitions were instituted within the context of *Yorùbá* people to guide and protect human life especially that of the leaders because of the value attached to it. After installation or coronation, it was a taboo for *the Oba* (the king) to prostrate to anybody again. He must also not see a dead body any longer. If he breaks any of these, calamities like strange diseases will happen either to Oba himself or his family or his entire domain.[403] More so, it was a taboo for anybody to have sexual intercourse with Oba's wife during the pre-colonial time, even till now. The crime is punishable by death. The prohibition was put in place because whoever had carnal knowledge of this kind would automatically live a miserable life for life. Generally speaking, incest is a taboo in Yorubaland because a sexual relationship of this kind offends the gods and the ancestors. It could also divide the family and bring about certain calamities such as abnormal births, defects in delivery and diseases.[404]

b. Taboos guiding against Accident

The writer also considers some of the taboos governing against possible accidents or death in this section since the concern of this paper is on the sanctity of human life. First, *aboyun ko gbodo dobale sun; ki omo re mo baa ku* ("a woman must not sleep on the stomach with pregnancy so that the child will not die"). This prohibition is to protect the life of the unborn child from possible death or any form of accidents since it is natural that the child may die of suffocation if the mother sleeps on her stomach. Second, *okunrin ko gbodo ba alaboyun lo po bi oyun re ba ti too bi; ki okunrin naa ma baa tosi* (a man must not have sexual intercourse with a pregnant woman whose day of delivery is near so that he would not be poor). This taboo is also to protect the foetus from any deformity and contacting possible diseases like gonorrhoea.

Third, *omode ko gbodo fi igi fa ila sile; bi eera ba ko si oju ila naa, iya omo naa yoo ku* (it is forbidden for a child to draw a line with stick on the ground; if ants should enter the line, the mother of the child will die). This taboo is to prevent children from playing with a stick. Its use may accidentally cause injury on the eyes of the child, and its attendant troubles may cause such a child's invalid mother untimely death. Fourth, *a ko gbodo gun igi ibepe; eni naa yoo ku* (it is a taboo to climb pawpaw tree, whoever does so will die). The basis of this prohibition is on the

---

[402] Ibid, 97-98.
[403] Ibid, 99.
[404] Ibid, 100.

feebleness of the pawpaw tree; it may break while jumping on it and causing bodily injury which may lead to death.[405]

c. Taboos relating to Crime Control

Murder and suicide are two prominent prohibitions relating to crime control in Yorubaland. It is generally a taboo to murder in the land. The crime is punishable by death for it is a sin against both the gods and humanity. In this regard, it is on record that kings in the Old Oyo Empire, as mighty as they were, could not even take human life anyhow. M.O. Ogunmola, the incumbent *Otun Alaafin* of Oyo, cites the case of *Alaafin* Jayin who became rejected by his subjects and eventually committed suicide for terminating the life of his son who committed adultery with his step-mother.[406] According to Ogunmola, an *Ifa* Corpus, called *Odu Ifa Idinse*, completely prohibits termination of life and the people of old observed this prohibition because they would sentence the culprits to death. However, the people later reduced the punishment to regular payment of fine since the time of King Arinlo.[407]

Similarly, suicide was not a common phenomenon among *Yorùbá* people. Whoever committed suicide must have indulged in a high crime or broken one taboo or the other as exemplified by *Alaafin* Jayin's case, the consequence of which the king was avoiding. Because of the gravity of this crime, the body of the one who hanged would have to be handed over to the priest for unique burial.[408] The interment might involve certain rituals to appease the gods for the sake of the living.

d. Taboos Relating to Cleanliness

One of the prohibitions cited by Omobola relates to the protection of human life by keeping good hygiene. *A ko gbodo subu ni baluwe, ki iru eni bee ma ba ku* (it is forbidden for anyone to fall within the toilet in other not to die). This taboo is to ensure carefulness with the use of the bathroom because of its general slippery nature when not adequately kept. The purpose is to prevent an accident which may lead to death.[409]

e. Taboos Relating to Moral Values

Some taboos relate to moral values, violations of which may lead to the termination of one's life. *A ko gbodo jeun ni idubule, ki ounje ma baa pa wa lori* (it is a taboo to eat while lying down so that the food will not go to our head). This prohibition is to teach the ethical value of having table manner. Violation of this moral principle may lead to any problem such as death.[410]

---

[405] Omobola, 224.

[406] M.O. Ogunmola, *A New Perspective to Oyo Empire History: 1530-1944* (Alagbon Oyo: Samuel Ayoade Reformed Press, 1985), 78.

[407] Ibid, 78-79.

[408] Afe, 105.

[409] Omobola, 225.

[410] Ibid.

f. Taboos concerning Children

There are some prohibitions placed on children in Yorubaland. It was a taboo for children to urinate into a mortal. The claim is that any child that violated this taboo would have one's mother dead. Since children are fond of their mothers so much that they would not want them to die, no one among them would, therefore, violate the taboo by this love. This prohibition taught good moral and similarly brings to the fore the worth that an ideal *Yorùbá* child placed on the life of his or her mother.[411]

g. Taboo concerning Women

Observance of *opo* (widowhood) right after the departure of one's husband is prominent among the taboos relating to women. This rite was observed usually for eight days. After the people might have buried the deceased husband, the woman would begin her widowhood immediately and would be asked to sit on "local mat" called *eni-ore* for seven days with her hair loosed. The people regard these days as a period of mourning and sober reflection. However, on the eighth day, the woman's cloth and the mat would be burnt after she had taken her bath. Another three months of restrictions from going to market and her family house would follow this period. The basis of this restriction is that the woman was not allowed to sleep outside her husband's house during her period of widowhood. All through this period, the woman must be in a black dress. The essence of widowhood in the wisdom of the *Yorùbá* was to prevent the children of the *opo* from an untimely death.[412]

Although this taboo brings the worth that an average *opo* attached to the lives of her children to the fore, this practice raises certain questions. Why are widowers (husbands who are bereaved of their wives) exonerated from this rite? Again, why should the suffering for children be limited to women while their children are busy enjoying life freely? The submission of this writer in this regard is that women were traditionally believed to be second fiddles generally in the society and property to their husbands. This understanding was the basis for charging them with murder upon their husbands' death. Thus, widowhood is a reflection of the low estimate of life attached to female children or women generally in the traditional setting of the Yorùbá.

h. Taboos on Things Difficult to Explain

There are some of these taboos which relate to things or circumstances that are difficult to explain. One of the social prohibitions in this category is: *A ko gbodo fi owo gbe ojo, ki aara ma baa san pa eni naa* (It is prohibited for anyone to collect rainwater with bare hand while it is raining so that one will not be struck dead by thunder). Although this is difficult to explain and scientists have not proven it, anything can happen to whoever does this.[413] In Africa, thunder strike is a possibility.

When these various categories of taboos are clearly understood, one will discover that the worth given human lives is with mixed feelings. On the one hand,

---

[411] Afe, 102.
[412] Ibid, 103-104.
[413] Omobola, 226.

many of these prohibitions are put in place to preserve human beings because of their sacredness. On the other hand, human life is lowly esteemed by the people today. A vivid example of ways by which the people manifest this violation is in gender discrimination as exhibited in the observance of *opo* (widowhood) rite. This rite is limited to women while men who experience bereavement are free. Hence, the lives of women are less esteemed among the people. This practice is not limited to Yorubaland but extends to some other people groups on the continent of Africa for most of their cultures are patriarchal.

6. Sanctity of Human Life in *Yorùbá* Politics

The worth of life among *Yorùbá* people can be understood further when one considers the nature of their politics before and after independence. *Yorùbá* remained autonomous until 1861 when they lost their sovereignty to the British control. What informed this situation were several civil wars fought by the people under the influence of local and international politics of the time. Many variables marked this politics, of which "divide and rule policies" of the British Colonial Master was prominent.[414] The results of these policies were two elements that later characterised the politics of the people before independence down to the period under investigation. These elements were the opposition politics advanced by the followers of Obafemi Awolowo called "the Awoists" and what is called "a high degree of institutionalization."[415]

The period of the year 2000 – 2003 marked the decline of *Yorùbá* politics. The opposition politics of the *Yorùbá* against the Hausa/Fulani hegemony of the north over the political terrain of the Nigerian nation at the national level greatly paid off for the people. This situation included internal politics within Afenifere socio-political group and Alliance for Democracy (AD) and politics at the national level until the year 2000 when trouble broke out within the house of Oduduwa. According to Olarinmoye, this crisis essentially was the basis for the decline of *Yorùbá* politics. Although strong factionalism characterises politics among the *Yorùbá*, there was a "close interaction between the struggle for the political leadership of *Yorùbá* ethnic group and intense factionalism of the dominant political grouping, the Awoists that the explanation for the decline of *Yoruba* opposition politics emerges."[416] The resultant effect of this interaction was a new form of stronger factionalism within the group of the Awoists core over agitation for who would be in control of the ethnic movement between Abraham Adesanya (leader of Afenifere group) and Bola Ige (deputy leader of Afenifere).

This situation began in the early year 2000 and led to breaking the tie between the movement (Afenifere) and the party (AD) into two different entities. This opposition within the Awoists was much more around Ige than Adesanya. The situation equally resulted in the expansion of the leadership of the party to include non-*Yorùbá* groups. The efforts of these politicians were to gain recognition at the

---

[414] Olarinmoye, 020-021.
[415] Ibid, 021-022.
[416] Ibid, 026.

national level with necessary potentials to fund Ige's presidential ambition. Therefore, Ige agreed to work with Olusegun Obasanjo, the then president, to promote the agenda of Afenifere. The situation led to some problems both within the people and the nation at large; one of which is the weakening of the political culture of Afenifere and its influence in Yorubaland. It also led to the assassination of Ige on December 23, 2001.[417]

The position of this writer on the death of Ige whose mastermind remains unknown to date is that his death is a top secret. As much as the writer is not saying that his *Yorùbá* kin murdered ige, his death cannot be without the involvement of any of Ige's *Yorùbá* political associates. The writer's claim is on the premise of a *Yorùbá* adage which says, *"Bi iku ile o ba pani, t'ode o le pani"* (If there are no collaborators within, one cannot die from outside). He was assassinated in his residence at daytime despite heavy security attached to his life.

By implication, the death of a high profile politician of Ige's status points to a low estimate of human life among the people. Similarly, another *Yorùbá* adage says, *"Araba tunramun, odo ngb'Arere"* (*Araba* tree should be cautious for *Arere* tree is being carried away by the river). This proverbial saying implies that if the life of a person like Ige could be so cheaply terminated, other persons of lower rank should be careful. On the one hand, *Arere* is a healthy tree which cannot be easily driven by anything, and the writer likens the person of Ige unto this. On the other hand, although *Araba* is equally significant, its size and weight are not like that of *Arere*. If the river is now carrying *Arere* away with ease, what then is the fate of *Araba* which symbolises the rest of the people who are not of Ige's rank?

7. Presentation and Analysis of Responses to Interview Questions

The writer takes three main steps in this section. They are the following: presentation of the procedure of the interview, analysis of the population sample, and a summary of the responses obtained from respondents.

a. Presentation of Interview Procedure

The writer designed the first section of the interview guide used for data collection tagged "Personal Profile," for self-identification of those interviewed; their names, towns of residence, genders, professions, and educational qualifications. The writer also administered the same after introducing the subject of the study with its purpose. The design of the second section aims to obtain the candid opinions of the respondents on various areas and ideas that would help in getting an adequate understanding of the concept of the sanctity of human life in *Yorùbá* worldview.

b. Analysis of Population Sample

The writer analyses the first section of the guide in such a way that all various items under it are separately accounted for and specifically noticed. The writer interviewed 22 people. They were all *Yorùbá* people living in four States of the Yorubaland; namely, Oyo, Osun, Ogun, and Lagos. 13 of the respondents were living at

---

[417] Ibid.

Ogbomoso, two at Oyo Alaafin, and two at Oko; all these are prominent places in Oyo State. Two of the respondents mentioned above are traditional title-holders in both Oyo and Osun States while one is holding titles in three States; namely, Oyo, Osun, and Lagos. Similarly, one respondent is living at Agbado, Ogun State, while four of them are living in various places in Lagos State; namely, Ijaye-Ojokoro, Idimu, Meiran, and Ilashamaja. One of the 22 respondents is female while the rest are male. Their selections were not purposeful since the purpose of the study is not gender-sensitive. Those interviewed were randomly selected.

Moreover, 11 of the respondents were practising *Ifa* priests and some other traditional groups such as *Osun* worship; nine of whom are holding prominent titles in *Awo* (*Ifa* divination). These titles are the following; namely, *Araba-Oluawo, Araba-Awo, Akoda-Awo, Bashorun-Awo, Awoko-Orunmila, Asiwaju-Awo, Egbeji, Akogun, Aroni-Ifalase, Adifala,* and *Elewi-Awo*. According to Abimbola, *Araba* is the highest religious title of all worshippers of *Ifa* Cult in any lands, of which Ogbomosoland is an example. Next to *Araba* are his assistant chief priests called *Oluwo* or *Oluawo,* each of whom is for a village, settlement or town.[418]

Since there are many towns and villages in Ogbomosoland, therefore, the highest title in the land is *Araba-Oluawo*. Also added to this title by this prominent figure who occupies the office is JP (Justice of Peace) as awarded by the Oyo State Government. More so, one of the respondents is the leader of all *Osun* worshippers in Ogbomosoland, called *Oba-Olomitutu*. Similarly, one of them is the *Araba-Awo* of Oko and its environment. In addition to all this, another interviewee is a practising herbalist (Native Doctor).

The need for the dominance given the diviners among various population samples consulted is on the basis that they are the custodians of the *Yorùbá* worldview. The idea of Philip M. Peek advanced is handy at this juncture:

> Throughout Africa - whether in the city or in the country, no matter the religion, sex, or status of the individual–questions, problems, and choices arise for which everyday knowledge is insufficient and yet action must be taken. The information necessary to respond effectively is available, but often only through a diviner. That is why divination continues to provide a trusted means of decision making, a basic source of vital knowledge.[419]

In other words, although answers to the questions to which the interviewees were to respond did not require acts of divination of any form, only well-versed individuals in *Yorùbá* language and custom could thrive in this enterprise, of which *Ifa* practitioners are viewed by the researcher to be the type. This reality becomes evident by the fact that the intricacy of *Yorùbá* language has its bedrock in *Ifa* Corpus. According to Abimbola, *Ifa* is regarded by the *Yorùbá* people as "the great authority on their mythology, history and philosophy."[420] Again, the scholar also captioned *Ifa* as "the

---

[418] Abimbola, *Sixteen Great Poems of Ifa*, 6.
[419] Philip M. Peek, "The Study of Divination, Present and Past," in *African Divination Systems: Ways of Knowing*, eds., Philip M. Peek et al (Indianapolis: Indiana University Press, 1991), 1-2.
[420] Abimbola, *Sixteen Great Poems of Ifa*, iii.

unwritten text-book" of the culture of the *Yorùbá* people.[421] Similarly, Elebuibon argues that the corpus is "an encyclopaedia of *Yorùbá* knowledge."[422] The logic here is that since *Ifá* is so esteemed by the majority of the people, to say the least, its diviners must possess the repertoires of knowledge of the various aspects of the life of the people.

Furthermore, seven of the respondents are clergymen. Five of these were still in active service; one of whom was lecturing in the Department of Theology of the NBTSO, specifically in the field of World Religions. Also, two of these clergymen had their background in YTR. Out of these two, one was a practising herbalist who rose in rank to become a title holder in *Awo* before his conversion to Christianity. Again, one of the seven was an 80-year-old Archbishop Emeritus in Methodist Church, Nigeria. He was one of the two elder statesmen directly interviewed in Oyo State. The other one was the incumbent *Otun Alaafin* of Oyo, a former Nigerian High Commissioner to the Republic of Zambia and Malawi between late 1981 and early 1984 and a former history teacher. Another respondent was a secondary school teacher while the last one was the *Bobagunwa* of Elebeland.

The range of the academic qualifications of the respondents is vast, from PhD Degree to those who do not have formal education at all. Three of the respondents were PhD holders in biblical Studies and World Religions, and one had a PhD Degree in view. Again, one of them had D.Min. Degree while one still had the degree in view. More so, one of the respondents had a double Masters Degree (M.A and M.Th.). Similarly, three of them had a First Degree, one of whom had B.A (Manchester) in English and History while the other two had B.Ed. in Yorùbá. Also, one of them obtained NCE, two were Secondary School leavers, and three were with the Primary School Leaving Certificate.

Furthermore, two of the respondents dropped out of primary school as a result of their parents' belief that the concerned individuals were destined to become *Ifá* priests. Also, four of them had no secular education partly because of the similar idea and the crude nature of the time they were born. On the one hand, 16 of the respondents gave verbal responses, most especially all of those who did not have a former education. They were all contacted in person. On the other hand, seven of them gave written responses. Six of these were approached by proxy while one of them responded both orally and in written form. The oral responses in *Yorùbá* were both translated and transcribed into English by the researcher. Likewise, a few of them preferred to give their answers both in *Yorùbá* and English. The writer presents the list of the primary sources as an appendix.

c. **Summary of Responses**
The interview guide contains 10 questions numbering 1-10. The aim behind question one to nine is to elicit responses on various areas of interest relating to the concept of the sacredness of human life. However, item 10 is open for other related ideas from

---

[421] Ibid.
[422] Elebuibon, *Ifá: the Custodian of Destiny*, viii.

the respondents which the interviewer might not have envisaged to address in the process. The researcher gave all respondents freedom to express themselves in either English language or Yorùbá. This step became necessary in ensuring the free expression of the intent of their minds to the various questions. The researcher, however, made efforts required to transcribe and translate ideas expressed in *Yorùbá* into the English language. To ensure originality of thoughts on various coverage areas, the researcher made no attempt to pass judgment on any of the responses obtained. Instead, the writer presents each of the 10 issues as a table including an analysis of the various reactions in percentages since the data collected are enumerative or non-parametric scores.

Table 1: *Yorùbá* Understanding of Sanctity of Human Life in *Ifa* Corpus

This part aims at obtaining specific ideas from the respondents on what makes human beings unique, distinct, different, and of significant worth than all other creatures like animals in *Ifa* Corpus.

S/N	Sanctity of Human Life in *Ifa* Corpus	No. of Respondents	% of Respondents
1.	Possessing good characters as contained in *Orosu-Ogunda* Corpus such as the following: good relationship, helping others, patience, contentment, faith in *Olodumare*, appreciating others, acts of goodness, hospitality, caring for others, praising *Olodumare*, being truthful, obedience, humility, following peace with others, keeping law and order, preserving human lives and property, and other godly cultural values	12	54.5
2.	The image, being or breath of God in humankind. This concept manifests itself as any of the following: God's creative power in man to invent or create things and the ability to will freely and exercise willpower	5	22.7
3.	The nature of human life is priceless. According to *Oyeku-Meji* Corpus, death must be averted for human being solely belongs to God.	2	9.1
4.	God places man at the centre of His mind and actions	2	9.1
5.	God's mercy and grace in humankind	1	4.5

The table suggests five main ideas which reflect the *Yorùbá* understanding of the sanctity of human life. These ideas are not exhaustive but suggest key among what the people believe to be the basis of the worth or sacredness of man.

Table 2: Markers of Sanctity of Human Life in *Yorùbá* Vocabulary

The basis of this item is to have a listing of specific ideas, proverbs and wise sayings expressing the worth of human life in *Yorùbá* vocabulary. This step goes a long way in gaining an adequate understanding of the concept in *Yorùbá* vocabulary.

S/N	Suggested *Yorùbá* Ideas, Proverbs and Wise Sayings	No. of Respondents	% of Respondents
1.	Owo funfun ni, ko to eniyan (Giving out of money is not as much important as the availability of humans)	2	9.1
2.	Awo b'owa (Flesh covers human characters)	2	9.1
3.	Omo ya j'owo (Children are more worth than money)	2	9.1
4.	Iwa l'ewa omo eniyan (Character is the beauty of human beings)	2	9.1
5.	Eni mi o s'eni, eniyan mi o s'eniyan, a ko ni fi we alaroo l'asan (My kinsman is not human enough, and my people are not humane either, we cannot compare them with a foreigner).	1	4.5
6.	Omo ki i pa omo j'aiye (No child kills another child to make a living)	1	4.5
7.	A ki i pa okan ke okan (We do not kill one to nurture another)	1	4.5
8.	Oyun ki i se idaniloju pe ire nbo l'ona (Pregnancy is not an evidence that good fortune is coming on the way)	1	4.5
9.	Igbati omo iya meji ba fi ija p'eta d'oju iku, alaroo ni n fi dukia won se ifa je (Whenever two siblings fight to the point of death, it is ordinary neighbours that enjoy their possessions)	1	4.5
10.	Iku ti n pa ojugba eni, owe nla ni n pa fun ni (Death that kills one's relatives is giving one a strong signal)	1	4.5
11.	Ore ni n gba ni n'igba isoro, fi owo re mejeeji di ojulowo ore mu (It is a friend that delivers one at the time of troubles, use your two hands to retain a good one)	1	4.5

12.	Ko si digi to dara bi ojulowo ore (No mirror is as good as a good friend)	1	4.5
13.	T'aba mu ragba ta ragba, iwa, t'aba mu ragba ta ragba, iwa ohun la nwa (If we join one with another, it is a character; if we join one with the other, it is the character that we long to see)	1	4.5
14.	Eni ba ni eniyan, ko mo l'ohun o lowo, toripe eni eni a maa boni lara ju aso lo, eniyan ni ise alatileyin eniyan. Bi eniyan ba ri nkan ibanuje, bi ko ba l'eniire l'odo yo sise (Whoever has people should not say he/she does not have money for one's own covers one's nakedness more than cloth. It is human beings that support one another. When one experiences something that brings sorrow, one makes mistakes if he/she is deficient of good supporters)	1	4.5
15.	Eke o kun ni, iwa ika o ye omo eniyan. Bi agba ba nyo ile da, ohun buburu abenu a maa yo iru won se (Falsehood is not profitable; wickedness is unfit for any man. When an adult is betraying, evil things always happen to them underneath)	1	4.5
16.	Onise ko ni f'ise re e le re ibi, arinrinajo t'ohun t'iwa, adifa fun Iwalapo t'ise omo oba ni Ado-Ewi (No businessman will abandon his/her business and go on a journey, travellers with their characters. Ifa divination was performed for Iwalapo, a prince to them at Ado-Ewi)	1	4.5
17.	Eniyan l'omo eniyan (Mankind gives birth to their kind)	1	4.5
18.	Bi eera ba fini pe igi, eniyan a won danu (If an insect takes us for a tree, we throw it away)	1	4.5
19.	Eni a fe l'amo a ko mo eni to fe ni (We know those we love, we do not know those who love us)	1	4.5
20	Ajeje owo kan ko gberu d'ori (Only one hand	1	4.5

	is not able to put the load on the head)		
21.	Ki i buru titi ko ma ku enikan mo ni, eni ti yoo ku lao mo (No matter what, one will be left with somebody. Those that will remain we do not know)	1	4.5
22.	A ki i j'aye oba ka su s'ara (We do not make fun like kings and defecate on the body)	1	4.5
23.	Alainirun ni idi iyawo, ki i ise ejo alarina (Lack of hair at the private part of the wife is not the problem of the go-between)	1	4.5
24.	Ara l'amo, a o mo inu (We only identify the body, we cannot see the mind)	1	4.5
25.	Eniyan ni aso mi, bi mo ba r'eniyan ara mi a ya gaga (Human beings are my garments, anytime I see humankind I become joyful)	1	4.5
26.	Ti ki i ba se aso, oniruuru idi l'aba maa ri (If not for cloth, we could have been seeing different buttocks)	1	4.5
27	Ko s'eniyan mo, k'areni barin l'oku (There are no human beings again, what we have are mere companions)	1	4.5
28.	Iwa ni f'oniwa han (Character is the identifier of the one who possesses it)	1	4.5
29.	Eefin n'iwa (Character is smoke)	1	4.5
30.	Suuru ni baba iwa, agba t'oni suuru ohungbogbo l'oni (Patience is the height of character, an adult with patience has everything)	1	4.5
31.	Omo eniyan dun ju omo eranko lo (Human beings have more worth than animals)	1	4.5
32.	Omo j'oro lo (Children are worth more than riches)	1	4.5
33.	Olomo lo l'aye (Those with children possess the earth)	1	4.5
34.	Eniyan s'owon, ka reni barin lo ku (Human beings are rare to find, what we have are mere	1	4.5

	companions)		
35.	A ki i fi agbalagba s'ori Ijoko lo (We do not leave the aged sitting and walk away)	1	4.5
36.	Suuru le se okuta jinna (Patience can cook a stone)	1	4.5
37.	Ibi o ju ibi, b'ati b'eru l'abi omo (There is no difference in delivery, just as we give birth to a slave we do for a child)	1	4.5
38.	Opo eniyan l'ogun (Much people are the secret of winning a battle)	1	4.5
39.	Ara eniyan l'oore wa (Blessings are part of having people)	1	4.5
40.	Owo omode ko to pepe, t'agbalagba ko wo akeregbe (Children's hand does not reach the roof rack, that of the aged does not enter the gourd)	1	4.5
41.	Bi a ko ba ku, omo ni i isin ni (If we do not die, it is children that will bury us)	1	4.5
42.	Bi a ba se oni, a o se ola (If we spend today, we shall spend tomorrow)	1	4.5
43.	Bi a ba n ja, bi k'aku ko (If we are fighting, it is not to the point of death)	1	4.5
44.	Eke o dara, odale o sun an (Falsehood is bad, betrayal is evil)	1	4.5
45.	Eni to bere to n wo idi omonikeji, Alahurabi n wo ti e lehin (Whoever bends and looks at another person's buttocks, God is behind looking at his/her own)	1	4.5
46.	Eni to n de isa okete, Olorun n de tire naa lehin (Whoever is hunting for a bush rat in its hole, God is behind hunting for his/her own)	1	4.5
47.	Eni to n se nkan ikoko, oju Olorun to o (Whoever is committing a secret sin, God's eyes are on him/her)	1	4.5
48.	Ire gbogbo, l'owo iwa l'owa (All manners of	1	4.5

	blessing depend on one's character)		
49.	Iberu Oluwa ni ipilese ogbon (The fear of the LORD is the beginning of wisdom)	1	4.5
50.	Eni to jin si koto, o ko araiyoku l'ogbon (Whoever enters into the ditch teaches others a lesson)	1	4.5

The number of *Yorùbá* ideas, proverbs and wise sayings suggested by the respondents is not absolute. However, the volume obtained indicates that the people have several expressions by which they bring the sacred nature of human life to the fore in their feelings. Similarly, the availability of these ideas in large number also pictures the value attached to the worth of human life by the people.

Table 3: General Understanding of Human Sacredness among *Yoruba* People
This portion aims at obtaining a list of general ideas that depict the sacredness of human life among *Yoruba* people. The listing will further give meaning to the understanding of the *Yorùbá* on the subject of the sanctity of human life.

S/N	General Understanding of Sacredness of Human Life among *Yorùbá* People	No. Of Respondents	% of Respondents
1.	Possessing *awon iwa rere* (good characters) such as the following: *Iberu Olorun* (the fear of God), *idariji elomiran* (forgiving other people), *didupe l'owo ara eni* (appreciating one another), *irele* (humility), *iwa-tutu* (gentleness), *isokan* (unity), *ife* (love), *jije olotito* (being truthful or honest), *pipa ofin mo* (being law abiding), *iwa pele* (gentleness), *igboran* (obedience), *jije eni t'ose fi okan tan* (trustworthiness), *eni ti ki i mu imukumu* (not a smoker), *sise abojuto awon ara* (caring for fellow human beings), *lilepa alaafia ni awujo* (maintaining peace and tranquillity in the society), *sise imototo* (maintaining good hygiene), *ibasepo t'o gunrege* (human relationship) and *imule* (brotherhood)	14	63.6
2.	Human life is a valuable gift to the entire created order. Thus, the life is precious, and we should prevent it from possible hurt or termination	5	22.7
3.	God's life given to humankind to reason or think creatively and exercise willpower	2	9.0
4.	God created human beings for a divine	1	4.5

138

| | purpose | | |

These four ideas further portray what *Yorùbá* generally has in mind on the concept of the sanctity of human life in their worldview. These ideas corroborate other ideas identified in Tables 1 and 2.

Table 4: *Yorùbá* Practices Depicting Worth of Human Life

This table sets to obtain a list of practices that depict the worth of human life among *Yorùbá* people. The step further strengthens readers' understanding of the concept of the sacredness of human life in *Yorùbá* worldview.

S/N	*Yorùbá* Practices Depicting Worth of Human Life	No. of Respondents	% of Respondents
1.	*Igbe aye otito* (Life of truthfulness)	9	40.9
2.	*Nini Iberu Olorun* (Having a fear of God)	9	40.9
3.	*Isoore* (Act of goodness)	5	22.7
4.	*Iteriba fun awon agba* (Respect for elders)	5	22.7
5.	*Sise ibojuto awon elomiran* (Caring for others)	5	22.7
6.	*Bibowo fun awon eewo ile Yorùbá* (Keeping *Yorùbá* cultural taboos)	4	18.2
7.	*Ibowo fun awon ti owo to si* (Giving honour to whom honour is due)	3	13.3
8.	*Iwa irele* (Act of humility)	3	13.3
9.	*Yiyago fun imotara-eni-nikan, elesin-mesin ati eleya-meya* (Abstaining from self-centeredness, religious bigotry, and tribalism)	2	9.1
10.	*Nini suuru fun elomiran* (Being patient with others)	2	9.1
11.	*Imura ni iwontunwonsi* (Modest dressing)	2	9.1
12.	*Iranlowo elomiran* (Helping others)	2	9.1
13.	*Jije olododo tabi eni to se f'okan tan* (Being faithful or dependable)	2	9.1
14.	*Fifi eniyan se irubo paapaa fun awon oba, bii apere ti awon "Abobaku* (Human sacrifice especially for king's sake in practice called "Dying with kings")	2	9.1

15.	*Isin bi i Igbeyawo, orin, ati ikomo* (Worship such as the wedding, music, and naming, etc.)	2	9.1
16.	*Yiyago fun ife owo* (Abstaining from the love of money)	1	4.5
17.	*Yiyago fun egbekegbe* (Abstaining from bad influence)	1	4.5
18.	*Didupe oore* (Being appreciative)	1	4.5
19.	*Jije alakikanju* (Being brave)	1	4.5
20.	*Fifi ife han* (Showing love)	1	4.5
21.	*Diduro lori imule* (Keeping the brotherhood)	1	4.5
22.	*Kiki awon eniyan* (Greeting fellow human beings)	1	4.5
23.	*Gbigbo ati siso ede Yorùbá* (Understanding and speaking the *Yorùbá* language)	1	4.5
24.	*Yiyago fun lilo owo osi fun awon agba* (Abstaining from the use of the left hand for elders)	1	4.5
25.	*Sise igboran si awon agba* (Being obedient to elders)	1	4.5
26.	*Bibebe fun asise* (Apologising to others for mistakes committed)	1	4.5
27.	*Sisa fun iwa ipaniyan* (Abstaining from killing fellow human beings)	1	4.5
28.	*Sise imototo* (Keeping good hygiene)	1	4.5
29.	*Pipa awon aje ati emere* (Killing witches and wizards)	1	4.5
30.	*Biba awon eniyan miran soro l'ona to dara* (Good communication)	1	4.5

The variety of practices suggested by the respondents as collated in this table is not exhaustive. However, the items depict actions and practices that are capable of making anyone gain acceptability among *Yorùbá* people.

Table 5: Factors Promoting Violation of Sacredness of Life among *Yorùbá*

This segment aims to have a list of factors that promote violations of the sacredness of human life among *Yorùbá* people at this contemporary time.

S/N	Factors Promoting Violation of Human Sacredness among *Yorùbá*	No. of Respondents	% of Respondents
1.	*Ife owo, agabra, ipo ati obinrin* (Love of money, power, position, and women)	9	40.9
2.	*Iwa wobia/ okanjuwara* (Greediness)	7	31.8
3.	*Jije ewoo ti ile Yorùbá* (Breaking of cultural taboos)	5	22.7
4.	*Elesin-mesin* (Religious bigotry)	4	18.2
5.	*Ojukokoro/ ojukokuro* (Covetousness)	4	18.2
6.	*Aini Iberu Olorun* (Lack of the fear of God)	4	18.2
7.	*Igbagbo awon Yorùbá ninu isepataki eje eniyan* (Worth of human blood)	4	18.2
8.	*Sise igbelaruge awon ajeji asa* (Promotion of foreign cultures)	3	13.3
9.	*Aini-ife-ara-eni-d'enu* (Lack of brotherly love)	3	13.3
10.	*Imotara-eni-nikan* (Selfishness)	3	13.3
11.	*Ogun* (War)	2	9.1
12.	*Pipadanu awon iwa omoluabi* (Erosion of good cultural values)	2	9.1
13.	*Iro pipa/ eke sise* (Falsehood)	2	9.1
14.	*Ohun ti a o je ati ohun ti a o je* (Desires for what to eat and aspiration for what to be)	2	9.1
15.	*Ijekuje ati imukumu* (Drugs and Drinking)	2	9.1
16.	*Olaju nipase eto-eko awon Oyibo* (Civilisation through western education)	2	9.1
17.	*Igberaga* (Pride)	2	9.1
18.	*Aileko idile* (Unrestricted and untaught family members)	2	9.1
19.	*Awon igbagbo-asan* (Superstitions)	2	9.1
20.	*Iko-ara-eni-sile ninu idile* (Divorce)	2	9.1
21.	*Asise awon eniyan* (Human errors)	1	4.5
22.	*Wahala ti eto oselu* (Political crisis)	1	4.5
23.	*Iwa-ika* (Wickedness)	1	4.5
24.	*Aini* (Poverty)	1	4.5
25.	*Imungbooro ise* (Business expansion)	1	4.5
26.	*Idunkokomoni lati odo awon ojugba-eni tabi ilu* (Peer pressure or Community influence)	1	4.5
27.	*Abokameji/ Agabangebe* (Double standard)	1	4.5
28.	*Pipo awon eniyan lai ni aala* (Uncontrolled	1	4.5

	population)		
29.	*Aimooko-moka* (Illiteracy)	1	4.5
30.	*Aini suuru* (Impatience)	1	4.5
31.	*Ede-ko-yede laarin awon* Yorùbá (Misunderstanding among *Yorùbá* people)	1	4.5

This list of 31 factors that are promoting the violation of human sacredness among *Yorùbá* in Table 5 above is not exhaustive but brings to the fore areas where the people should intensify efforts to curb various violations. The effort will go a long way in making Yorubaland a better place to be if the people take necessary actions.

Table 6: Types of Violation of Sanctity of Human Life among *Yorùbá*

This table aims at generating a list of some of the types of violation of the sanctity of human life among Yoruba people as obtained today. The step will further enhance the comprehensive understanding of the subject matter among the people.

S/N	Types of Violation to the Sanctity of Human Life among Yoruba People	No. of Respondents	% of Respondents
1.	*Ipaniyan fun awon idi kan bi i fun igbenipa ati igbenisowo* (Killing for certain purposes such as ritual killing and kidnapping)	9	40.9
2.	*Iro-pipa/ eke-sise* (Falsehood)	9	40.9
3.	*Pipaniyan lai ro tele* (Killing of a human being in error)	8	36.4
4.	*Ole-jija* (Stealing)	6	27.3
5.	*Agbere ati Pansaga* (Fornication and Adultery)	5	22.7
6.	*Ile-dida* (Covenant-breaking)	3	13.6
7.	*Ije-wobia* (Greediness)	3	13.6
8.	*Imutipara* (Drunkenness)	2	9.1
9.	*Owo-eru* (Slavery)	2	9.1
10.	*Mo-daru* (Sabotage)	2	9.1
11.	*Titabuku elomiran* (Slander)	2	9.1
12.	*Magomago/ didabaru eto idibo* (Election rigging)	1	4.5
13.	*Etan* (Deceit)	1	4.5
14.	*Aibowo fun agba* (Lack of respect for elders)	1	4.5
15.	*Sisi agabra lo* (Abuse of power)	1	4.5
16.	*Tete-tita* (Gambling)	1	4.5
17.	*Iwa-ika* (Acts of wickedness)	1	4.5
18.	*Oyun-sise* (Abortion)	1	4.5
19.	*Egbe okunkun* (Cultism)	1	4.5
20.	*Imukumun* (Taking to drugs)	1	4.5
21.	*Aini-imototo* (Lack of good hygiene)	1	4.5

22.	*Ailojutiti* (Shamelessness)	1	4.5
23.	*Odi-yiyan* (Keeping malice)	1	4.5
24.	*Ikorira eniyan* (Hatred)	1	4.5
25.	*Imo-tara-eni-nikan* (Selfishness/ Self-centeredness)	1	4.5
26.	*Ifipabanilopo* (Sexual abuse or Rape)	1	4.5
27.	*Ojukokoro/Ojukokuro* (Covetousness)	1	4.5

Various violations of the sacredness of human life in Table 6 above clearly show that human beings are often at risk among *Yorùbá* people. This situation depicts the level of appreciation given to human lives in the land and where concerted efforts should be placed among the people to enhance their understanding of human sacredness.

Table 7a: Effects of Violations to Sanctity of Human Life on the Victims
This table aims at having a possible list of some of the effects of violations of the sanctity of human life on the victims.

S/N	Effects of violations of Sanctity of Human Life on the Victims	No. of Respondents	% of Respondents
1.	The destiny (*ayanmo*) of the victims will still come to pass. This situation sometimes happens in the family-line. If the death is untimely, the victims will re-incarnate in another environment to complete their earth-life	8	36.4
2.	They could suffer an untimely death	5	22.7
3.	The killers violate the victims' rights and also endanger their worth	5	22.7
4.	They could incur loss, indebtedness, poverty, lack of respect, stigmatisation or be under perpetual fear	4	18.2
5.	They could be wounded, maimed and intimidated.	3	13.6
6.	They will be vindicated and compensated in the end if not guilty	2	9.1
7.	The victims could imbibe negative characters such as hatred, malice, and wickedness, etc.	2	9.1
8.	Violations may teach them better ways of doing things through experience, knowledge, and wisdom obtained	1	4.5
9.	Their wives/husbands and children could become widows/widowers and orphans respectively	1	4.5

This table shows some of the suggested possible consequences or effects of violations of the sanctity of human lives on the victims. The gravity of the impact brings to the fore various degrees of pains and trauma many people are passing through in the society as a result of one violation or the other either directly against their lives or the lives of their loved ones.

Table 7b: Effects of Violations to Sanctity of Human Life on the Family

This part aims at obtaining a list of possible effects of violations of the sanctity of human life on the family system.

S/N	Effects of violations of Sanctity of Human Life on the Family	No. of Respondents	% of Respondents
1.	Many families are facing retribution. Many parents are irritating to their children for lack of proper home training, and many families are suffering from breaking cultural taboos. This most of the time leads to a cycle called the generational curse	7	31.8
2.	The family generally is worst off for various violations as a result of attendant hunger, indebtedness, unfaithfulness, and conflict, etc.	4	18.2
3.	The family system could become unstable for multiple reasons	3	13.6
4.	African traditional arrangement with its values have collapsed	3	13.6
5.	Sorrow, trouble, emotional trauma and stigmatisation attend to many families today	2	9.1
6.	Many families are wiped off the earth already as a result of communal conflicts, pipeline vandalism and ritual killings	2	9.1
7.	African system of the community has given way for western individualism in most families	2	9.1
8.	There could be a loss of the integrity of family members with its attendant rewards	1	4.5
9.	The family could abandon law and order	1	4.5
10.	Many families are suffering for crimes they never committed	1	4.5

This table shows various degrees of effects of violations of human sacredness on the family among *Yorùbá* people. The sad aspect of it is the claim that many families are indirectly suffering today in the land for crimes they never committed.

Table 7c: Effects of Violations of Sanctity of Human Life on the Society

This table aims at obtaining a possible list of suggested effects of violations of the sanctity of human life on the society. This list will bring to the fore the general situations facing the majority of the people.

S/N	Effects of violations of Sanctity of Human Life on the society	No. of Respondents	% of Respondents
1.	A complete collapse of the social system and its values. The people do not follow law and order any longer	6	27.3
2.	Retribution has taken over the land. The society is suffering and is troubled	5	22.7
3.	Lack of security, and peace and tranquillity	5	22.7
4.	The community becomes unstable. Thereby, considerable progress becomes unrealistic. There is an increase in the unemployment rate, economic challenges, an outbreak of diseases, and poverty rate, etc.	4	18.2
5.	Increase in crime rate, lawlessness moral decadence and cultism	4	18.2
6.	God does not answer prayers again the way He used to do for people are preoccupied with their problems instead of God's interest	1	4.5
7.	Genuine love has become a mirage to find	1	4.5
8.	Inter-tribal war or communal conflicts	1	4.5
9.	A problem of underdevelopment	1	4.5

This table suggests that many people living within the territory of Yorubaland are suffering. The suffering is in different categories, many of which are effects of the various violations of the sanctity of human lives on them.

Table 7d: Effects of Violations of Sanctity of Life on Younger Generation

This part aims at having a possible list of some of the effects of violations of the sanctity of human life on the younger generation.

S/N	Effects of Violations to Sanctity of Human Life on Younger Generation	No. of Respondents	% of Respondents
1.	Their future is bleak for their psyche is being ruined	6	27.3
2.	They are vulnerable to bad influences and evil practices today as they teach negative values such as the following: assassination,	5	22.7

	kidnapping, raping, and drug abuse, etc.		
3.	The bulk of societal problems are on them as they have more of them to grapple with, an example of which is unemployment	4	18.2
4.	Life expectancy rate is becoming shorter for them as many of them cannot survive the challenges	4	18.2
5.	Life is growing increasingly difficult for them by the day	3	13.6
6.	They are devastated; their life perception (worldview) is perverted, and they are growing more corrupt and depraved daily	3	13.6
7.	Failure has become the order of the day for them	1	4.5
8.	The crime rate is on the increase among them for life has lost its meaning and value to them	1	4.5
9.	There may not be any progress for them	1	4.5

The contents of this table are the challenges and societal risks facing the life of today's generation in Yorubaland. This situation shows the rate at which the people appreciate human life and possible consequences to them at large shortly if they fail to check the trend.

Table 8a: Responses of Governments to Human Life Violations among Yorùbá
This table seeks to obtain a possible list of responses of governments to various violations of the worth of human life within the context of the *Yorùbá* people. The step aims at making governments at all levels identify possible areas where they are doing well and those they are neglecting.

S/N	Responses of Governments to Violations of Human Worth among Yoruba	No. of Respondents	% of Respondents
1.	Nonchalant attitude towards various violations	8	36.4
2.	Most leaders are self-centred, greedy, corrupt, and wicked. They are liars and thieves	6	27.3
3.	Promoting various violations in their favour and to their benefits most of the time	6	27.3
4.	Leaders fail to put in place sound policies on education, economy, and security	2	9.1
5.	Placing a premium on western education and	2	9.1

S/N		No. of Respondents	% of Respondents
	foreign culture to the neglect of the cultural values of the land		
6.	Leaders are not united. They fail to speak with one voice	1	4.5

The responses of the representative samples indicate that there is a wide gap between the leaders who are at the helm of affairs and the masses they govern. The situations on the ground, therefore, demand urgent attention from governments to check the trend and forestall possible consequences.

Table 8b: Responses of Religious Bodies to Life Violations among *Yorùbá*

This table seeks to obtain a possible list of responses of the religious organisations to various violations of the worth of human life among *Yorùbá* people. This list identifies potential areas of strength and weaknesses of the different bodies in the land.

S/N	Responses of Religious Bodies to Violations of Human Worth among *Yorùbá*	No. of Respondents	% of Respondents
1.	Good adherents of YTR do not support human sacrifice. They are exemplary in the moral aspects of life. *Ifa* does not demand human sacrifice, but *Esu* divinity does	5	22.7
2.	Fake and untaught *Ifa* practitioners promote the shedding of human blood. These people are followers of *Esu* divinity for various reasons	4	18.2
3.	Many religious leaders are not any better than political leaders. They do not challenge the governments to perform better	4	18.2
4.	Evil and corrupt adherents of all religious bodies in the land indulge in violations like killing. They also sabotage one another	4	18.2
5.	Some religious leaders are fraudulent and deceptive. They bury the truth and practice money ritual	3	13.6
6.	YTR practitioners promoted human sacrifice in the ancient time, especially among the warriors. However, this has stopped today	3	13.6
7.	Almost all religions support the sanctity of human life by opposing bloodshed	2	9.1
8.	Religious leaders fail to promote good moral	2	9.1

	values in their teaching		
9.	Religious bodies are more concerned about family and societal matters. They preach and teach on how peace and tranquillity could be in society. However, they are lagging in post-marital counselling	2	9.1
10.	The gods demand human sacrifices sometimes when people break *eewo* (taboos) in the land	1	4.5
11.	Many Christian and Islamic leaders are collaborators in bloodshed for ritual purposes	1	4.5

The table above shows responses of the various religious bodies in Yorubaland to the matter of the sanctity of human life. It is evident from the table that if the society is to experience a meaningful change in this regard, religious leaders have a lot to do in stemming the tide of the various violations taking place within their domains.

Table 8c: Responses of the Family to Life Violations among *Yorùbá* People

This table aims to obtain a possible list of the responses of the family to the various violations of the worth of human life within the context of *Yorùbá* people.

S/N	Responses of Family to Violations of Human Worth among *Yorùbá*	No. of Respondents	% of Respondents
1.	The *Yorùbá* family has generally abandoned training of children in their cultural values and practices	6	27.3
2.	The *Yorùbá* family is typically weak in the teaching of good cultural values and traditions. The situation may be as a result of a polygamous system of marriage and single-parenting	3	13.6
3.	Some *Yorùbá* families are still committed to their roles of raising children in good cultural values and practices	3	13.6
4.	Many parents encourage their wards to seek money at all cost. They want to get rich quickly	3	13.6
5.	There is a complete breakdown of order in the family system in Yorubaland. Most families are individualistic, and many of the parents have lost authority. Their children are disobedient and fail to take care of them at old	3	13.6

S/N		No.	%
	age		
6.	Many children are proud and deviant to parents' instructions. They are preoccupied with money making	2	9.1
7.	Most families prefer to promote foreign cultures at the expense of that of Yorùbá	2	9.1
8.	Many parents are disinterested in raising children against violations of the sanctity of human life	1	4.5

The various responses are the respondents' suggestions on family responses to the violation of the sanctity of human life among Yorùbá. These are quite revealing.

Table 9: Appropriate Measures to Curtail the Sanctity of Human Life Violations
This item aims at prescribing appropriate measures to curtail various violations to the sanctity of human life among *Yorùbá* people.

S/N	Appropriate Measures to Violations of Sanctity of Human Life	No. of Respondents	% of Respondents
1.	Governments should wake up to their responsibilities in the following ways: creating jobs for the jobless, creating awareness on security of life and property, providing adequate protection and punishing the offenders, making sound education readily available and affordable, making people's votes count, and strengthening extant laws and enacting new ones against violation of human sacredness, etc	12	54.5
2.	Parents should intensify on training and teaching good values at home	9	40.9
3.	Religious leaders should be exemplary in their approaches to life and emphasise good moral values in their preaching and teaching	7	31.8
4.	Cultivating the fear of God, allowing God's Spirit to lead in all situations and praying for divine intervention	6	27.3
5.	Reverting to Yorùbá cultural heritage and religious practices such as respect for elders, a culture of greeting and keeping good hygiene	4	18.2
6.	Human right advocacy is needed to sensitise	4	18.2

	the public on the worth of human life and teaching the younger generation on the acceptable way of life. This step can take the form of a seminar, workshop, and conference by corporate bodies.		
7.	Parents should be exemplary in all their dealings, most importantly at home	2	9.1
8.	Common focus and joint efforts by all leaders at all levels and strata are needed to correct wrong values	2	9.1
9.	Change of value system from the love of money to good moral values of Yorùbá culture	1	4.5
10.	Movies that promote a culture of naked-dressing and robbery should be prohibited	1	4.5

Various measures identified in the table above are all-encompassing. The governments, religious bodies and families have specific roles to play. These must be adequately considered and implemented for the sanctity of human life to gain a better appreciation and become a culture in Yorubaland.

Question 10:
The basis of this question is to elicit some other vital information that could bring about adequate understanding and correct low appreciation of the sanctity of human life among Yorùbá people. First of these ideas is the need to refine the Yorùbá value system about the sacredness of human life. The need becomes necessary as there are parts of the cultural elements which cannot match the challenges of this time in Yorùbá worldview. Similarly, the basis of Yorùbá value system has to undergo redefinition. This demand is imperative because anything done by monetary gain against the love of it will not last; it will be bereft of quality. Again, if the subject of the sanctity of human life will become a culture, religions should be contextualised in the land. In this way, stakeholders must carefully fuse both religion and culture for a better understanding of religious tenets in the local context of the people.

More so, the cultural elements of patience and contentment, which have become almost non-existent in the lives of most of the people today, especially the younger generation, need to be reintegrated into the moral values of the land. The people need to teach the values into the minds of the younger generation. Also, the culture of a communal system of living that Africa, most importantly Yorubaland, was once known for should be reintroduced into the educational system of the younger generation beginning from home to school. Again, the value of the family should be part of the psyche of the younger ones. This need becomes imperative because charity begins at home.

8. Analysis of *Yorùbá* Understanding of Sanctity of Human Life

This section is set to bring to the fore the summary of the understanding of the concept of the sacredness of human life among *Yorùbá* people. Five main elements characterise this understanding from the preceding discussion, and they reflect the various dimensions of the existence and practices of the people as analysed above; namely, their philosophy, rituals, vocabulary, social relations and political life.

a. Sanctity of Human Life is about Human Characters

From the various responses of the representative samples analysed above, the subject of the sanctity of life among *Yorùbá* people is about a man sharing certain characters with God. Some of these characters are the following as contained in Table 1: patience, contentment, appreciating others, human relations, helping others, faith in *Olodumare*, acts of goodness, hospitality, caring for others, praising *Olodumare*, being truthful, obedience, humility, following peace with others, being law-abiding, and preserving God's created order (human lives in particular). Others mentioned in Table 3 are these: having a fear of God, forgiving other people, gentleness, being in one accord with fellow human beings for good reasons, love, truthfulness or honesty, not being a smoker or drug addict, keeping good hygiene, and keeping the brotherhood.

According to this writer, these characters are various ways by which man projects the relational part of God to other created beings in the universe. Similarly, they are evidence of God's approval of the life of whoever possesses them that such a person is indeed human. The reflection is because not all in human form are human beings in the understanding of *Yorùbá* people but only those who have characters. In another sense, the measure of these attributes in one shows the quality of such a person's humanness.

This understanding has its reflections on the life and practices of an average individual. In *Yorùbá* philosophy, there is a traditional belief in reincarnation, transmigration, retribution, and future judgment. The story told by S.T. Ola. Akande of a man who claimed to have been born three times aforetime is a reflection of transmigration.[423] Another is the story of a new baby boy born in the exact copy of his grandfather.[424] *Yorùbá* people believe that there is a repayment of whatever evil or right which was previously done anytime one comes to earth-life again. According to this belief-system, future judgment is by the characters that an individual manifested or practices displayed during one's earth-life. Some of the good customs that could earn one a right place in heaven with the ancestors are contained in Table 4 while Table 6 shows examples of evil practices. Similarly, Table 2 displays some of the ideas, proverbs and wise sayings that bring the need to live right to the fore.

---

[423] S.T. Ola. Akande, *Miracles, Mysteries, Death and Dying, and Other Supernatural Events in Nigeria* (South Carolina: CreateSpace Independent Publishing Platform, 2013), 254-255.
[424] Ibid, 256-257.

b. Sacredness of Human Life is About God's Image in Mankind

In *Yorùbá* metaphysics, *Yorùbá* people believe that the basis of human sacredness is the breath of Olodumare passed into the human body, the lump of clay moulded by all of the *orisa* (deities). This breath is the Spirit of God in man which accounts for the various godly characters expected of an ideal human being in Table 1 and different good practices expected of an average person in Table 4. This breath is the soul of a man that also gives an individual ability to relate well with God.

c. Human Worth relates to *Yorùbá* Practice of Death Aversion

It is part of the philosophy of Yorùbá people that human life is a valuable gift from Olodumare and must be averted from death whenever there is an opportunity. In other words, the being of man is so precious that people should prevent it from possible hurt or termination. On this basis, an average *Yorùbá* person can go extra miles to avert a possible death. One area where this idea comes to play is in the *Yorùbá* understanding of the concept of the good life. They believe that life is very precious and should be enjoyed by accumulating wealth and riches and fulfilling one's destiny. Not only this, but a good life is also that of pleasure.

The mindset of life-enjoyment by kings in the ancient time accounted for the sacrifice of the *Abobaku* (Dying for kings) as obtained in item 14 of Table 4. This ordinance was usually performed as a rite of passage whenever any deceased king was to be committed to the grave to join the ancestors. Another example of rituals of this kind is the sacrifice of a human being for anyone who desired for the longevity of life. This practice was widespread among the warriors of old in Yorubaland. All these traditions are by the worth of human blood as expressed in item 7 of Table 5.

d. Human Sanctity relates to Man Created for Divine Purpose

One other basis for the *Yorùbá* understanding of the sacredness of human life is that God sets human beings at the centre of His mind, activities, and actions. The people believe that God created human beings primarily as God's co-creators and partners. This situation is evident in their ability to think creatively and exercise their God-given willpower. The various scientific discoveries, space expeditions, and explorations and giant strides made in technology are practical testimonies to bolster this idea. These are some of the ways by which human beings express their functional ability as God's co-regents on earth.

More so, another one by *Yorùbá* metaphysics is the engagement of all deities in the moulding of the human body by all of the 401 gods before *Olodumare* would sanction individual's *ayanmo* (destiny) in heaven. An additional dimension to this understanding is the engagement of different *Irunmole* (divinities), environmental powers and ancestors by an average individual in the land through rituals to obtain fulfilment of destiny. Examples of these ecological powers as discussed above in this chapter are spirits inhabiting certain environmental objects such as the following: highlands and hills; rivers, lagoons and, the sea temples; thick and abundant vegetation of trees; certain animals; and earth or land.

e. Worth of Human Life relates to God's Mercy and Grace in Mankind

Yorùbá believe that human beings are unique and special. They also think that what accounts for this exceptionality is God's special mercy obtained and grace released upon human life. As a result of this, man is different from animals and every other created being. This understanding reflects in almost all aspects of life.

In their philosophy, this grace reflects in the choice of *ayanmo* (destiny) to determine one's course of earth-life in the pre-incarnated state. It also expresses itself in man's given ability to reason creatively and understand God's mind and purpose. An example of this is the investigation of the *Ikose w'aye* ('stepping into the world')[425] of any newborn child in the traditional *Yorùbá* setting. In this way, the parents would consult with *Ifa* priests demanding for the choices the child had made before coming for earth-life.

Similarly, God gives humankind the grace to ward off evil in fulfilling one's destiny in *Yorùbá* rituals. This potential is with the help of the deities through sacrifice. Thus, a man could enjoy a good life and reach out to Olodumare with the help of the gods and ancestors. A man also receives grace to communicate intelligibly with *Olodumare* and fellow human beings through the power of the spoken words. These are just a few examples by which God's grace manifests in an average human being expressing the *Yorùbá* understanding of the sacredness of human life.

---

[425] Drewal, 54.

CHAPTER FIVE

SANCTITY OF HUMAN LIFE IN NUMBERS 35:9-34 AND *YORÙBÁ* WORLDVIEW: A COMPARATIVE ANALYSIS

The focus of this section is to compare the understanding of the sanctity of human life in the context of Numbers 35:9-34 and *Yorùbá* worldview. This step brings to the fore possible areas of harmony and conflict between the two settings. In the end, the writer draws the necessary implications by the identified elements. .

1. Nexus between Numbers 35:9-34 and *Yorùbá* Worldview

As part of the fifth objective of this study, it is on the imperative to identify necessary areas of unity which Numbers 35:9-34 has in common with the *Yorùbá* people. This step is with the aim of adding to knowledge in the field of comparative study with specific references to cultural values and world religions.

a. Ethnic Correlations

The first part of the nexus is in the area of ethnic correlations between ancient Israel and the *Yorùbá*. The United Kingdom of Israel occupied the land on the Mediterranean Sea which roughly corresponds to the State of modern Israel. According to Joshua J. Mark, the ancient region where this kingdom belonged was at different times known and referred to as Canaan, Phoenicia and later as Palestine. The area also assumed another nomenclature after the Hebrew patriarch called Jacob (also known as *Yisrae'el*)[426] at the time of Joshua's conquest about 1250 BCE. According to Niels Peter Lemche, it is a tribal society in its pre-national period consisting of 12 tribes unified by a shared monotheistic religion which centred on the worship of Yahweh.[427] Israel developed into a state with loosed confederacy after the conquest of the land, resulting in a displacement of indigenous people which affected the whole of the region.[428]

According to Mark S. Smith, scholars presented monotheism as the "worship and belief in Yahweh and disbelief in the reality of other deities."[429] In addition to this definition, Harold B. Hunting advances that Prophet Isaiah presents Yahweh not only as the God of Israel and Judah but as that of the entire universe. Thus, Yahweh is the God of all humanity, and His reign has no limit. Hunting regards this as the beginning

---

[426] Joshua J. Mark, "Israel," *Ancient History Encyclopedia, http://www.ancient.eu/israel/* (accessed April 13, 2017).

[427] Niels Peter Lemche and Frederick Cryer, trans., "Israel, History (Archaeology and the Conquest)," *The Anchor Bible Dictionary*, Volume 3, ed., David Noel Freedman (New York: Doubleday, 1992), n.p.

[428] Mark, n.p.

[429] Mark S. Smith, *The Early History of God: Yahweh and the Other Deities in Ancient Israel*, Second Edition (Grand Rapids, Michigan/ Cambridge, U.K: William B. Eerdmans Publishing Company, 1990, 2002), 24.

of the true religion of monotheism, "the religion of the one All-Father."[430] Given this, this writer asserts that parts of Yahweh's designations among *Yorùbá* people could be *Olodumare* since He is the Father of all nations and peoples, assuming different names from one land to the other.

Equally, the term 'Yorùbá' is an ethnic group in Nigeria. It is a term used for people of this way of life in Diaspora like Republic of Benin, Togo, Cuba, and Brazil with a common origin and progenitor in the ancient town of Ile-Ife and *Oduduwa* respectively. The people are also of a common culture. However, they are different in dialects with five subgroups as analysed in chapter four. The philosophical, ethical, and religious aspects of the corporate life of the people are all contained in *Ifa* Corpus. On account of this similarity, there are attempts to connect the *Yorùbá* race with the Jews or Arabs.

b. Basis of Sanctity of Human Life

Another element central to the two contexts is the similarity in the basis of the sacredness of life. In the context of OT, especially in Numbers 35:9-34, the sanctity of life is by the concept of *Imago Dei* which reveals a biblical system of justice in the preservation of God's image in humankind. In chapter three, the writer described this concept as the components of God which make humans what they are. These components can be substantive, dealing with man's innate capacities for emotion and exercise of willpower. It can also be relational, depicting God's ability in humans for effective communication with God. More so, the concept could be functional with the explicit purpose of humanity exercising God's rule and dominion over God's creation. Thus, termination of human life is not only a sin against the victim but also against God. This is not because the killer has deprived the victim of the right to enjoy the inherent divine qualities alone but that the killer has destroyed God's image also.

Likewise, the sacredness of human life in *Yorùbá* philosophy is by the breadth of *Olodumare* passed into the human body moulded by the deities as analysed in chapter four. In other words, the man became a living soul on account of the God-given breath. Because of this, *Olodumare's* inspiration is man's innate ability to perform or act as God's co-creators, vice regents or partners. All of these activities are projected for others to see using individual's characters and ethical practices.

Thus, the Jewish understanding of the concept of *Imago Dei* is supported by that of *Olodumare's* breath in *Yorùbá* thought. Individual's characters and practices, therefore, determine whether God's image is still active in one or not. In this way, it is possible for one to forfeit this innate ability going by the *Yorùbá* understanding of life. This reality is because it is not all people in human appearance that are human indeed; some of them are animals, some of them are evil spirits while some are other beings. The people express this idea in their adage that says, *Ara l'amo, a ko mo inu* (It is the body we see, no one knows the content). *Yorùbá* people manifest the exercise of an individual's willpower of the substantive Jewish form of God's image through characters. Similarly, the writer also expressed both functional and relational

---

[430] Harold B. Hunting, *Hebrew Life and Times* (New York: Nashville, MCMXXI), 44.

155

structures using godly characters as identified in Tables 1 and 3 and good practices in Table 4. Given all this, characters and holy conducts are one main basis for expressing the sanctity of human life in *Yorùbá* worldview.

c. High Appreciation for Human Worth

High appreciation for the value of the sanctity of human life is another element of note as contained in the ethical standards of the two cultural groups of people. On the one hand, the OT law codes, especially the Ten Commandments, have provided a primary body of legal formulations outlining fundamental principles of virtue and justice. According to R.E. Clements, there was a more comprehensive picture of the rise and development of law and systems of justice in the ancient world with the recovery of law codes from the ancient Near East in the 19th century, an example of which is the Code of Hammurabi. The law codes were meant to promote a healthy and acceptable social order. The prophets in the OT were empowered as reformers and innovators to uphold and defend the laws or ethical conducts thereby leaving a strong moral legacy.[431] A vivid aspect of these conducts is the biblical reference for the worth of human life in the context of Numbers 35:9-34 which brings to the fore that the sanctity of human life in the OT is not racial, gender, social, economic and cultural biases. Yahweh's law governing the administration of the cities of refuge was not limited to the children of Israel alone; the provision was also for the sojourners and aliens among them. Thus, there is a good ethical standard for the sacredness of life in the chosen text.

On the other hand, there are considerable ways by which *Yorùbá* people honour the worth of human life in their worldview. The people go about these through their cultural values and practices. The first of these is about names given to the newborn children. This is one reality that reflects the people's general and specific value which they attach to names. *Yorùbá* people name their children on the basis of the perceived worth of the child either to itself as a person or to others like the family, community and, entire world.

Furthermore, the people consider many things to identify their worth for human life; namely, the day the child was born, the manner by which the child was born, the time the child was born, the circumstances surrounding the birth, and the destiny of the child. Also, children are so named based on the expectations of their parents. Most of the time, an average traditional *Yorùbá* parent would consult the gods to understand the child's destiny. These parents, especially the father, also engage some of the members of the extended families in the process. There are three possible categories of names in the land from which a child may receive two at most; namely, *Amutorunwa* (the name with which the child is born), *Abiso* ("the christening names"), and *Oriki* (the Cognomen, Attributive or Pet names). The writer expounded these three categories in chapter four of this work.

---

[431] R.E. Clements, ed., *The World of Ancient Israel: Sociological, Anthropological and political Perspectives* (Cambridge: Cambridge University Press, 1989), 9-10.

Again, some other forms by which the value of the sanctity of life reflects in *Yorùbá* cultural practices and ethical standard include *Yorùbá* proverbs and administration of *eewo* (taboos). Traditionally, the following activities are *eewo* in the Yorubaland; namely, murder, cannibalism, incest, swearing, the use of foul languages, and cursing. Besides, taboos are guiding the following: personal hygiene or general cleanliness, accident and death, crime control, and teaching and keeping moral values. Explicitly, it is forbidden to murder for the action is a crime against the gods and humanity and is punishable by death.

Moreover, the sanctity of human life reflects in the *Yorùbá* system of beliefs. The lives and practices of *Yorùbá* people are by these beliefs. Prominent among them are these: belief in *Olodumare* or *Olorun* as the Maker of the universe, and in the existence of many *Orisa* (deities) as intermediaries between the people and their Maker. They also believe in the future judgment, invocation of the spirits of the ancestors regarded as the living dead, and transmigration (rebirth). Pre-incarnation is another, a belief in the pre-existence of humankind as analysed in chapter four. All of these are in addition to the value attached to good characters which the people expect from human beings.

d. Violations of the Sacredness of Life

One other area of harmony is the existence of the violations of the sacredness of human life within the two settings. The writer established this in chapter three that killing was a common phenomenon within the context of the OT. This claim is partly due to the various Hebrew words employed in the Hebrew Bible with a general connotation of this idea and the volume of times the OT people used each of these vocabularies. Again, the violations are equally attested to by the amount of the evidence obtained within the contexts of the Law, Prophets, and Writings as analysed in the third chapter of study.

Violations of this kind were in diverse categories such as constant warfare which often led to humiliation, degradation, mutilation, and murder. Gender inequality is another for the culture of the ancient Near East was generally patriarchal. The exercise of political hegemony of the dominant powers at the expense of the weaker ones was another form of violation. Internal conflicts were others of which palace coup is an example. Also, pollution of the political atmosphere of the ancient world, especially within the context of the OT, is another reflection. Hence, violations of the sanctity of human life were real in the OT despite the given sound biblical system of justice.

Similarly, it is a fact that related violations are one reality that does not take place in the life and practices of the *Yorùbá* people only but is deeply rooted in their understanding of the world around them also. This situation reflects in the rating of man in the hierarchy of beings. *Yorùbá* believe in the existence of a hierarchical kind of living which places a premium on all spirit beings at the expense of humankind as analysed in chapter four. On this basis is the worship of all kinds of spirits and sacred objects among the people. Worship of certain environmental objects like mountains, rivers, hills, land, thunder and lightning, big trees in thick forests, and animals like monkey, reptile, and crocodile are by the people's understanding that these are the abodes of the gods. Sometimes, human beings are offered at some of these shrines as sacrifices to appease the gods.

Violations of this kind also take the form of worship of the ancestor by an average traditional Yorùbá. Apart from the fact that a typical *Yorùbá* person attaches more significant value to the departed ones, the manifestations of this practice are often at the expense of the living. This value might be the basis for why *Yorùbá* people regard their ancestors as 'the living dead.' The people borrow money to give their departed ones a befitting burial. Again, they practice libation by offering some portion of drink on the ground while they have not fed the living among them adequately. They also present the first portion of their food on the ground to the deities.

Again, violations of the worth of human life among the people are also by their understanding of the concept of the good life which relates to a life of pleasure and happiness. This life, in turn, is by the volume of riches and wealth in one's possession. The spate of killing for various purposes in the land is possibly in connection with this belief. A violation of this kind also takes the form of war expeditions which ravaged the lives of many people, especially at the earliest times. Most of these conflicts aimed at achieving the desires for power, position, and wealth by some *Yorùbá* leaders. Drewal expresses some of these factors as she reflected on the strength of rituals among their performers in Yorubaland:

> Performers succeed in influencing their situations, although they cannot always determine the consequences. In part this is because, in a highly competitive society of operationally strong individuals, everybody is engaged in the same exercise to alter their current conditions, seizing opportunities, jockeying for position, extending their power and influence, 'playing' situations to turn them to their own advantage, in short, 'making things happen.' As the oft-seen adage painted on trucks and lorries in Nigeria asserts, 'NO CONDITION IS PERMANENT.'[432]

In other words, many people in the land take to rituals to change bad situations with them for the better. Additionally, gender discrimination is another manifestation of violations of this kind. This situation is evident in the practice of *Opo* (widowhood) rite made compulsory for only female widows. Thus, the value attached to the essence and existence of human life about the spirit beings (such as the deities with their sacred objects and ancestors) and material possessions is low.

The writer made mention of some of the types of violations in Table 6 above as they were suggested by the respondents. The first on the list of these is murder expressed as killing for certain purposes. Two examples of the killing of this form are killing for ritual purposes and kidnapping. Similarly, next to wilful termination of human life are the following: falsehood, unpremeditated murder, stealing, fornication and adultery, covenant-breaking, greediness, drunkenness, slavery, and sabotage.

---

[432] Drewal, xix.

Some others are; namely, slander, election rigging, deceit, lack of respect for elders, abuse of power, gambling, acts of wickedness, and abortion. The list also consists of cultism, drug addiction, lack of proper hygiene, shamelessness, keeping malice, hatred towards fellow human beings, covetousness, sexual abuse such as rape, and selfishness/self-centeredness.

e. Punitive Measures against Killing

Necessary punitive measures against killers are one other element that connects the two contexts. In the setting of the Jews, the editor of the Book of Numbers prescribes two kinds of punishment, and each of them is for a specific category of killers in the chosen text. Capital punishment is imposed on murderers while imprisonment is for those guilty of manslaughter. The two penal codes are made available in Numbers 35:9-34 through which the people exclusively purged the land of blood. Thus, capital punishment is biblical. The same applies to the cultural practice of imprisonment. The divine command in the text is altogether an essential expression of God's care not only for the lives of His covenant people in ancient Israel but also for others whom the editor depicts as aliens and sojourners among the people. Also, the OT prohibits payment of ransom to avert punishment over the termination of human life. No ransom must be collected either for the murderer or one guilty of manslaughter, but the person would have to face a mandatory penalty.

In a similar vein, capital punishment is part of the worldview of the *Yorùbá* people. This reality is specifically against anyone who murdered one's fellow being. The death penalty is measured against the murderer because the crime is against the gods and humanity. The case of *Alaafin* Jayin who was rejected by his subjects and committed suicide in the end for terminating the life of his son is an example.[433] In *Yorùbá* worldview, the ethical rules given the 401 divinities are aimed at making the earth worthwhile and are for proper conducts on earth. The people regard these as Natural Laws, the basis of all ethical behaviours as expanded in chapter four. If the Laws are followed, therefore, to murder fellow human beings will be impossible. Hence, failure to follow the divine code of Olodumare is a basis for violations of these kinds among the people, and the society has the duty of enforcing the laws by awarding appropriate disciplinary measures to the offenders.

f. Culture of Brotherhood

The culture of brotherhood among the Jews is quite close to that of the Yorùbá. In the former, it is the cultural practice of 'Kinsman-Redeemer.' A kinsman-redeemer in ancient Israel used to be a close relative to the victim of murder or manslaughter. He had the role of avenging the death of his deceased brother on the killer. He also had the role of redeeming his brother's name if he died without a child. He performed the latter role by getting married to his deceased brother's wife and giving her children, the first of whom would continue with the name of his late brother. The redeemer of blood in ancient Israel was God's provision for the execution of the divine mandate

---

[433] Ogunmola, 78.

on behalf of the family and society. The basis of this is the sacredness of human life, violation of which demands retribution.

Likewise, the culture of communal living characterises *Yorùbá* people in their traditional setting. An instance of this is the cultural practice of *Opo* (widowhood) among the people and is similar to the concept of kinsman-redeemer among the Jews. Whenever a brother is dead within a family, it is the right of the nearest kinsman to get married to his late brother's wife to preserve the deceased's name or heritage. Although this practice is on the decline at this contemporary time, it is still in vogue within the traditional setting.

2. Dissonance between Numbers 35:9-34 and *Yorùbá* Worldview

Identification of areas of differences between the two contexts of the study is of equal importance to this paper just like the immediate past section. This rationale provides opportunities for cultural transformation, especially among the Yorùbá.

a. Practice of Cities of Refuge

The practice of cities of refuge identified among the Jews in the chosen text is one main area of difference. The primary function of the cities was to offer maximum protection for any manslayer that killed in error from possible danger of death by the redeemer of blood. The manslayer would continue enjoying this offer long after the assembly had proved his or her innocence until the demise of the serving high priest. Yahweh saddled the Levites with the enforcement of this law to keep the sacredness of human life intact. However, this provision is lacking within the context of the *Yorùbá* people, although today's prisons perform some of the roles attributed to this provision in the context of the Jews.

b. Right of Asylum

The right of asylum is another element to consider. The concept was a commonplace in ancient time, especially in the OT. It was not just for anybody but exclusively for those who killed in error. The right expired when the accused stood before the assembly for judgment. This opportunity is not common among the *Yorùbá* people, especially at this contemporary time.

c. System of purging of Land from Blood Pollution

Cultural purging of the land from possible blood pollution using the practice of atonement is another area of difference. This feature was a usual practice in the OT as evident in the laws guiding the cities of refuge in Numbers 35:9-34. The need for atonement is on the imperative at all times, and its purpose was to preserve God's created order. This is not well defined among the *Yorùbá* as it was in the Bible world.

Two specific ways are identified in the chosen text by which atonement was practiced in ancient Israel. In the case of intentional killing, the land could be atoned exclusively by shedding the blood of the murderer on the ground. This is regarded as capital punishment. The second was through the death of the anointed high priest who was a type of Christ Jesus in the NT. The holiness of God is evident in these two requirements in ancient Israel since blood pollution was capable of sending Yahweh away from among His people.

d. Enhancement of Quality of Earth-Life

The quality of life during one's earth-life is another different area. According to *Yorùbá* worldview, the quality of the existence of an individual during the earth-life depends on certain factors. The kind of wishes presented to Olodumare by the person which eventually turned out to become one's destiny or fate on earth is one - either *Ori-rere* (good fortune) or *Ori-buruku* (evil destiny). Various inhibitions to good life from the 200 minor and malevolent spirit beings are among others. Others are from *Elenini*, a deity who is privy to the choice of an individual's destiny, *Esu* (Satan), and *Iku* (Death). The main activity of these divinities is to make everybody's desire for good life impossible except necessary sacrifices are paid.

However, this worldview is strange to the Jews. The Israelites believe that Yahweh is the sole Maker of the heavens and earth. The proclamation of God in Genesis 1:26, "Then God said, "Let us make man in our image," is an expression of the divine majesty of the Godhead. This declaration does not imply that God was inviting any deities for assistance. Similarly, man does not exist before the time of his biological delivery, and no deity was involved in the moulding process. Nonetheless, the two cultures have a similar understanding that the being of humankind is a combination of the soil from the ground and breath that comes from God in line with the Yahwehist creation narrative in Genesis 2 and *Yorùbá* cosmology. Thus, there is nothing like good and bad destinies; all things that God made were good. Again, the Satan of the *Yorùbá* worldview tends to be similar to that of the Hebrew Bible. However, Satan of the Jewish cosmology is one of the angels whose number is innumerable. This is against the 401 deities of the *Yorùbá* worldview.

3. Implications of the Nexus and Dissonance of the Two Contexts

By the various contextual elements identified as areas of harmony and dissonance between the setting of the chosen text and *Yorùbá* context, this writer draws necessary implications on the subject of the sanctity of human life. Adequate understanding and application of these implications will bring about a better appreciation of the worth of human life, especially among *Yorùbá* people.

a. Implications for Cultural Partnership and Tourism

The Jews and *Yorùbá* have common potentialities to explore based on similar cultural heritage. This cultural similarity can be attested to by their common ethnic dynamics. God has endowed both the Jews and *Yorùbá* with well-structured ethnicity with clearly defined geographical locations. The Jews occupy the land of Palestine while *Yorùbá* people predominantly live in Nigeria and some are in Diaspora.

Again, the nomenclatures of both people groups are well defined. The children of Israel were initially called Hebrew while in Egypt until they became Israel in the wilderness as declared by Yahweh at Horeb (Gen. 19-20). They maintained this designation until the southern kingdom went to exile in Babylon where they became Jews. The location of northern Israel remains unknown till date since their deportation by the Assyrians in 722 BC.[434] At the moment, the children of Israel of the Bible time are named Israelis or the Zionists, the terminology they assumed since 1948.[435] Similarly, the other people group is called *Yorùbá* both as an ethnic group and language.

Another dimension to the ethnicity is the nature of their tribes, origin, and progenitor. On the one hand, OT people were of 12 tribes who became an ethnic group upon occupying the land of Canaan dated 13th century BCE as evident in Merenptah's script. All of these tribes have a common progenitor in Abraham. They also have shared monotheistic religion and the sacred Book called Hebrew Bible. By its three components; namely, *Torah* (Law), *N^{e}bhiim* (Prophets) and *Kethubhim* (Writings), the holy Book is called *TaNaKh*. On the other hand, *Yorùbá* people are of many dialects but adopted that which Ajayi Crowther used for his *Yorùbá* Bible published in 1884 as the standard language. They all have their origin in Ile-Ife and Oduduwa as their common progenitor with a universal religion of YTR and *Ifá* Corpus as their sacred book.

All of these cultural dynamics can enhance the bilateral relationship between the two people groups in particular and Israel and Nigeria in general. Similarly, these are right avenues for educational, social and cultural tourism when explored. Research can also be carried out on these two people groups to ascertain the level of this affinity. This opportunity for further study is with the specific purpose of verifying whether or not the *Yorùbá* people are part of the lost 10 tribes of northern Israel as speculated in some quarters.

b. Implications for Right to Life

The greatest of the rights conferred on every human being by God is the right to life. This submission by the writer is on the premise of the latent image of God in all lives according to the biblical injunction in Genesis 1:26-28, notwithstanding the later attended effects of sin on humanity.

The right to life is global in content and scope of which Nigerian situation is an instance. In this nation, this right is the first provision among various fundamental human rights that every citizen must enjoy as enshrined in the 1979 Constitution of the Federal Republic of Nigeria as amended. In this provision, "Every person has a right to life, and no one shall be deprived intentionally of his life, save in execution of the sentence of a court in respect of a criminal offence of which he has been found guilty in Nigeria."[436] In other words, there is no provisional justification for intentional termination of the life of any Nigerian citizen other than proper execution of a court order when such a citizen is guilty of a criminal offence like murder. This claim follows that the right of any Nigerian citizen to life terminates upon a legal conviction that such a person has become a murderer. This understanding is not alien

---

[434] Hunting, 40.

[435] Benny Morris, *The Birth of the Palestinian Refugee Problem Revisited* (Cambridge: Cambridge University Press, 2004), n.p.

[436] Section 33 (1), "Chapter IV: Fundamental Rights," of the *Constitution of the Federal Republic of Nigeria*, 1979.

to the context of the OT as every killer had the right to seek asylum in any of the cities of refuge. However, the redeemer of blood must execute the killer upon the conviction that he or she was guilty.

There are certain other provisions attached to the human right of every Nigerian citizen. Each citizen should enjoy respect for the dignity of one's very person.[437] This right is irrespective of one's social, political or economic standing in the society. More so, every citizen entitles to one's freedom without any deprivation as permitted by law.[438] This provision also covers the following: a right to privacy,[439] and freedom of thought, religion, and conscience.[440] The liberty of every citizen also extends to the following: expression, association, movement, and owing immovable property anywhere in the country.[441]

c. Implications for Judicial System

Prohibition of payment of ransom for killing in the two contexts has legal implications for the contemporary people of Israel and Yorùbá. In Numbers 35:9-34, the leaders of the Assembly of God's people must hand the murderer over to the redeemer of blood to be put to death while they had to return the one guilty of manslaughter to the city of refuge. The offender must be made to pay for the crime committed whether it is murder or manslaughter. Similarly, murder was a taboo in Yorubaland in ancient time for it is a sin against the gods and the ancestors. Therefore, the murderer must be put to death.

This is against the culture of impunity of the contemporary time in Yorubaland where anybody can kill at will. Extra-judicial killing is also the order of the day specifically within the context of Yorùbá people and in Nigeria at large. The death penalty, called capital punishment, is the standard measure against murder both in the chosen text and traditional Yorùbá setting. In the first context, the purpose for this was not only to serve as a deterrent to other people who might have the presentiment for this crime but also to atone for the land from blood pollution. A similar view obtains in the second context among the Yorùbá. Hence, this sound justice system must not be jettisoned today but should be promoted especially in Yorubaland.

d. Implications for Christian Missions

The generality of Yorùbá people, most especially Christians among them, stand a better chance to understand and appreciate human life better than others as required in Numbers 35:9-34. This claim has its footing on the profound cultural similarity between the Jews and Yorùbá people concerning the subject matter. In both worldviews, human life is sacred and should be honoured, protected, and appreciated.

Yorùbá people traditionally have value for the sacredness of life in their cultural beliefs and practices just like the Jews. In the OT, this value system is on the

---

[437] Ibid, Section 34 (1).
[438] Ibid, Section 35 (1).
[439] Ibid, Sections 37.
[440] Ibid, Section 38 (1).
[441] Ibid, Sections 39 (1), 40, 41 (1), and 43.

concept of *Imago Dei* (Image of God) while it is by the breadth of Olodumare passed into the human body of clay moulded by the deities. The value is also on the foundation of sound ethical standards contained in the *Decalogue* (Ten Commandments) within the context of the Jews. A similar one is part of the *Yorùbá* moral standard called 'Natural Laws' as reflected in *Yorùbá* vocabularies, names, proverbs, wise sayings, and taboos. It also reflects in some of the tables above. Table 1 shows a fivefold-basis of the sanctity of human life among *Yorùbá* people while Table 3 depicts the general understanding of this concept. These two tables with some of the practices held in high esteem among the people in Table 4 are handy to assist Christians in making a difference in their practical Christian living and mission enterprise to their non-Christian people. Just as Yahweh gave the role of keeping the standard to the Levites and Prophets in the Jewish settings, the task of practical enforcement of the same should be championed by Christians among the *Yorùbá*.

This understanding and appreciation of human sacredness will throw more light on the system of animal sacrifice of the Jews, types, and essence of OT blood covenants, and the basis of Israel's election. Thus, *Yorùbá* readers will develop better value for the reading of the Hebrew Bible and gain an adequate understanding of its contents. The basis of this claim is that the areas are some of the main themes of the OT. Similarly, this understanding and appreciation will also help *Yorùbá* people understand and appreciate NT better concerning the essence of the sacrifice of Jesus the Messiah. Again, the understanding and appreciation of human sacredness gained will motivate *Yorùbá* Christians to demonstrate a better commitment to missions.

e. Implications for Security of Lives and Properties

Appreciation for the worth of human life is with mixed feelings in the two contexts. This situation could serve as a threat to the growth and development of Yorubaland. This claim is by the various analyses considered in chapters three and four. It is also contingent on the information obtained on the field within the context of Yorubaland.

The quantum of the Hebrew vocabularies employed in the Hebrew Bible depicting the ideas of killing and murder and the number of times these words appear are on the high side. This situation attests to the fact that OT people were familiar with violations of the sacredness of life in various forms of which termination of life is prime. Also, there is gender inequality, an undue exercise of power, internal conflicts and pollution of the political environment within the two contexts.

Similarly, human lives are at the bottom of the table in the *Yorùbá* ranking of the value of beings involving the following: spirits, ancestors (the living dead), and revered environmental objects. Violations of the sacredness of human life in Yorubaland are also part of the belief system of the people as the standard for good life resides in the quests for pleasure and happiness. The violation also takes the form of gender inequality, an example of which is the practice of *Opo* (widowhood) rite and war expeditions. More so, this violation reflects in *Yorùbá* names given to the firstborn among any twins. They call the firstborn *Taiwo* (i.e. "*To-aiye-wo*" meaning have the first taste of the world) while the one who came last is named *Kehinde* (One who lags at delivery). The question is: why should *Kehinde* be regarded as the elder under the guise that he is the one who lags in taking the pre-eminence? This cultural practice is extraneous to the OT and has caused some troubles in many families.

Because of these situations, the growth and development of Yorubaland are grossly under serious threats. This argument is fundamental because the socio-economic growth and development of any land largely depend on the availability of peace and security. It also depends on the political state of the people as no investor will put money to use where the future for such an investment is bleak. Thus, the primary driving force for growth and development of any land is the value for the sacredness of life. This point is a reality of all times to understand by all people.

f. Implications for Cultural Transformation

There is a need for cultural transformation in *Yorùbá* worldview. This study should review certain cultural beliefs and practices for necessary change. The first area is in gender inequality. The custom of *Opo* (widowhood) should not only be discouraged but wholly abolished. The practice is not human. This writer considers it a reflection of the modern-day slavery. Next to this is the need to review *Yorùbá* metaphysics especially in the area of ranking of the value of beings. If humankind is so sacred by the presence of the spiritual component (the breath of *Olodumare*) why should any other creature or object be more valuable? Something is fundamentally wrong with this understanding and requires urgent attention.

More so, since the sanctity of human life is an established belief among Yorùbá, the practice of human sacrifice for various ritual purposes is unimaginable and is cannibalistic. The authority should check this practice and bring the offenders to face the wrath of the law. The basis of the good life in *Yorùbá* ethics on pleasure and happiness is also misleading. It is capable of inciting young ones to go diabolical to become rich and wealthy overnight. Lastly, the sentiment of *Yorùbá* people against *Taiwo* the first born twin also needs to be reviewed. The writer regards this as a day-light robbery against a particular set of people in the land.

CHAPTER SIX

SUMMARY, CONCLUSION, AND RECOMMENDATIONS

The thrust of this study is the quest to obtain a comparative understanding of Numbers 35:9-34 and *Yorùbá* worldview of the sanctity of human life. Historical-critical and grammatical method of biblical hermeneutics is employed to unravel the concept in the chosen text within the general context of the world of the OT. The writer did this from the viewpoints of grammar, literature, and exegesis. Similarly, the writer investigated the sanctity of human life in *Yorùbá* worldview with special considerations on the philosophy, rituals, vocabulary, social relations and political life of the *Yorùbá* people. In the preceding chapter, the writer made efforts to compare the various identified elements of the subject matter within the two contexts of the study intending to bring to the fore areas of agreement and disagreement. At this juncture, efforts are made to summarise and conclude the investigation. The writer also makes necessary recommendations to the appropriate authorities.

1. Summary

In chapter three, Yahweh gave two main orders against the termination of human life in Numbers 35:9-34. The first of these provisions is the establishment of six cities of refuge while the redeemer of blood who is the nearest kinsman to the deceased fellow is the other. There is a profound reality to note with the shedding of human blood in this Law. Anywhere anybody sheds human blood; the land where the crime was committed shall demand atonement. The reason for this is that human life is so sacred and valuable to God that its termination causes guilt upon the ground, the cleansing of which is by the blood of the killer. Bloodshed is the highest form of pollution in ancient Israel just as it is in any land. However, there is another way by which God's people could atone for the ground apart from shedding the blood of the murderer. In the case of manslaughter, when the killing took place in error, atonement is done through the blood of the anointed high priest upon his death. OT High priests were a prototype of the coming Messiah whose death could atone for the sins of the whole world. This provision is a pure disposition of grace upon those who killed in error and upon the world at large.

Numbers 35:9-34 is a divine order that God's people must obey in all of the generations of Yahweh's covenant people. There are indeed other things to note with the element of the "cities of refuge" in this Law. The children of Israel must know that the towns were exclusively for manslayers, not murderers. More so, the cities were to be central to the entire community of God's people, and the people must keep the roads to them from all obstacles. Again, the people were to cite the cities on hills within the territory of the tribal inheritance of the Levites and priests. Besides, each of the six towns appointed was unique in meaning, serving as references to the coming Messiah. They located three of them on the east of the Jordan; namely, Bezer (a

166

stronghold or fortified place), Ramoth (high or exalted) and Golan (joy or revelation). The rest three were on the west in Canaan land; namely, Kedesh (holy or set apart), Shechem (shoulder) and Hebron (fellowship).

The analysis of the chosen text shows the worth of human life from God's perspective and the divine standard against those who violated this innate sanctity. However, what is this sacredness in human life about that God demands such a high standard in Numbers 35:9-34 against the violator? The writer and editor of the Books of the Pentateuch addressed this question. In this biblical literature, the basis of human sanctity is on the concept of *Imago Dei* (Image of God). There are three views to this concept; namely, the substantive view, the relational view, and the functional view. All of these observe the idea differently but in a complementary manner. The substantive view holds that the image of God in man is the God-given ability for humankind to exercise their willpower rightly.

Similarly, the relational view considers *imago Dei* as the supernatural ability given to man for a meaningful relationship with God and fellow human beings. Lastly, the functional aspect is about the divine quality in humankind to carry out the activities of ruling God's creation and exercising dominion over it. Thus, the basis of the sanctity of human life in the OT is on the concept of *Imago Dei*.

Furthermore, the choice of the context of Numbers 35:9-34 became necessary by the grammatical content of רָצַח which is one out of the 11 vocabularies that express the general idea of killing in the Hebrew Bible. Out of all of these words, it is this verb that has the greatest lexical power for termination of human life. The editor of the Book of Numbers used it exclusively for the cessation of human life or shedding of human blood, never for animals. Again, the verb has a dual rendering for premeditated murder and accidental manslaughter. This reality is unlike the rest of the vocabularies, none of which expressly suggests the idea of murder. Also, this verb has a special and unique usage in the Hebrew Bible. It is employed only in two contexts; the context of the *Decalogue* (Exod. 20:13; Deut. 5:17) and Numbers 35 where it appears in not less than 18 times. At each time, the editor used the verb with a direct link to God. Thus, murder is not only a sin against the victim but also against God the Creator.

Moreover, it is abundantly clear from the various analyses made that people significantly violated the sanctity of human life in the OT. This situation is evident in OT grammar based on the quantum of the Hebrew vocabularies employed for the general idea of the termination of life either premeditatedly or involuntarily. The number of times these words appear is also handy. Besides, both the prophetic Corpus and Writings also attest to this fact with overwhelming supports from archaeological findings. The world of the OT was that of constant war where stronger nations were switching roles and weaker ones were disappearing from the scene.

Similarly, the understanding of the concept of the sanctity of life in the context of *Yorùbá* people is both similar and complementary to that of the Israelites. This reality is the focus of chapter four. The writer identified five unique elements in this study marking the understanding of the people on the concept covering their philosophy, rituals, vocabulary and social-political aspects of life.

First, the concept stands on the foundation of human characters. In the *Yorùbá* understanding of human life, each person exhibits his or her God-given humanness by the characters displayed. Those who have good characters are believed to be human beings while those whose characters are evil are viewed to have either lost their humanness or never been part of human beings at all. In this belief system, there are various creatures among human beings. Whoever is naturally dirty are regarded as pigs while those who are of the habit of flirting around are called dogs. Snakes are the deceptive and misleading kind of people. Murderers are not human beings at all for it is unrealistic for a sane person to terminate the life of a fellow being in *Yorùbá* worldview. Therefore, human characters are natural means by which fellow human beings could identify each person.

The situations expressed above are not strange to *Yorùbá* people in their traditional setting for cases of human beings turning to birds, animals or any other creatures at night are common phenomena among them. There were records of events when some of these happenings took place in broad daylight. Akande's book, *Miracles, Mysteries, Death and Dying, and Other Supernatural Events in Nigeria* is handy here to understand many of these mysteries. When one considers the lifestyles of those who are in the know among these people, they are often discovered to be evil in the natural sense of it. The writer identified some examples of the characters that an average *Yorùbá* person expects from a normal human being in Tables 1, 3 and 4 above.

Second, a sacred life carries the divine breath of *Olodumare*, the *Yorùbá* name for Almighty God. This breath is the divine presence in human beings which manifests as characters that project the person of God. Thus, characters are ways by which fellow human beings identify real human beings among them and through which Olodumare sanctions their humanness. Characters are God's logo or stamp in the life of humankind. Part of the belief system of this people group is that one cannot run away from one's characters as expressed in some of their wise sayings. Two out of several ideas available about human characteristics in the philosophy and vocabulary of *Yorùbá* people are *"Eefin ni iwa"* (characters are like smoke) and *"Iwa ki i fi oni iwa s'ile"* (one's character does not detach itself from one). Table 2 above contains 50 of these ideas, proverbs and wise sayings.

Third, the people also express the sanctity of human life in the *Yorùbá* practice of death aversion. The most challenging thing for an average *Yorùbá* to do is to commit suicide. This claim is not saying that people are not doing so these days but the practice was strange in the olden days for life was sweet even when there is nothing to live by. One can find an expression of this idea in this *Yorùbá* wise saying, *"Nigbati emi ba wa, ireti nbe"* (Once there is life, there is hope). Given this, an average *Yorùbá* person can go extra miles traditionally to avert death even when it is imminent. On account of this, warriors and influential people of old were of the habit of sacrificing human beings as a ransom to avert imminent death facing them.

Fourth, an average traditional *Yorùbá* holds to the belief that human life is sacred because God created it for a divine purpose. In their worldview, every other created being is created for man's use because human beings are at the centre of God's mind, actions, and purposes. In this study, the writer examined this idea from different perspectives of the people's worldview. On this basis, they believe that man is God's vice-regent, co-creator, and partner. This is manifested in various scientific discoveries and inventions achieved by man in science and technology. Humanity also has many achievements of this kind in all other fields such as the health sector and space exploration.

Fifth, the sanctity of human life in *Yorùbá* understanding also relates to the disposition of God's mercy and grace to humankind. The people believe that the exalted position of man in God's creation and the giant strides achieved in all fields of knowledge are altogether manifestations of God's special grace to man. This grace manifests in their creative reasoning, and the ability to tame and put other creatures under check. It is also evident in man's ability to ward off evil and control spirit beings with the use of systems of sacrifice.

Furthermore, the writer identified certain elements showing areas of harmony and conflict between the contexts of Numbers 35:9-34 of the world of OT and *Yorùbá* worldview in chapter five. The writer after that drew necessary implications by the identified elements. On the one hand, the following are areas where there are agreements between the two contexts: ethnic components, the basis of the sanctity of human life, appreciation of the worth of human beings, violations of the sacredness of life, punitive measures against killing, and cultural brotherhood. On the other hand, the two contexts are at variance in some areas; namely, the practice of cities of refuge is limited to the setting of Numbers 35:9-34, right of asylum is not pronounced among *Yorùbá* like it was among the Israelites, and there was a system by which the people could purge the land from blood pollution among the people. This element is not well defined in the *Yorùbá* setting. More so, there was a system by which the people could ritually enhance the quality of one's earth-life in the context of the *Yorùbá*. This cultural practice was not available in the other context as it was Yahweh's exclusive right to determine.

Lastly, the writer drew some implications in this study which consist of the following: beneficial partnership and tourism especially in the area of cultural affinity, right to life, the judicial system, missions and evangelism, security of lives and property, and cultural transformation. All this covers some areas of human life; namely, culture, tourism, human rights, the judicial system, religion, and security.

2. Conclusion

It is the writer's position that the spate of incessant killings that pervades Yorubaland and various dehumanising treatments to which some human elements subject the lives of their fellow beings in their day-to-day activities calls *Yorùbá* worldview to question on the subject of the sanctity of human life. The worrisome part of the problem is the paucity of studies conducted in this area, more importantly from a comparative point of view in the biblical context of the Book of Numbers 35:9-34 and *Yorùbá*

169

worldview. This makes the need for this study obvious, pertinent and imperative. Efforts made in this study are not only aimed at identifying the existing anomaly but also at correcting the deviant practices among *Yorùbá* people. This is one area where the study contributes to knowledge.

Furthermore, biblical expositions and expositors of the Book of Numbers 35:9-34 that would make meaning within the context of *Yorùbá* people must put certain things into consideration. This work therefore concludes that, first, the complementary role of the value of human characters which is one major basis of the idea of the sanctity of life among the people must be brought into meaningful contextualisation. Asides, any biblical exposition from OT that underestimates the value of morality while dealing with the question of the sacredness of human life will not appeal to the sense of the understanding of the people.

Second, on the basis of the apparent dissonance between what the *Yorùbá* hold as the ideal on human life sanctity and the observable practices among the people, *Yorùbá* ideas, proverbs and wise sayings on the subject of the study must be aptly contextualised if an adequate understanding of the message and contents of Numbers 35:9-34 will be obtained by the people. *Yorùbá* has very rich vocabularies to express their ideas relating to the way they view the world. If one is to gain an adequate understanding of any of these concerns, the need to have a proper understanding of their language, especially their proverbial sayings, is on the imperative.

Third, the would-be biblical expositors of Numbers 35:9-34 must prioritise certain aspects of *Yorùbá* practices. The need for this consideration is high for such expositors to gain the audience of the people in the first place. Relevant in this area is the *Yorùbá* mode of greetings. Respect for the elders is paramount in the fabric of their culture to which biblical expositors must be exposed. These modes of salutation are gender-sensitive and are still conscious of the time of the day and the age of the person to be greeted. All of these are considered necessary ingredients of being cultured. The people also hold a relationship with others in high esteem, and biblical scholars must give it a priority. Biblical expositors who default in any of these areas would be considered aliens even if they are born and bred in the land and christened in *Yorùbá* names.

3. Recommendations

At this juncture, it is pertinent and imperative to forward important recommendations to different and appropriate authorities for necessary actions. This effort will go a long way in correcting the various deviant practices among the *Yorùbá* people.

First, governments at all levels in the Yorubaland should put appropriate mechanisms in place in correcting the deviant practices against the sanctity of life. They need to check the laid-back attitude of various occupants of leadership positions in government offices towards various violations if the situations on the ground would not lead to further crises. This step becomes necessary because the states of the affairs of the people are tense already. Again, there should be appropriate mechanisms to check the self-centeredness, greediness, corruption, and wickedness of some of the leaders leading to their complete apathy to the plight of the masses. Also, necessary measures should be put in place to checkmate various ways by which some of these leaders go about promoting various violations to their benefits especially during the time of elections.

Similarly, government should prioritise education, economy, and security by putting necessary policies in place that could drive all these developmental apparatuses. One major cause of these deviant practices is the priority placed on western education at the expense of good cultural values of the *Yorùbá* people. This practice must be corrected for it is a misplacement of priority. *Yorùbá* people cannot afford to lose their good heritage to the promotion of foreign cultures, much of whose practices are also alien to the biblical standard of the sanctity of human life. More so, the Federal government needs to create a forum whereby leaders at all levels could come together periodically to address issues of regional and national concerns, irrespective of the political affiliations of these leaders.

Second, the next set of recommendations is for the various religious bodies in the land. It is very pertinent at this point to establish the fact that there is nothing wrong with most of these religions in the area of the sanctity of human life. Almost all of them promote the sacredness of life by opposing bloodshed. They are equally concerned about family and societal matters in their teachings. However, the problem lies with most of their leaders. Therefore, religious leaders should emphasise the aspect of post-marital counselling and be exemplary in all their approaches to life and situations. This effort will go a long way in being different and challenging political leaders and government officials to perform better and holding them accountable for their actions.

Moreover, the various leaders of each of the religious bodies should be empowered to checkmate the indulgences of the corrupt adherents of their respective affiliations. An example of the leadership of this kind is that of the Christian faith, called the Christian Association of Nigeria (CAN). These bodies should also see to the issue of sabotage that breeds rivalry amongst the various religious organisations in the land. They should also address the problems of corruption and deceit among leaders and apathy to sound teaching on moral values as a matter of urgency.

Similarly, the claim that Orunmila, and essentially *Ifa* worshippers, do not support human sacrifice except the worshippers of *Esu* divinity should be further investigated. Governments should bring these fake and untaught practitioners to book, and the practice should be completely discouraged. Also, any gods that demand human sacrifices for violating *eewo* (taboos) in the land are not worth celebrating. This writer makes this position because God has given human beings an elevated position in His created order and this is second to none of the idols. Moreover, the evil practices of the collaborators in bloodshed for ritual purposes among Christian and Islamic leaders need to be addressed by the appropriate authorities. This recommendation demands adequate and necessary sanitisation of the religious bodies.

Third, the writer must also make some recommendations on the aspect of roles that the people traditionally enshrine for the family in Yorubaland. This writer recommends curriculum review at the level of primary and secondary education such that will encourage the revival of training of children in their cultural languages, values, and practices. This should be replicated on the home-front and the parents should champion this. Again, the havoc caused by single-parenting to the violation of the sacredness of life today is unquantifiable. Therefore, parents should intensify on training in the area of marriage. They should also make themselves exemplary in this area. In addition to all this, parents should discourage their wards from being conscious of money at this tender age for the love of money is the root of all evils. This step will go a long way to discourage getting-rich-quickly and at-all-cost syndrome.

More so, the breakdown of order in the family system as a result of factors like the individualistic tendency of many parents and the sick economy of the home is a serious concern to well-meaning *Yorùbá* people. Given this, adequate and necessary teachings should be embarked upon by parents on human relations, care of the aged, and the value of community for which *Yorùbá* people were once known. It will also put rebellious behaviours at home under check. Parents should also control the influx of foreign cultural practices at home which can endanger the lives of their wards.

APPENDIX 1

LOCATION AND TRANSLATION OF NUMBERS 35:9-34

9 וַיְדַבֵּ֥ר יְהֹוָ֖ה אֶל־מֹשֶׁ֥ה לֵּאמֹֽר׃

10 דַּבֵּר֙ אֶל־בְּנֵ֣י יִשְׂרָאֵ֔ל וְאָמַרְתָּ֖ אֲלֵהֶ֑ם כִּ֥י אַתֶּ֛ם עֹבְרִ֥ים אֶת־הַיַּרְדֵּ֖ן אַ֥רְצָה כְּנָֽעַן׃

11 וְהִקְרִיתֶ֤ם לָכֶם֙ עָרִ֔ים עָרֵ֥י מִקְלָ֖ט תִּהְיֶ֣ינָה לָכֶ֑ם וְנָ֣ס שָׁ֗מָּה רֹצֵ֕חַ מַכֵּה־נֶ֖פֶשׁ בִּשְׁגָגָֽה׃

12 וְהָי֤וּ לָכֶם֙ הֶעָרִ֣ים לְמִקְלָ֔ט מִגֹּאֵ֑ל וְלֹ֤א יָמוּת֙ הָרֹצֵ֔חַ עַד־עָמְד֥וֹ לִפְנֵ֥י הָעֵדָ֖ה לַמִּשְׁפָּֽט׃

13 וְהֶעָרִ֖ים אֲשֶׁ֣ר תִּתֵּ֑נוּ שֵׁשׁ־עָרֵ֥י מִקְלָ֖ט תִּהְיֶ֥ינָה לָכֶֽם׃

14 אֵ֣ת׀ שְׁלֹ֣שׁ הֶעָרִ֗ים תִּתְּנוּ֙ מֵעֵ֣בֶר לַיַּרְדֵּ֔ן וְאֵת֙ שְׁלֹ֣שׁ הֶעָרִ֔ים תִּתְּנ֖וּ בְּאֶ֣רֶץ כְּנָ֑עַן עָרֵ֥י מִקְלָ֖ט תִּהְיֶֽינָה׃

15 לִבְנֵ֣י יִשְׂרָאֵ֗ל וְלַגֵּ֤ר וְלַתּוֹשָׁב֙ בְּתוֹכָ֔ם תִּהְיֶ֛ינָה שֵׁשׁ־הֶעָרִ֥ים הָאֵ֖לֶּה לְמִקְלָ֑ט לָנ֣וּס שָׁ֔מָּה כָּל־מַכֵּה־נֶ֖פֶשׁ בִּשְׁגָגָֽה׃

16 וְאִם־בִּכְלִ֨י בַרְזֶ֥ל׀ הִכָּ֛הוּ וַיָּמֹ֖ת רֹצֵ֣חַֽ ה֑וּא מ֥וֹת יוּמַ֖ת הָרֹצֵֽחַ׃

17 וְאִ֡ם בְּאֶ֣בֶן יָד֩ אֲשֶׁר־יָמ֨וּת בָּ֥הּ הִכָּ֛הוּ וַיָּמֹ֖ת רֹצֵ֣חַֽ ה֑וּא מ֥וֹת יוּמַ֖ת הָרֹצֵֽחַ׃

18 א֡וֹ בִּכְלִ֣י עֵץ־יָד֩ אֲשֶׁר־יָמ֨וּת בּ֥וֹ הִכָּ֛הוּ וַיָּמֹ֖ת רֹצֵ֣חַֽ ה֑וּא מ֥וֹת יוּמַ֖ת הָרֹצֵֽחַ׃

19 גֹּאֵ֣ל הַדָּ֔ם ה֥וּא יָמִ֖ית אֶת־הָרֹצֵ֑חַ בְּפִגְעוֹ־ב֖וֹ ה֥וּא יְמִיתֶֽנּוּ׃

20 וְאִם־בְּשִׂנְאָ֖ה יֶהְדָּפֶ֑נּוּ אֽוֹ־הִשְׁלִ֥יךְ עָלָ֛יו בִּצְדִיָּ֖ה וַיָּמֹֽת׃

21 א֣וֹ בְאֵיבָ֞ה הִכָּ֣הוּ בְיָד֗וֹ וַיָּמֹת֙ מֽוֹת־יוּמַ֣ת הַמַּכֶּ֔ה רֹצֵ֖חַ ה֑וּא גֹּאֵ֣ל הַדָּ֗ם יָמִ֛ית אֶת־הָרֹצֵ֖חַ בְּפִגְעוֹ־בֽוֹ׃

22 וְאִם־בְּפֶ֥תַע בְּלֹא־אֵיבָ֖ה הֲדָפ֑וֹ אוֹ־הִשְׁלִ֥יךְ עָלָ֛יו כָּל־כְּלִ֖י בְּלֹ֥א צְדִיָּֽה׃

23 א֣וֹ בְכָל־אֶ֜בֶן אֲשֶׁר־יָמ֥וּת בָּ֙הּ֙ בְּלֹ֣א רְא֔וֹת וַיַּפֵּ֥ל עָלָ֖יו וַיָּמֹ֑ת וְהוּא֙ לֹא־אוֹיֵ֣ב ל֔וֹ וְלֹ֥א מְבַקֵּ֖שׁ רָעָתֽוֹ׃

24 וְשָֽׁפְטוּ֙ הָֽעֵדָ֔ה בֵּ֚ין הַמַּכֶּ֔ה וּבֵ֖ין גֹּאֵ֣ל הַדָּ֑ם עַ֥ל הַמִּשְׁפָּטִ֖ים הָאֵֽלֶּה׃

25 וְהִצִּ֨ילוּ הָעֵדָ֜ה אֶת־הָרֹצֵ֗חַ מִיַּד֮ גֹּאֵ֣ל הַדָּם֒ וְהֵשִׁ֤יבוּ אֹתוֹ֙ הָֽעֵדָ֔ה אֶל־עִ֖יר מִקְלָט֑וֹ אֲשֶׁר־נָ֣ס שָׁ֑מָּה וְיָ֣שַׁב בָּ֗הּ עַד־מוֹת֙ הַכֹּהֵ֣ן הַגָּדֹ֔ל אֲשֶׁר־מָשַׁ֥ח אֹת֖וֹ בְּשֶׁ֥מֶן הַקֹּֽדֶשׁ׃

26 וְאִם־יָצֹ֥א יֵצֵ֖א הָרֹצֵ֑חַ אֶת־גְּבוּל֙ עִ֣יר מִקְלָט֔וֹ אֲשֶׁ֥ר יָנ֖וּס שָֽׁמָּה׃

173

27 וּמָצָ֣א אֹתוֹ֒ גֹּאֵ֣ל הַדָּ֗ם מִחוּץ֙ לִגְב֣וּל עִ֣יר מִקְלָט֔וֹ וְרָצַ֞ח גֹּאֵ֤ל הַדָּם֙ אֶת־הָ֣רֹצֵ֔חַ אֵ֥ין ל֖וֹ דָּֽם׃

28 כִּ֣י בְעִ֤יר מִקְלָטוֹ֙ יֵשֵׁ֔ב עַד־מוֹת֙ הַכֹּהֵ֣ן הַגָּדֹ֔ל וְאַחֲרֵי֙ מוֹת֙ הַכֹּהֵ֣ן הַגָּדֹ֔ל יָשׁוּב֙ הָרֹצֵ֔חַ אֶל־אֶ֖רֶץ אֲחֻזָּתֽוֹ׃

29 וְהָי֨וּ אֵ֧לֶּה לָכֶ֛ם לְחֻקַּ֥ת מִשְׁפָּ֖ט לְדֹרֹתֵיכֶ֑ם בְּכֹ֖ל מוֹשְׁבֹתֵיכֶֽם׃

30 כָּל־מַ֙כֵּה־נֶ֔פֶשׁ לְפִ֣י עֵדִ֔ים יִרְצַ֖ח אֶת־הָרֹצֵ֑חַ וְעֵ֣ד אֶחָ֔ד לֹא־יַעֲנֶ֥ה בְנֶ֖פֶשׁ לָמֽוּת׃

31 וְלֹֽא־תִקְח֥וּ כֹ֙פֶר֙ לְנֶ֣פֶשׁ רֹצֵ֔חַ אֲשֶׁר־ה֥וּא רָשָׁ֖ע לָמ֑וּת כִּי־מ֖וֹת יוּמָֽת׃

32 וְלֹא־תִקְח֣וּ כֹ֔פֶר לָנ֖וּס אֶל־עִ֣יר מִקְלָט֑וֹ לָשׁוּב֙ לָשֶׁ֣בֶת בָּאָ֔רֶץ עַד־מ֖וֹת הַכֹּהֵֽן׃

33 וְלֹא־תַחֲנִ֣יפוּ אֶת־הָאָ֗רֶץ אֲשֶׁ֤ר אַתֶּם֙ בָּ֔הּ כִּ֣י הַדָּ֔ם ה֥וּא יַחֲנִ֖יף אֶת־הָאָ֑רֶץ וְלָאָ֣רֶץ לֹֽא־יְכֻפַּ֗ר לַדָּם֙ אֲשֶׁ֣ר שֻׁפַּךְ־בָּ֔הּ כִּי־אִ֖ם בְּדַ֥ם שֹׁפְכֽוֹ׃

34 וְלֹ֧א תְטַמֵּ֣א אֶת־הָאָ֗רֶץ אֲשֶׁ֤ר אַתֶּם֙ יֹשְׁבִ֣ים בָּ֔הּ אֲשֶׁ֥ר אֲנִ֖י שֹׁכֵ֣ן בְּתוֹכָ֑הּ כִּ֚י אֲנִ֣י יְהוָ֔ה שֹׁכֵ֖ן בְּת֥וֹךְ בְּנֵ֥י יִשְׂרָאֵֽל׃ פ[442]

Location and Translation of Words

Verse 9

וַיְדַבֵּ֣ר vav consecutive *and, also, even, then, with, and in addition, and indeed, namely, or, but, whether, then,*[443] prefixed to verb piel imperfect 3ms from דבר meaning *he spoke, talked, threatened, promised, commanded*[444]; hence, **then he commanded.**

יְהוָה noun proper no gender no number no state meaning *Yahweh, the proper name of the God of Israel*[445]; hence, **Yahweh.**

אֶל־מֹשֶׁה particle preposition *to, into, toward* in construct relationship to noun proper no gender no number no state meaning *Moses*; hence, **to Moses.**

לֵאמֹר׃ prefixed ל preposition *to, towards, until, at, in, of, about, into, in (regard to), concerning, according to, by, in relation to, in the direction of, for, because of*[446] prefixed to verb qal infinitive construct from אָמַר meaning *to say*; hence, **to say of.**

Rough Translation: Then he commanded Yahweh to Moses to say of.

Smooth Translation: Then Yahweh commanded Moses saying,

---

[442] A. Schenker, A. Alt, O. EiBfeldt, P. Kahle ediderat, R. kittel, adjuvantibus H. Bardtke, W. Baumgartner et al, eds., "Numbers 35:9-34," *Biblia Herbraica Stuttgartensia* (BHS) (Nordlingen: Deutsche Forschungsgemeinschaft, 1997), 280-81.

[443] Holladay, 85.

[444] Ibid, 67.

[445] BDB, 219.

[446] Holladay, 169.

Verse 10

דַּבֵּר verb piel imperative singular from דבר meaning he *spoke, talked, threatened, promised, commanded*[447]; hence, **command**.

אֶל־בְּנֵי אֶל particle preposition *to, into, toward* in construct relationship to noun common masculine plural construct from בֵּן meaning *son, descendant*; hence, **to the sons of.**

יִשְׂרָאֵל noun proper no gender no number no state meaning Israel (etymologically implying *El persists* while in jussive means *Let El persists*)[448]; hence, **Israel.**

וְאָמַרְתָּ vav consecutive *and, also, even, with, and in addition, and indeed, namely, or, but, whether, then*, prefixed to verb qal perfect 2ms from אָמַר meaning he *said, uttered, promised, commanded*[449]; hence, **and you will say.**

אֲלֵהֶם אֶל particle preposition *to, into, toward* suffixed with 3mp, meaning *them*; hence, **to them.**

כִּי particle conjunction meaning *that, for, when*[450]; hence, **when.**

אַתֶּם pronoun independent 2mp meaning *you*[451]; hence, **you.**

עֹבְרִים verb qal participle masculine plural absolute from עָבַר meaning *passing from one side (or end) to the other, passing through, going through*; hence meaning **passing from one side to the other.**

אֶת־הַיַּרְדֵּן אֶת particle direct object marker in construct relationship to definite article *the* prefixed to noun proper no gender no number no state meaning *Jordan*; hence **the Jordan.**

אַרְצָה[452] noun common feminine singular absolute from אֶרֶץ meaning *ground, piece of land, territory, land, earth, underworld*[453]; hence, **a land.**

כְּנָעַן: noun proper no gender no number no state meaning *Canaan*[454]; hence, **Canaan.**

Rough Translation: Command to the sons of Israel and you will say to them when you passing from one side to the other side the Jordan a land Canaan.

Smooth Translation: "Command the children of Israel and say to them: 'when you pass from the Jordan to the land of Canaan,

Verse 11

וְהִקְרִיתֶם vav consecutive *and, also, even, with, and in addition, and indeed, namely, or, but, whether, then*, prefixed to verb hiphil perfect 2mp from קרה meaning he/it *ordained, directed, selected*[455]; hence, **and you will cause to ordain.**

---

[447] Ibid, 67.

[448] BDB, 976.

[449] Ibid, 56.

[450] Ibid, 475.

[451] Holladay, 31.

[452] A critical issue is discussed about the Hebrew word אַרְצָה under textual analysis of verse 10.

[453] Holladay, 28.

[454] Ibid, 160.

[455] Ibid, 325.

לָכֶם לְ preposition meaning *to, towards, until, at, in, of, about, into, in (regard to), concerning, according to, by, in relation to, in the direction of, for, because of* prefixed to pronominal suffix 2mp meaning you; hence, ***for you.***

עָרִים noun common feminine plural absolute from עִיר meaning *city, quarter, population;* hence, ***cities.***

עָרֵי noun common feminine plural construct from עִיר meaning *city, quarter, population;* hence, ***cities of.***

מִקְלָט noun common masculine singular absolute meaning *refuge, asylum;* hence, ***refuge***[456].

תִּהְיֶינָה verb qal imperfect 3fp from meaning *to be, become, take place, happen, occur*[457]; hence, ***they will become.***

לָכֶם לְ preposition meaning *to, towards, until, at, in, of, about, into, in (regard to), concerning, according to, by, in relation to, in the direction of, for, because of* suffixed by 2mp meaning you; hence, ***for you.***

וְנָס vav consecutive *and, also, even, with, and in addition, and indeed, namely, or, but, whether, then,* prefixed to verb qal perfect 3ms from נוּס meaning *he fled, escaped, slipped away;* hence, ***and he will flee.***

שָׁמָּה particle adverb meaning *there, then;* hence, ***there.***

רֹצֵחַ[458] verb qal participle masculine singular absolute from רָצַח meaning *murder, manslayer* (both with intent and without intent)[459]; hence, ***a murderer.***

מַכֵּה־נֶפֶשׁ[460] verb hiphil participle masculine singular construct from נָכָה meaning *he smote, struck, beat, killed unintentionally, slayed, exterminated, destroyed*[461] in construct relationship to noun common feminine singular absolute from נֶפֶשׁ meaning *soul, living being, life, self, person, desire, appetite, emotion, and passion;* hence, ***he causing to smite a person.***

בִּשְׁגָגָה: בְּ preposition meaning *in, at or by, (together) with*[462] prefixed with noun common feminine singular absolute from שְׁגָגָה meaning *sin of error, inadvertence;* hence, ***in a sin of error.***

Rough Translation: And you will cause to ordain for you cities cities of refuge they will become for you and he will flee there a murderer he causing to smite a person in a sin of error.

Smooth Translation: you will ordain for yourselves cities which will become cities of refuge for you; any manslayer who has smitten a person in error may flee there.

---

[456] Ibid, 212.

[457] Ibid, 79.

[458] There is a critical issue about the Hebrew word רָצַח as discussed under textual analysis of verse 11.

[459] BDB, 954.

[460] There is a critical issue about מַכֵּה־נֶפֶשׁ as discussed under textual analysis of verse 11.

[461] BDB, 646.

[462] Ibid, 91.

Verse 12

וְהָיוּ   vav consecutive *and, also, even, with, and in addition, and indeed, namely, or, but, whether, then*, prefixed to verb qal perfect 3cp from הָיָה meaning *he/it fell out, came to pass, became, was*[463]; hence, **and they will be.**

לָכֶם לְ   preposition meaning *to, towards, until, at, in, of, about, into, in (regard to), concerning, according to, by, in relation to, in the direction of, for, because of* suffixed by 2mp meaning you; hence, **for you.**

הֶעָרִים   particle article the prefixed to noun common feminine plural absolute from עִיר meaning *city, quarter, population*; hence, **the cities.**

לְמִקְלָט לְ   preposition meaning *to, towards, until, at, in, of, about, into, in (regard to), concerning, according to, by, in relation to, in the direction of, for, because of* prefixed to noun common masculine singular absolute from מִקְלָט meaning *refuge, asylum*; hence, **for refuge.**

מִגֹּאֵל[464] מִן   preposition meaning *from, out of*[465] prefixed to verb qal participle masculine singular absolute from גָּאַל meaning he/it *redeemed, delivered, ransomed, laid claim to*[466]; hence, **from a redeemer.**

וְלֹא   vav consecutive *and, also, even, with, and in addition, and indeed, namely, or, but, whether, then*, prefixed to particle negative *no, not*; hence, **and not.**

יָמוּת[467]   verb qal imperfect 3ms from מוּת meaning *to die, dying, dead, finally kill, give the death-blow, slay, kill*; hence, **he will execute.**

הָרֹצֵחַ   particle definite article the prefixed to verb qal participle masculine singular absolute from רָצַח meaning *he murdered, slayed*; hence **the murderer.**

עַד־עָמְדוֹ   particle preposition *as far as, until, while, during, toward, up to, forever* in construct relationship to verb qal infinitive construct from עָמַד meaning *to stand, take one's stand, stay*; hence, **as far as to stay.**

לִפְנֵי לְ   preposition meaning *to, towards, until, at, in, of, about, into, in (regard to), concerning, according to, by, in relation to, in the direction of, for, because of* prefixed to noun common both plural construct from פָּנֶה meaning *face, surface, front, before, in the face of, in front of*[468]; hence, **until (the) presence of.**

הָעֵדָה   definite article the prefixed to noun common feminine singular absolute from עֵדָה meaning *congregation, company, assemblage*; hence, **a congregation.**

לְמִשְׁפָּט: לְ   preposition meaning *to, towards, until, at, in, of, about, into, in (regard to), concerning, according to, by, in relation to, in the direction of, for,*

---

[463] Ibid, 228.

[464] A critical issue is discussed about the Hebrew word מִגֹּאֵל under textual analysis of verse 12.

[465] Ellis, 376.

[466] Holladay, 53.

[467] A critical issue is discussed on this word under textual analysis of verse 12.

[468] Holladay, 294.

because of prefixed to definite article *the* prefixed to noun common masculine singular absolute meaning *judgment, place or court seat of judgment, case or cause presented for judgment, sentence, decision of judgment, ordinance promulgated, decision of the case of law*[469]; hence, **for the judgment.**

Rough Translation: And they will be for you the cities for refuge from a redeemer and not he will execute the murderer as far as to stay until (the) presence of an assembly for the judgment.

Smooth Translation: They will be a refuge from a redeemer of the blood and he will not execute the killer as far as he stays in any of the cities until he appears before the assembly for judgment.

Verse 13

וְהֶעָרִים vav consecutive *and, also, even, with, and in addition, and indeed, namely, or, but, whether, then,* prefixed to definite article the prefixed to noun common feminine plural absolute meaning *cities, quarters, populations*; hence, **and the cities.**

אֲשֶׁר particle relative pronoun meaning *who, which, that, because, when, since*; hence, **which.**

תִּתְּנוּ verb qal imperfect 2mp from נָתַן meaning *he gave, put, set*[470]; hence, **you will give.**

שֵׁשׁ־עָרֵי numeral cardinal feminine singular absolute from שֵׁשׁ meaning *six*[471] in construct relationship to noun common feminine plural construct meaning *cities of*; hence, **six cities of.**

מִקְלָט noun common masculine singular absolute from מִקְלָט meaning *refuge, asylum*; hence, **refuge.**

תִּהְיֶינָה verb qal imperfect 3fp from הָיָה meaning *he/it fell out, came to pass, became, was*; hence, **they will be.**

לָכֶם: לְ preposition meaning *to, towards, until, at, in, of, about, into, in (regard to), concerning, according to, by, in relation to, in the direction of, for, because of* prefixed to pronominal suffix 2mp meaning *you*; hence, **for you.**

Rough Translation: And the cities which you will give six cities of refuge they will be for you.

Smooth Translation: And the cities which you will give will be for you six cities of refuge.

Verse 14

אֵת untranslatable direct object marker.

שְׁלֹשׁ numeral cardinal feminine singular construct from שָׁלֹשׁ meaning *three, triad*[472], hence, **three of.**

הֶעָרִים definite article *the* prefixed to noun common feminine plural absolute meaning *cities*; hence, **the cities.**

תִּתְּנוּ verb qal imperfect 2mp meaning *he gave, put, set*; hence, **you will give.**

---

[469] BDB, 1049.
[470] Ibid, 681.
[471] Ibid, 995.
[472] Ibid, 1026.

מֵעֵבֶר מִן preposition meaning *out of, away from, far away, just after, after, because of, from, against, without*[473] prefixed to noun common masculine singular construct from עֵבֶר meaning *one of two sides (opposite each other), over there, on one side and on the other, side, edge, bank, shore, opposite side, over*[474]; hence, ***out of a side.***

לַיַּרְדֵּן לְ preposition meaning *to, towards, until, at, in, of, about, into, in (regard to), concerning, according to, by, in relation to, in the direction of, for, because of* prefixed to definite article *the* prefixed to noun proper no gender no number no state from יַרְדֵּן meaning *Jordan*; hence, ***of the Jordan.***

וְאֵת vav conjunction *and* prefixed to untranslatable direct object marker; hence, ***and.***

שְׁלֹשׁ numeral cardinal feminine singular construct from שָׁלֹשׁ meaning *three, triad*, hence, ***three of.***

הֶעָרִים definite article *the* prefixed to noun common feminine plural absolute meaning *cities quarters and populations*; hence, ***the cities.***

תִּתְּנוּ verb qal imperfect 2mp meaning *he gave, put, set*; hence, ***you will give.***

בְּאֶרֶץ בְּ preposition meaning *in, at or by, (together) with* prefixed to noun common feminine singular construct from אֶרֶץ meaning *ground, piece of land, territory, land, earth, depths of the earth, underworld*; hence, ***in a territory of.***

כְּנַעַן noun proper no gender no number no state from כְּנַעַן meaning *Canaan*; hence, ***Canaan.***

עָרֵי noun common feminine plural construct meaning ***cities of.***

מִקְלָט noun common masculine singular absolute from מִקְלָט meaning *refuge, asylum*; hence, ***refuge.***

תִּהְיֶינָה: verb qal imperfect 3fp from הָיָה meaning *he/it fell out, came to pass, became, was*; hence, ***they will be.***

Rough Translation: Three of the cities you will set out of a side of the Jordan and three of the cities you will set in a territory of Canaan cities of refuge they will be.

Smooth Translation: You will give three of these cities on this side of the Jordan and three in the territory of Canaan as cities of refuge.

Verse 15

לִבְנֵי לְ preposition meaning *to, towards, until, at, in, of, about, into, in (regard to), concerning, according to, by, in relation to, in the direction of, for, because of* prefixed to noun common masculine plural construct from בֵּן meaning *son, descendant*; hence, ***for the descendants of.***

יִשְׂרָאֵל noun proper no gender no number no state meaning *Israel*; hence, ***Israel.***

וְלַגֵּר vav conjunction *and* prefixed to לְ preposition meaning *to, towards, until, at, in, of, about, into, in (regard to), concerning, according to, by, in relation to, in the direction of, for, because of* prefixed to definite article *the* prefixed to noun common masculine singular absolute from גֵּר meaning *sojourner,*

---

[473] Holladay, 201.
[474] Ibid, 264.

temporary dweller, new-comer (no inherited rights); hence, **and for the sojourner.**

וְלַתּוֹשָׁב vav conjunction *and* prefixed to לְ preposition meaning *to, towards, until, at, in, of, about, into, in (regard to), concerning, according to, by, in relation to, in the direction of, for, because of* prefixed to definite article *the* prefixed to noun common masculine singular absolute from תּוֹשָׁב meaning *alien*; hence, **and for the alien.**

בְּתוֹכָם בְּ preposition meaning *in, at or by, (together) with* prefixed to noun common masculine singular construct from תָּוֶךְ meaning *midst of, middle of* prefixed to pronominal suffix 3mp meaning *them*; hence, **in (the) midst of them.**

תִּהְיֶינָה verb qal imperfect 3fp from הָיָה meaning *he/it fell out, came to pass, became, was*; hence, **they will be.**

שֵׁשׁ־הֶעָרִים numeral cardinal feminine singular construct meaning *six of* in construct relationship to definite article *the* prefixed to noun common feminine plural absolute meaning *cities*; hence, **six of the cities.**

הָאֵלֶּה definite article the prefixed to demonstrative adjective both plural no state from meaning *these*[475]; hence; **the these.**

לְמִקְלָט לְ preposition meaning *to, towards, until, at, in, of, about, into, in (regard to), concerning, according to, by, in relation to, in the direction of, for, because of* prefixed to noun common masculine singular absolute meaning *refuge*; hence, **for refuge.**

לָנוּס לְ preposition meaning *to, towards, until, at, in, of, about, into, in (regard to), concerning, according to, by, in relation to, in the direction of, for, because of* prefixed to verb qal infinitive construct from נוּס meaning *to flee, escape, slip away*; hence, **into (which) to flee.**

שָׁמָּה particle adverb directional from שָׁם meaning *there, then*; hence, **there.**

כָּל־מַכֵּה־נֶפֶשׁ noun common masculine singular construct from כֹּל meaning *the whole, all*[476] in construct relationship to verb hiphil participle masculine singular construct from נָכָה meaning *he/it smote* in construct relationship to noun common feminine singular absolute from נֶפֶשׁ meaning *soul, living being, life, self, person, desire, appetite, emotion and passion*; hence, **all of (the) causing to smite a person.**

בִּשְׁגָגָה: בְּ preposition meaning *in, at or by, (together) with* prefixed to noun common feminine singular absolute from שְׁגָגָה meaning *sin of error, inadvertence*; hence, meaning **in inadvertence.**

Rough Translation: For the descendants of Israel and for the sojourner and for the alien in (the) midst of them they will be six of the cities the these for refuge into (which) to flee there all of (the) causing to smite a person in inadvertence.

Smooth Translation: These six cities will be for refuge for the children of Israel, the sojourner and the alien living among them; anyone that smites a person unintentionally may flee there.

---

[475] Ibid, 16.
[476] BDB, 483.

Verse 16

וְאִם־בִּכְלִי   וְ vav conjunction *and* prefixed to אִם particle conjunction *if*[477] in construct relationship to בְּ preposition meaning *in, at or by, (together) with* prefixed to noun common masculine singular construct from כְּלִי meaning *article, utensil, vessel of*; hence, ***and if with a vessel of.***

בַּרְזֶל   noun common masculine singular absolute from בַּרְזֶל meaning *iron*[478]; hence, ***iron.***

הִכָּהוּ   verb hiphil perfect 3ms from נָכָה meaning *he/it smote* prefixed to pronominal suffix 3ms meaning *him/ it*; hence, ***he caused to smite him.***

וַיָּמֹת   וְ vav consecutive *and* prefixed to verb qal imperfect 3ms from מוּת meaning *to die, dying, dead*; hence, ***and he died.***

רֹצֵחַ   verb qal participle masculine singular absolute from רָצַח meaning *murder, manslayer* (both with intent and without intent); hence, ***a murderer.***

הוּא   pronoun independent 3ms meaning ***he/ it.***

מוֹת   verb qal infinitive absolute meaning ***to die.***

יוּמַת   verb hophal imperfect 3ms meaning *he/ it was caused to die*; hence, ***he will be caused to die.***

הָרֹצֵחַ:   definite article *the* prefixed to verb qal participle masculine singular absolute from רָצַח meaning *murderer, manslayer* (both with intent and without intent); hence, ***the murderer.***

Rough Translation: And if with a vessel of iron he caused to smite him and he died a murderer he/ it to die he will be caused to die the murderer.

Smooth Translation: 'If a man smites another man with an iron object and the person dies, he is a murderer; the murderer shall be made to die.

Verse 17

וְאִם   וְ vav conjunction *and* prefixed to אִם particle conjunction *if*; hence, ***and if.***

בְּאֶבֶן   בְּ preposition meaning *in, at or by, (together) with* prefixed to noun common feminine singular construct from meaning *stone, plummet, weight*[479]; hence, ***with a stone of.***

יָד   noun common feminine singular absolute meaning *forearm, hand*[480]; hence, ***a hand.***

אֲשֶׁר־יָמוּת   particle relative pronoun meaning *who, which, that, because, when, since* in construct relationship to verb qal imperfect 3ms meaning *he/it will die of*; hence, ***which he will die of.***

בָּהּ   בְּ preposition meaning *in, at or by, (together) with* prefixed to pronominal suffix 3fs meaning *her/ it*; hence, ***by it.***

---

[477] Ibid, 50.
[478] Holladay, 48.
[479] Ibid, 3.
[480] Ibid, 128.

הִכָּהוּ verb hiphil perfect 3ms from נָכָה meaning *he smote, struck, beat, killed unintentionally, slayed, exterminated, destroyed* prefixed to pronominal suffix 3ms meaning *him/it;* hence, **he caused to smite him.**

וַיָּמֹת וַ consecutive *and* prefixed to verb qal imperfect 3ms from מוּת meaning *to die;* hence, **and he died.**

רֹצֵחַ verb qal participle masculine singular absolute from רָצַח meaning *murderer, manslayer* (both with intent and without intent); hence, **a murderer.**

הוּא pronoun independent 3ms meaning *he/ it.*

מוֹת verb qal infinitive absolute meaning *to die.*

יוּמָת[481] verb hophal imperfect 3ms meaning *he/ it was caused to die;* hence, **he will be caused to die.**

הָרֹצֵחַ: definite article *the* prefixed to verb qal participle masculine singular absolute from רָצַח meaning *murderer, manslayer* (both with intent and without intent); hence, **the murderer.**

Rough Translation: And if with a stone of a hand which he will die of by it he caused to smite him and he died a murderer he/ it to die he will be caused to die the murderer.

Smooth Translation: And if a man has a stone in his hand which could kill and he smites another man so that he dies, the man is a murderer; the murderer shall be made to die.

Verse 18

אוֹ[482] conjunction meaning *either ... or, whether ... or;* hence, **either ... or.**

בִּכְלִי בְ preposition meaning *in, at or by, (together) with* prefixed to noun common masculine singular construct meaning *article, utensil, vessel of;* hence, **with a vessel of.**

עֵץ־יָד noun common masculine singular absolute from עֵץ meaning *tree, trees, wood* in construct relationship to noun common feminine singular absolute from יָד meaning *hand;* hence, **a wood of a hand.**

אֲשֶׁר־יָמוּת אֲשֶׁר relative pronoun *who, which, that, because, when, since* in construct relationship to verb qal imperfect 3ms meaning *he/it will die, finally kill, give the death-blow, slay, kill;* hence, **which it will kill of.**

בּוֹ בְ preposition meaning *in, at or by, (together) with* prefixed to pronominal suffix 3ms meaning *him/it;* hence, **with it.**

הִכָּהוּ verb hiphil perfect 3ms from נָכָה meaning *he smote, struck, beat, killed unintentionally, slayed, exterminated, destroyed* prefixed to pronominal suffix 3ms meaning *him/it;* hence, **he caused to smite him.**

וַיָּמֹת וַ consecutive *and* prefixed to verb qal imperfect 3ms from מוּת meaning *to die;* hence, **and he died.**

רֹצֵחַ verb qal participle masculine singular absolute from רָצַח meaning *murderer, manslayer* (both with intent and without intent); hence, **a murderer.**

---

[481] There is a critical issue about יוּמָת and is discussed under textual analysis of verse 17.

[482] A critical issue is raised about אוֹ as discussed under textual analysis of verse 18.

הוּא pronoun independent 3ms meaning *he/ it.*

מוֹת verb qal infinitive absolute meaning *to die.*

יוּמַת verb hophal imperfect 3ms meaning *he/ it was caused to die;* hence, **he will be caused to die.**

הָרֹצֵחַ: definite article *the* prefixed to verb qal participle masculine singular absolute from רָצַח meaning *murderer, manslayer* (both with intent and without intent); hence, **the murderer.**

Rough Translation: Either … or with a vessel of a wood of a hand which it will kill of with it he caused to smite him and he died a murderer he/ it to die he will be caused to die the murderer.

Smooth Translation: Or if a man has a wooden object in his hand and smites another person with it so that the person dies; he is a murderer and the murderer shall be made to die.

Verse 19

גֹּאֵל verb qal participle masculine singular construct from גָּאַל meaning he redeemed, delivered, ransomed[483]; hence, **a redeemer of.**

הַדָּם definite article the prefixed to noun common masculine singular absolute meaning *blood*[184]; hence, **the blood.**

הוּא demonstrative pronoun 3ms meaning *this*; hence, **this.**

יָמִית verb hiphil imperfect 3ms from מוּת meaning *to die, dying, dead, finally kill, give the death-blow, slay, kill*; hence, **he will cause to die.**

אֶת־הָרֹצֵחַ untranslatable direct object marker in construct relationship to definite article the prefixed to verb qal participle masculine singular absolute from רָצַח meaning *murderer, manslayer* (both with intent and without intent); hence, **the murderer.**

בְּפִגְעוֹ־בוֹ [485] בְּ preposition meaning *in, at or by, (together) with* prefixed to verb qal infinitive construct from פָּגַע meaning *to meet, encounter, reach* prefixed to pronominal suffix 3ms meaning him/it in construct relationship to בְּ preposition meaning *in, at or by, (together) with* prefixed to pronominal suffix 3ms meaning *him/it*; hence, **in to meet him by him.**

הוּא demonstrative pronoun 3ms meaning *this*; hence, **this.**

יְמִיתֶנּוּ: verb hiphil imperfect 3ms from מוּת meaning *to die, dying, dead, finally kill, give the death-blow, slay, kill* prefixed to pronominal suffix 3ms meaning him/it; hence, **he will cause to kill him.**

Rough Translation: A redeemer of the blood this he will cause to die the murderer in to meet him by him this he will cause to kill him.

Smooth Translation: The redeemer of blood shall put this murderer to death as he meets him, he shall put him to death.

---

[483] Holladay, 53.

[484] BDB, 197.

[485] There is a critical issue raised by Schenker on the Hebrew word בְּפִגְעוֹ־בוֹ which is textually analysed in verse 19.

Verse 20

וְאִם־בְּשִׂנְאָה vav conjunction *and* prefixed to אִם particle conjunction *if* in construct relationship to בְ preposition meaning *in, at or by, (together) with* prefixed to noun common feminine singular absolute from שִׂנְאָה meaning *hating, hatred*[486]; hence, ***and if with hatred.***

יֶהְדָּפֶנּוּ verb qal imperfect 3ms from הָדַף meaning *he thrust, pushed, drove*[487] prefixed to pronominal suffix 3ms meaning *him/it*; hence, ***he will thrust him.***

אוֹ־הִשְׁלִיךְ conjunction meaning *either ... or, whether ... or* in construct relationship to verb hiphil perfect 3ms from שָׁלַךְ meaning *he caused to throw, fling, cast*[488]; hence, ***or caused to throw.***

עָלָיו עַל preposition meaning *upon, on the ground of, according to, on account of, on behalf of, concerning, beside, in addition to, together with, beyond, above, over, by, on to, towards, to, against*[489] prefixed to pronominal suffix 3ms meaning *him/it*; hence, ***upon him.***

בִּצְדִיָּה בְ preposition meaning *in, at or by, (together) with* prefixed to noun common feminine singular from צְדִיָּה meaning *ambush, malice aforethought*[490]; hence, ***in ambush.***

וַיָּמֹת: וְ consecutive *and* prefixed to verb qal imperfect 3ms from מוּת meaning *to die*; hence, ***and he died.***

Rough Translation: And if with hatred he will thrust him or caused to throw upon him in ambush and he died.

Smooth Translation: And if any man with hatred thrusts another person or throws something upon him intentionally and the person dies.

Verse 21

אוֹ conjunction meaning *either ... or, whether ... or*; hence, ***or.***

בְאֵיבָה בְ preposition meaning *in, at or by, (together) with* prefixed to noun common feminine singular from אֵיבָה meaning *enmity, hostile intention*; hence, ***in enmity.***

הִכָּהוּ verb hiphil perfect 3ms from נכה meaning *he smote, struck, beat, killed unintentionally, slayed, exterminated, destroyed* prefixed to pronominal suffix 3ms meaning *him/it*; hence, ***he caused to smite him.***

בְיָדוֹ בְ preposition meaning *in, at or by, (together) with* prefixed noun common feminine singular construct meaning *hand* prefixed to pronominal suffix 3ms meaning *him/it*; hence, ***with (the) hand of him.***

וַיָּמֹת וְ consecutive *and* prefixed to verb qal imperfect 3ms from מוּת meaning *to die*; hence, ***and he died.***

[486] BDB, 972.
[487] Ibid, 213.
[488] Ibid, 1021.
[489] Ibid, 759.
[490] Holladay, 303.

מוֹת־יוּמַת verb qal infinitive absolute meaning *to die, dying, dead, finally kill, give the death-blow, slay, kill* in construct relationship verb hophal imperfect 3ms meaning *he/ it was caused to die;* hence, **to die of he will be caused to die.**

הַמַּכֶּה definite article *the* prefixed to verb hiphil participle masculine singular absolute from נָכָה meaning *he/it smote;* hence, **the one cause to smite.**

רֹצֵחַ verb qal participle masculine singular absolute from רָצַח meaning *murderer, manslayer* (both with intent and without intent); hence, **a murderer.**

הוּא demonstrative pronoun 3ms meaning *this;* hence, **this.**

גֹּאֵל verb qal participle masculine singular construct from גָּאַל meaning *he redeemed, delivered, ransomed*[491]; hence, **a redeemer of.**

הַדָּם definite article the prefixed to noun common masculine singular absolute meaning *blood*[492]; hence, **the blood.**

יָמִית verb hiphil imperfect 3ms from מוּת meaning *to die, dying, dead, finally kill, give the death-blow, slay, kill;* hence, **he will cause to die.**

אֶת־הָרֹצֵחַ untranslatable direct object marker in construct relationship to definite article the prefixed to verb qal participle masculine singular absolute from רָצַח meaning *murderer, manslayer* (both with intent and without intent); hence, **the murderer.**

בְּפִגְעוֹ־בוֹ: בְּ preposition meaning *in, at or by, (together) with* prefixed to verb qal infinitive construct from פָּגַע meaning *to meet, encounter, reach* prefixed to pronominal suffix 3ms meaning *him/it* in construct relationship to בְּ preposition meaning *in, at or by, (together) with* prefixed to pronominal suffix 3ms meaning *him/it;* hence, **in to meet him by him.**

Rough Translation: Or in enmity he caused to smite him with (the) hand of him and he died to die of he will be caused to die the one cause to smite a murderer this a redeemer of the blood he will cause to die the murderer in to meet him by him.

Smooth Translation: or if in enmity he smites another person with his hand so that he dies, he is a murderer; the redeemer of blood will put the murderer to death when he meets him.'

Verse 22

וְאִם־בְּפֶתַע vav conjunction *and* prefixed to אִם particle conjunction *if* in construct relationship to בְּ preposition meaning *in, at or by, (together) with* prefixed to particle adverb from פֶּתַע meaning *instantly, suddenly*[493]; hence, **and if by suddenly.**

בְּלֹא־אֵיבָה בְּ preposition meaning *in, at or by, (together) with* prefixed to negative particle meaning *not, not only, without, no, rather, (whether) ... or if not, and if not, not with*[494] in construct relationship to noun common feminine singular absolute meaning *enmity, hostile intention;* hence, **with not enmity.**

---

[491] Ibid, 53.
[492] BDB, 197.
[493] Holladay, 301.
[494] Ibid, 170.

185

הֲדָפוֹ[495] verb qal perfect 3ms from הָדַף meaning *he thrust, pushed, drove* prefixed to pronominal suffix 3ms meaning *him/it*; hence, ***he thrust him.***

אוֹ־הִשְׁלִיךְ אוֹ conjunction meaning *either ... or, whether ... or* in construct relationship to verb hiphil perfect 3ms from שָׁלַךְ meaning *he caused to throw, fling, cast*[496]; hence, ***or caused to throw.***

עָלָיו עַל preposition meaning *upon, on the ground of, according to, on account of, on behalf of, concerning, beside, in addition to, together with, beyond, above, over, by, on to, towards, to, against*[497] prefixed to pronominal suffix 3ms meaning *him/it*; hence, ***upon him.***

כָּל־כְּלִי noun common masculine singular construct from כֹּל meaning *the whole, all* in construct relationship to noun common masculine singular construct from כְּלִי meaning *article, utensil, vessel of*; hence, ***the whole of (the) vessel of.***

בְּלֹא בְּ preposition meaning *in, at or by, (together) with* prefixed to negative particle meaning *not, not only, without, no, rather, (whether) ... or if not, and if not, not with*; hence, ***with not.***

צְדִיָּה: noun common feminine singular from צְדִיָּה meaning *ambush, malice aforethought*; hence, ***malice aforethought.***

Rough Translation: And if by suddenly with not enmity he thrust him or caused to throw upon him the whole of (the) vessel of with not malice aforethought.

Smooth Translation: '"But if without enmity someone suddenly thrusts another person or throws an object upon him unintentionally.

Verse 23

אוֹ conjunction meaning *either ... or, whether ... or*; hence, ***or.***

בְּכָל־אֶבֶן[498] בְּ preposition meaning *in, at or by, (together) with* prefixed to noun common masculine singular construct from כֹּל meaning *the whole, all* in construct relationship to אֶבֶן noun common feminine singular construct from meaning *stone, plummet, weight*; hence, ***by the whole of stone of.***

אֲשֶׁר־יָמוּת אֲשֶׁר relative pronoun *who, which, that, because, when, since* in construct relationship to verb qal imperfect 3ms meaning *he/it will die, finally kill, give the death-blow, slay, kill*; hence, ***which he will die of.***

בָּהּ בְּ preposition meaning *in, at or by, (together) with* prefixed to pronominal suffix 3fs meaning *her/ it*; hence, ***by it.***

בְּלֹא בְּ preposition meaning *in, at or by, (together) with* prefixed to negative particle meaning *not, not only, without, no, rather, (whether) ... or if not, and if not, not with*; hence, ***with not.***

---

[495] There is a critical issue raised on the Hebrew word הֲדָפוֹ as discussed under textual analysis of verse 22.

[496] Holladay, 1021.

[497] Ibid, 759.

[498] A critical issue is raised on the Hebrew word: בְּכָל־אֶבֶן and is discussed in the textual analysis of verse 23.

רְאוֹת verb qal infinitive construct from רָאָה meaning *to see, seeing*; hence, ***seeing.***

וַיַּפֵּל ו consecutive *and* prefixed to verb hiphil imperfect 3ms from נָפַל meaning *he fell (unintentionally), turned out, collapsed, be born, threw oneself down*[499]; hence, ***and caused to fall.***

עָלָיו עַל preposition meaning *upon, on the ground of, according to, on account of, on behalf of, concerning, beside, in addition to, together with, beyond, above, over, by, on to, towards, to, against*[500] prefixed to pronominal suffix 3ms meaning *him/it*; hence, ***upon him.***

וַיָּמֹת ו consecutive *and* prefixed to verb qal imperfect 3ms from מות meaning *to die*; hence, ***and he died.***

וְהוּא ו consecutive *and* prefixed to personal pronoun 3ms meaning *he*; hence, ***he.***

לֹא־אוֹיֵב לֹא particle negative meaning *not, not only, without, no, rather, (whether) ... or if not, and if not, not with* in construct relationship to verb qal participle masculine singular absolute from אָיַב meaning *he was hostile to, an enemy*; hence, ***not an enemy.***

לוֹ לְ preposition meaning *to, towards, until, at, in, of, about, into, in (regard to), concerning, according to, by, for, because of*[501], prefixed to pronominal suffix 3ms meaning *him/it*; hence, ***to him.***

וְלֹא ו consecutive *and* prefixed to particle negative meaning *not, not only, without, no, rather, (whether) ... or if not, and if not, not with*; hence, ***and not.***

מְבַקֵּשׁ verb piel participle masculine singular absolute from בָּקַשׁ meaning *seeking, requiring, trying to get, seeking to obtain, seeking prayer, pleading for*; hence, ***seeking.***

רָעָתוֹ: noun common feminine singular construct from meaning *evil, harm, wickedness, perverseness, crime, misery, trouble, disaster of* prefixed to pronominal suffix 3ms meaning *him/it*; hence, ***evil of him.***

Rough Translation: Or by the whole of stone of which he will die of by it with not seeing and caused to fall upon him and he died he not an enemy to him and not seeking evil of him.

Smooth Translation: or without seeing him, causes a heavy stone to fall on him so that he dies without being his enemy and seeking evil against him.

Verse 24

וְשָׁפְטוּ ו consecutive *and* prefixed to verb qal perfect 3cp from שָׁפַט meaning *he judged, governed*; hence, ***and they will judge.***

הָעֵדָה definite article *the* prefixed to noun common feminine singular absolute from עֵדָה meaning *congregation, assembly*; hence, ***the assembly.***

בֵּין בֵּין preposition meaning *interval, space between*; hence, ***between.***

הַמַּכֶּה definite article *the* prefixed to verb hiphil participle masculine singular absolute from נָכָה meaning *he smote*; hence, ***the one causing to smite.***

---

[499] Holladay, 242.
[500] Ibid, 759.
[501] Ibid, 169.

וּבֵין וְ consecutive *and* prefixed to בֵּין preposition meaning *interval, space between*; hence, **and between.**

גֹּאֵל verb qal participle masculine singular construct from גָּאֵל meaning he redeemed, delivered, ransomed[502]; hence, **a redeemer of.**

הַדָּם definite article the prefixed to noun common masculine singular absolute meaning *blood*[503]; hence, **the blood.**

עַל עַל preposition meaning *upon, on the ground of, according to, on account of, on behalf of, concerning, beside, in addition to, together with, beyond, above, over, by, on to, towards, to, against;* hence, **upon.**

הַמִּשְׁפָּטִים definite article *the* prefixed to noun common masculine plural absolute from מִשְׁפָּט meaning *judgment, place or court seat of judgment, case or cause presented for judgment, sentence, decision of judgment, ordinance promulgated, decision of the case of law;* hence, **the judgments.**

הָאֵלֶּה: definite article *the* prefixed to adjective both plural no state meaning the *these;* hence, **the these.**

Rough Translation: And they will judge the assembly between the one causing to smite and between a redeemer of the blood upon the judgments the these.

Smooth Translation: The assembly will judge between the accused person and the redeemer of blood according to these ordinances promulgated.

Verse 25

וְהִצִּילוּ וְ consecutive *and* prefixed to verb hiphil perfect 3mp from נָצִיר meaning *he rescued, saved, escaped;* hence, **and they will cause to escape.**

הָעֵדָה definite article *the* prefixed to noun common feminine singular absolute from עֵדָה meaning *congregation, assembly;* hence, **the assembly.**

אֵת־הָרֹצֵחַ[504] untranslatable direct object marker in construct relationship to definite article *the* prefixed to verb qal participle masculine singular absolute from רָצַח meaning *murderer, manslayer* (both with intent and without intent); hence, **the one guilty of manslaughter.**

מִיַּד מִן preposition meaning *from, out of* prefixed to noun common feminine singular construct meaning *a hand;* hence, **out of a hand of.**

גֹּאֵל verb qal participle masculine singular construct from גָּאֵל meaning he redeemed, delivered, ransomed[505]; hence, **a redeemer of.**

הַדָּם definite article *the* prefixed to noun common masculine singular absolute meaning *blood*[506]; hence, **the blood.**

וְהֵשִׁיבוּ וְ consecutive *and* prefixed to verb hiphil perfect 3cp from שׁוּב meaning he turned back, returned; hence, **and they will turn back.**

---

[502] Ibid, 53.

[503] BDB, 197.

[504] A very critical issue is raised on אֵת־הָרֹצֵחַ and is discussed under textual analysis of verse 25.

[505] Ibid, 53.

[506] BDB, 197.

אֹתוֹ   untranslatable direct object marker prefixed to pronominal suffix 3ms meaning *him/it*; hence, **him.**

הָעֵדָה   definite article *the* prefixed to noun common feminine singular absolute from עֵדָה meaning *congregation, assembly*; hence, **the assembly.**

אֶל אֶל־עִיר   preposition meaning toward, as far as, into, with regard to[507] in construct relationship to noun common feminine singular construct meaning *city, quarter, population*; hence, **into (the) city.**

מִקְלָטוֹ   noun common masculine singular construct meaning *refuge, asylum*; prefixed to pronominal suffix 3ms meaning *him/it*; hence, **refuge of him.**

אֲשֶׁר־נָס   particle relative pronoun meaning *who, which, that, because, when, since*; in construct relationship to verb qal perfect 3ms from נוּס meaning *he fled, escaped*; hence, **that he fled.**

שָׁמָּה   particle adverb directional meaning there; hence, **there.**

וְיָשַׁב   וְ consecutive and prefixed to verb qal perfect 3ms from יָשַׁב meaning *he sat, remained, dwelled*; hence, **and he will remain.**

בָּהּ   בְּ preposition meaning *in, at or by, (together) with* prefixed to pronominal suffix 3fs meaning *her/ it*; hence, **in it.**

עַד־מוֹת   particle preposition *as far as, until, while, during, toward, up to, forever* in construct relationship to noun common masculine singular construct from מָוֶת meaning death, dying, pestilence[508]; hence, **until (the) death of.**

הַכֹּהֵן   definite article *the* prefixed to noun common masculine singular absolute from כֹּהֵן meaning *priest, the high priest, Levitical priests*[509], hence, **the priest.**

הַגָּדֹל   definite article *the* prefixed to adjective masculine singular absolute from גָּדוֹל meaning great[510]; hence, **the great.**

אֲשֶׁר־מָשַׁח   particle relative pronoun meaning *who, which, that, because, when, since*; in construct relationship to verb qal perfect 3ms from מָשַׁח meaning *he smeared, anointed*; hence, **who he anointed of.**

אֹתוֹ   untranslatable direct object marker prefixed to pronominal suffix 3ms meaning *him/it*; hence, **him.**

בְּשֶׁמֶן   בְּ preposition meaning *in, at or by, (together) with* prefixed to noun common masculine singular construct from שֶׁמֶן meaning *oil, oleaster*[511]; hence, **with oil.**

הַקֹּדֶשׁ:   definite article *the* prefixed to noun common masculine singular absolute from קֹדֶשׁ meaning *a holy thing, votive gifts, offerings, holiness, holy area, something most holy*; hence, **the holy thing.**

Rough Translation: And they will cause to escape the assembly the one guilty of manslaughter out of a hand of a redeemer of the blood and they will turn back him the

---

[507] Holladay, 16.
[508] Ibid, 188.
[509] Ibid, 152.
[510] Ellis, 371.
[511] Holladay, 376.

assembly into (the) city refuge of him that he fled there and he will remain in it until (the) death of the priest the great who he anointed of him with oil the holy thing.

Smooth Translation: The assembly shall make the one convicted of manslaughter escape from the redeemer of blood by sending him back to the city of refuge where he had fled and he shall remain there until the death of the high priest who was anointed with the holy oil.'"

Verse 26

וְאִם־יָצֹא ‏ וְ vav conjunction *but* prefixed to אִם particle conjunction *if* in construct relationship to verb qal infinitive absolute from יָצָא meaning he went, came out[512]; hence, ***but if he comes out of.***

יֵצֵא verb qal imperfect 3ms meaning he will come out; hence, ***he will come out.***

הָרֹצֵחַ definite article *the* prefixed to verb qal participle masculine singular absolute from רָצַח meaning *murderer, manslayer* (both with intent and without intent); hence, ***the murderer.***

אֶת־גְּבוּל untranslatable direct object marker in construct relationship to noun common masculine singular construct from גְּבוּל meaning *border, boundary, territory*; hence, ***of (the) territory of.***

עִיר noun common feminine singular construct meaning city; hence, ***city of.***

מִקְלָטוֹ noun common masculine singular construct meaning *refuge, asylum*; prefixed to pronominal suffix 3ms meaning *him/it*; hence, ***refuge of him.***

אֲשֶׁר relative pronoun meaning which; hence, ***which.***

יָנוּס verb qal imperfect 3ms from נוּס meaning he fled, escaped; hence, ***he will flee.***

שָׁמָּה: particle adverb directional meaning there; hence, ***there.***

Rough Translation: But if he comes out of he will come out the murderer of (the) territory of city of refuge of him which there he will flee.

Smooth Translation: 'But if the one convicted of manslaughter goes out of the territory of the city of refuge where he fled

Verse 27

וּמָצָא ‏ וְ vav consecutive *and* prefixed to verb qal perfect 3ms from מָצָא meaning he attained to, found, came, arrived[513]; hence, ***and he will find.***

אֹתוֹ untranslatable direct object marker prefixed to pronominal suffix 3ms meaning *him/it*; hence, ***him.***

גֹּאֵל verb qal participle masculine singular construct from גָּאַל meaning he redeemed, delivered, ransomed[514]; hence, ***a redeemer of.***

הַדָּם definite article the prefixed to noun common masculine singular absolute meaning *blood*[515]; hence, ***the blood.***

---

[512] BDB, 425.
[513] Ibid, 594.
[514] Ibid, 53.
[515] BDB, 197.

מִן מֵחוּץ   preposition meaning *from, out of* prefixed to noun common masculine singular absolute from חוּץ meaning *the outside* (of a house, tent, city, camp), *abroad*; hence, ***from outside.***

לְ לִגְבוּל   preposition meaning *to, for, in regard to* prefixed to noun common masculine singular construct meaning *border, boundary, territory*; hence, ***to (the) territory of.***

עִיר   noun common feminine singular construct meaning *city*; hence, ***city of.***

מִקְלָטוֹ   noun common masculine singular construct meaning *refuge, asylum*; prefixed to pronominal suffix 3ms meaning *him/it*; hence, ***refuge of him.***

וְרָצַח   ו vav consecutive *and* prefixed to verb qal perfect 3ms from רָצַח meaning *murder, slay* (both with intent and without intent); hence, ***and he will murder.***

גֹּאֵל   verb qal participle masculine singular construct from גָּאַל meaning *he redeemed, delivered, ransomed*; hence, ***a redeemer of.***

הַדָּם   definite article *the* prefixed to noun common masculine singular absolute meaning *blood*[516]; hence, ***the blood.***

אֶת־הָרֹצֵחַ   untranslatable direct object marker in construct relationship to definite article *the* prefixed to verb qal participle masculine singular absolute from רָצַח meaning *murderer, manslayer* (both with intent and without intent); hence, ***the one guilty of manslaughter.***

אֵין   particle adverb meaning *absence, nothing, not there*; hence, ***not there.***

לוֹ   לְ preposition meaning *to, for, in regard to* prefixed to pronominal suffix 3ms meaning *him/it*; hence, ***for him.***

דָּם׃   noun common masculine singular absolute from דָּם meaning *blood*; hence, ***blood.***

Rough Translation: And he will find him a redeemer of the blood from outside to (the) territory of city of refuge of him and he will murder a redeemer of the blood the one guilty of manslaughter not there for him blood.

Smooth Translation: and the redeemer of blood finds him outside the border of the city of refuge; the redeemer of blood may kill him without being guilty of murder

Verse 28

כִּי   particle conjunction meaning *that, for, when*; hence, ***for.***

בְעִיר   בְּ preposition meaning *in, at, by* (together with) prefixed to noun common feminine singular construct meaning *city, quarter, population of*; hence, ***city of.***

מִקְלָטוֹ   noun common masculine singular construct meaning *refuge, asylum*; prefixed to pronominal suffix 3ms meaning *him/it*; hence, ***refuge of him.***

יֵשֵׁב   verb qal imperfect 3ms from יָשַׁב meaning *he sat, remained, dwelled*; hence, ***and he will remain.***

עַד־מוֹת   particle preposition *as far as, until, while, during, toward, up to, forever* in construct relationship to noun common masculine singular construct from מָוֶת meaning *death, dying, pestilence*; hence, ***until (the) death of.***

---

[516] BDB, 197.

הַכֹּהֵן definite article *the* prefixed to noun common masculine singular absolute from כֹּהֵן meaning *priest, the high priest, Levitical priests*[517], hence, **the priest.**

הַגָּדֹל definite article *the* prefixed to adjective masculine singular absolute from גָּדוֹל meaning great[518]; hence, **the great.**

וְאַחֲרֵי וְ conjunction *and* prefixed to אַחַר preposition meaning *behind him/it, afterwards, pursue a thing*[519]; hence, **and behind him.**

מוֹת noun common masculine singular construct from מָוֶת meaning *death, dying, pestilence*; hence, **death of.**

הַכֹּהֵן definite article *the* prefixed to noun common masculine singular absolute from כֹּהֵן meaning *priest, the high priest, Levitical priests*[520], hence, **the priest.**

הַגָּדֹל definite article *the* prefixed to adjective masculine singular absolute from גָּדוֹל meaning great[521]; hence, **the great.**

יָשׁוּב verb qal imperfect 3ms meaning he *sat, remained, dwelled*; hence, **he will remain.**

הָרֹצֵחַ definite article *the* prefixed to verb qal participle masculine singular absolute from רָצַח meaning *murderer, manslayer* (both with intent and without intent); hence, **the murderer.**

אֶל־אֶרֶץ particle preposition *to, into, toward* in construct relationship to noun common feminine singular construct from אֶרֶץ meaning *earth, land, piece of ground*[522], hence, **into (the) land of.**

אֲחֻזָּתוֹ: noun common feminine singular construct from אֲחֻזָּה meaning *possession, landed property, possession by right of inheritance* prefixed to pronominal suffix 3ms meaning *him/it*; hence, **possession of him.**

Rough Translation: For city of refuge of him and he will remain until (the) death of the priest the great and behind him death of the priest the great he will remain the murderer into (the) land of possession of him.

Smooth Translation: for he must remain within the city of his refuge until the death of the high priest. But after the death of the high priest the accused person may return to the land of his possession.

Verse 29

וְהָיוּ וְ consecutive and prefixed to verb qal perfect 3cp from הָיָה meaning *he/it fell out, came to pass, became, was*[523]; hence, **and they will be.**

אֵלֶּה adjective both plural no state meaning these; hence, *these.*

לָכֶם לְ preposition meaning *to, for, in regard to* prefixed to pronominal suffix 2mp meaning *you*; hence, **for you.**

[517] Ibid, 152.
[518] Ellis, 371.
[519] Holladay, 11.
[520] Ibid, 152.
[521] Ellis, 371.
[522] BDB, 76.
[523] Ibid, 228.

לְחֻקַּת **ל** preposition meaning *to, for, in regard to* prefixed to noun common feminine singular construct from חֻקָּה meaning something prescribed, enactment, statute; hence, *for a statute of.*

מִשְׁפָּט[524] noun common masculine singular absolute meaning *judgment, place or court seat of judgment, case or cause presented for judgment, sentence, decision of judgment, ordinance promulgated, decision of the case of law*; hence, *judgment.*

לְדֹרֹתֵיכֶם **ל** preposition meaning *to, for, in regard to* prefixed to noun common masculine plural construct from דּוֹר meaning *period, generation, dwelling* of prefixed to pronominal suffix 2mp meaning *you*; hence, *for generations of you.*

בְּכֹל **בּ** preposition meaning *in, at or by, (together) with* prefixed to noun common masculine singular construct from כֹּל meaning *the whole, all*; hence, *in all of.*

מוֹשְׁבֹתֵיכֶם: noun common masculine plural construct from מוֹשָׁב meaning *seat, assembly, dwelling-place, dwelling dwellers* prefixed to pronominal suffix 2mp meaning *you*; hence, *(the) dwelling-place of you.*

Rough Translation: And they will be these for you for a statute of judgment for generations of you in all of (the) dwelling-place of you.

Smooth Translation: '"These will be a standard of judgment for you forever for all of your generations in all of your dwelling-places.

Verse 30

כָּל־מַכֵּה־נֶפֶשׁ noun common masculine singular construct from כֹּל meaning *the whole, all*[525] in construct relationship to verb hiphil participle masculine singular construct from נכה meaning *he/it smote* in construct relationship to noun common feminine singular absolute from נֶפֶשׁ meaning *soul, living being, life, self, person, desire, appetite, emotion and passion*; hence, *all of (the) causing to smite a person.*

לְפִי **ל** preposition meaning *to, for, in regard to* prefixed to noun common masculine singular construct from פֶּה meaning mouth, edge, statement, decision, command of[526]; hence, *for (the) mouth of.*

עֵדִים noun common masculine plural absolute from עֵד meaning *witness*[527]; hence, *witnesses.*

יִרְצַח verb qal imperfect 3ms from רָצַח meaning *he murdered, slayed*; hence *he will murder.*

אֶת־הָרֹצֵחַ untranslatable direct object marker in construct relationship to definite article *the* prefixed to verb qal participle masculine singular absolute from

---

[524] A critical issue is raised about מִשְׁפָּט (judgment) and is discussed under textual analysis of verse 29.

[525] BDB, 483.

[526] Holladay, 289.

[527] Ibid, 265.

רָצַח   meaning *murderer, manslayer* (both with intent and without intent); hence, ***the murderer.***

וְעֵד   וְ conjunction *and* prefixed to noun common masculine singular absolute from עֵד meaning *witness;* hence, ***and a witness.***

אֶחָד   numeral cardinal masculine singular absolute meaning *one, another;* hence, ***one.***

לֹא־יַעֲנֶה   particle negative meaning *not, not only, no* in construct relationship to verb qal imperfect 3ms from עָנָה meaning *he answered, responded, testified;* hence, ***he will not testify.***

בְּנֶפֶשׁ   בְּ preposition meaning *in, at, by, (together) with* prefixed to noun common feminine singular absolute meaning *soul, living being, life, self, person, desire, appetite, emotion, and passion;* hence, ***in a person.***

לָמוּת: לְ preposition meaning *to, for, in regard to* prefixed to verb qal infinitive construct from מוּת meaning *he died, finally killed, gave the death-blow, slayed, killed;* hence, ***for to die of.***

Rough Translation: All of (the) causing to smite a person for (the) mouth of witnesses he will murder the murderer and a witness one he will not testify in a person for to die of.

Smooth Translation: Anyone who smites a person to death shall die as a murderer but only by the testimony of witnesses; no one is to be put to death upon the testimony of only one witness.

Verse 31

וְלֹא־תִקְחוּ   וְ conjunction *and* prefixed to particle negative meaning *not, no, without, less, rather, nothing, and if not* in construct relationship to verb qal imperfect 2mp from לָקַח meaning *he took, laid hold of, seized, received, acquired, fetched, brought, taken away*[528]; hence, ***and you will not take.***

כֹּפֶר   noun common masculine singular absolute from כֹּפֶר meaning *bribe*[529], *ransom;* hence, ***a ransom.***

לְנֶפֶשׁ   לְ preposition meaning *to, for, in regard to* prefixed to noun common feminine singular absolute meaning *soul, living being, life, self, person, desire, appetite, emotion, and passion;* hence, ***for a life.***

רֹצֵחַ   verb qal participle masculine singular absolute from רָצַח meaning *murderer, manslayer* (both with intent and without intent); hence, ***a murderer.***

אֲשֶׁר־הוּא   relative pronoun meaning *who, which, that, because, when* in construct relationship to personal pronoun 3ms meaning *he, it, himself, itself, that;* hence, ***who himself.***

רָשָׁע   adjective masculine singular absolute from רָשָׁע meaning *guilty, in the wrong, wicked, criminal;* hence, ***guilty.***

לָמוּת   לְ preposition meaning *to, for, in regard to* prefixed to verb qal infinitive construct meaning *to die, slay, kill;* hence, ***for to die of.***

---

[528] Ibid, 179.
[529] Ibid, 163.

כִּי־מוֹת כִּי conjunction meaning *that, for, when, in order that* in construct relationship to verb qal infinitive absolute meaning *to die, slay, kill*; hence, **in order that to die.**

יוּמָת: verb hophal imperfect 3ms meaning *he/ it died, slayed, killed*; hence, **he will be made to die.**

Rough Translation: And you will not take a ransom for a life a murderer who himself guilty for to die of in order that to die he will be made to die.

Smooth Translation: You must not collect a ransom for the life of a murderer who is guilty for he is to die; he must be put to death.

Verse 32

וְלֹא־תִקְחוּ וְ conjunction *and* prefixed to particle negative meaning *not, no, without, less, rather, nothing, and if not* in construct relationship to verb qal imperfect 2mp from לָקַח meaning *he took, laid hold of, seized, received, acquired, fetched, brought, taken away*[530]; hence, **and you will not take.**

כֹפֶר noun common masculine singular absolute from כֹפֶר meaning bribe, ransom[531]; hence, **a ransom.**

לָנוּס[532] לְ preposition meaning *to, towards, until, at, in, of, about, into, in (regard to), concerning, according to, by, in relation to, in the direction of, for, because of* prefixed to definite article *the* prefixed to verb qal infinitive construct from נוּס meaning *to flee, escape, slip away*; hence, **for the (which) to flee.**

אֶל־עִיר אֶל preposition meaning *toward, as far as, into, with regard to*[533] in construct relationship to noun common feminine singular construct meaning *city, quarter, population*; hence, **into (the) city.**

מִקְלָטוֹ noun common masculine singular construct meaning *refuge, asylum*; prefixed to pronominal suffix 3ms meaning *him/it*; hence, **refuge of him.**

לָשׁוּב לְ preposition meaning *to, towards, until, at, in, of, about, into, in (regard to), concerning, according to, by, in relation to, in the direction of, for, because of* prefixed to definite article *the* prefixed to verb qal infinite construct from שׁוּב meaning *to turn back, return*[534]; hence, **for the to turn back.**

לָשֶׁבֶת לְ preposition meaning *to, towards, until, at, in, of, about, into, in (regard to), concerning, according to, by, in relation to, in the direction of, for, because of* prefixed to definite article *the* prefixed to verb qal infinitive construct from יָשַׁב meaning he *sat, remained, dwelled*; hence, **for the to remain.**

בָּאָרֶץ בְּ preposition meaning *in, at or by, (together) with* prefixed to noun common feminine singular construct from אֶרֶץ meaning *ground, piece of land, territory, land, earth, depths of the earth, underworld*; hence, **in a territory of.**

---

[530] Ibid, 179.

[531] Ibid, 163.

[532] Another critical issue is raised about the Hebrew word לָנוּס (for [which] to flee) and is discussed under textual analysis of verse 32.

[533] Holladay, 16.

[534] BDB, 1000.

עַד־מוֹת particle preposition *as far as, until, while, during, toward, up to, forever* in construct relationship to noun common masculine singular construct from מוֹת meaning *death, dying, pestilence*; hence, ***until (the) death of.***

הַכֹּהֵן:[535] definite article *the* prefixed to noun common masculine singular absolute from כֹּהֵן meaning *priest, the high priest, Levitical priests*[536], hence, ***the priest.***

Rough Translation: And you will not take a ransom for the (which) to flee into (the) city refuge of him for the to turn back for the to remain in a territory of until (the) death of the priest.

Smooth Translation: You shall not collect ransom for anyone who has fled to the city of his refuge in order to bring him back; he must remain within the territory until the death of the high priest.

Verse 33

וְלֹא־תַחֲנִיפוּ conjunction *and* prefixed to particle negative meaning *not, no, without, less, rather, nothing, and if not* in construct relationship to verb hiphil imperfect 2mp from חָנֵף meaning *he polluted, profaned*[537]; ***and not you will not cause to pollute.***

אֶת־הָאָרֶץ untranslatable direct object marker prefixed to definite article the prefixed to noun common feminine singular absolute meaning *ground, piece of land, territory, land, earth, depths of the earth, underworld*; hence, ***the land.***

אֲשֶׁר particle relative pronoun meaning *who, which, that, because, when, since*; hence, ***which.***

אַתֶּם[538] pronoun independent 2mp meaning *you*[539]; hence, ***you.***

בָּהּ בְּ preposition meaning *in, at, by, (together) with* prefixed to pronominal suffix 3fs meaning *her/it*; hence, ***in her.***

כִּי כִּי conjunction meaning *that, for, when, in order that*; hence, ***that.***

הַדָּם definite article the prefixed to noun common masculine singular absolute meaning *blood*[540]; hence, ***the blood.***

הוּא personal pronoun 3ms meaning *he, it, himself, itself, that*; hence, ***himself.***

יַחֲנִיף verb hiphil imperfect 3ms from חָנֵף meaning *he polluted, profaned*; hence, ***he will cause to pollute.***

אֶת־הָאָרֶץ untranslatable direct object marker prefixed to definite article the prefixed to noun common feminine singular absolute meaning *ground, piece of land, territory, land, earth, depths of the earth, underworld*; hence, ***the land.***

---

[535] There seems to be an addition to the last Hebrew word of verse 32: הַכֹּהֵן (the priest).

[536] BDB, 152.

[537] Ibid, 338.

[538] There is an insertion of יֹשְׁבִים (you remaining) to אַתֶּם (you) just as it happens in verse 34. See textual analysis of verse 33.

[539] Holladay, 31.

[540] BDB, 197.

וְלָאָרֶץ וּ conjunction *and* prefixed to לְ preposition meaning *to, towards, until, at, in, of, about, into, in (regard to), concerning, according to, by, in relation to, in the direction of, for, because of* prefixed to definite article *the* prefixed to noun common feminine singular absolute meaning *ground, piece of land, territory, land, earth, depths of the earth, underworld*; hence, **and for the land.**

לֹא־יְכֻפַּר particle negative meaning *not, no, without, less, rather, nothing, and if not* in construct relationship to verb pual imperfect 3ms from כָּפַר meaning he covered over, atoned[541]; hence, **he (it) will not be atoned.**

לַדָּם לְ preposition meaning *to, towards, until, at, in, of, about, into, in (regard to), concerning, according to, by, in relation to, in the direction of, for, because of* prefixed to definite article *the* prefixed to noun common masculine singular absolute meaning *blood*; hence, **for the blood.**

אֲשֶׁר particle relative pronoun meaning *who, which, that, because, when, since*; hence, **which.**

שֻׁפַּךְ־בָּהּ verb qal pass perfect 3ms from שָׁפַךְ meaning *he poured out, spilled, shed* in construct relationship to בְּ preposition meaning *in, at, by, (together) with* prefixed to pronominal suffix 3fs meaning *her/it*; hence, **he poured out in her.**

כִּי־אִם conjunction meaning *that, for, when, in order that* in construct relationship to אִם particle conjunction *if*; hence, **for if.**

בְּדַם בְּ preposition meaning *in, at, by, (together) with* prefixed to prefixed to noun common masculine singular absolute meaning *blood*; hence, **in blood.**

שֹׁפְכוֹ: verb qal participle masculine singular construct from שָׁפַךְ meaning *he poured out, spilled, shed* prefixed to pronominal suffix 3ms; **pouring it out.**

Rough Translation: And not you will not cause to pollute the land which you in her that the blood himself he will cause to pollute the land and for the land he (it) will not be atoned for the blood which he poured out in her for if in blood pouring it out.

Smooth Translation: You must not pollute the land where you are living for blood pollutes the land. Atonement cannot be made for the land on which blood has been poured except by the blood of the person who poured it.'"

Verse 34

וְלֹא וּ conjunction *and* prefixed to particle negative meaning *not, no, without, less, rather, nothing, and if not*; hence, **and not.**

תִטַּמֵּא[542] verb piel imperfect 2ms from טָמֵא meaning *he was or became unclean*; hence, **you will become grossly unclean.**

אֶת־הָאָרֶץ untranslatable direct object marker prefixed to definite article the prefixed to noun common feminine singular absolute meaning *ground, piece of land, territory, land, earth, depths of the earth, underworld*; hence, **the land.**

אֲשֶׁר particle relative pronoun meaning *who, which, that, because, when, since*; hence, **which.**

---

[541] Ibid, 498.

[542] A critical issue is raised on this Hebrew word תִטַּמֵּא as explained under textual analysis of verse 34.

אַתֶּם pronoun independent 2mp meaning *you*[543]; hence, **you.**

יֹשְׁבִים verb qal participle masculine plural absolute from יָשַׁב meaning he *sat, remained, dwelled*; hence, **you remaining.**

בָּהּ בְּ preposition meaning *in, at, by, (together) with* prefixed to pronominal suffix 3fs meaning *her/it*; hence, **in it.**

אֲשֶׁר particle relative pronoun meaning *who, which, that, because, when, since*; hence, **which.**

אֲנִי pronoun independent 1cs meaning I; hence, **I.**

שֹׁכֵן verb qal participle masculine singular absolute from שָׁכֵן meaning *he submitted, settled (to live), stayed, stopped, inhabited, lived in, sojourned*[544]; hence, **living in.**

בְּתוֹכָהּ בְּ preposition meaning *in, at, by, (together) with* prefixed to noun common masculine singular construct from תָּוֶךְ meaning *midst, middle of*[545] prefixed to pronominal suffix 3fs meaning *her/it*; hence, **in (the) midst of her.**

כִּי conjunction meaning *that, for, when, in order that*; hence, **that.**

אֲנִי pronoun independent 1cs meaning I; hence, **I.**

יְהוָה noun proper no gender no number no state meaning *Yahweh, the proper name of the God of Israel*; hence, **Yahweh.**

שֹׁכֵן verb qal participle masculine singular absolute from שָׁכֵן meaning *he submitted, settled (to live), stayed, stopped, inhabited, lived in, sojourned*[546]; hence, **living in.**

בְּתוֹךְ בְּ preposition meaning *in, at, by, (together) with* prefixed to noun common masculine singular construct from תָּוֶךְ meaning *midst, middle of*; hence, **in (the) midst of.**

בְּנֵי noun common masculine plural construct from בֵּן meaning *son, descendant*; hence, **children of.**

פ יִשְׂרָאֵל: noun proper no gender no number no state meaning Israel (etymologically implying *El persists* while in jussive means *Let El persists*); hence, **Israel.**

Rough Translation: And not you will become grossly unclean the land which you you remaining in it which I living in in (the) midst of her that I Yahweh living in in (the) midst of children of Israel.

Smooth Translation: Do not defile the land on which you are living for I Yahweh live in the midst of the children of Israel."

---

[543] Holladay, 31.
[544] Ibid, 370.
[545] Ibid, 387.
[546] Ibid, 370.

APPENDIX 2

LIST OF PRIMARY SOURCES

Abimbola, Grace Taiwo 2018. Interview by proxy, Real Care Model College, Ope-Ilu, Agbado, Ogun State, B.Ed. (Yorùbá), Teacher, July 20.

Adigun, S. (Bobagunwa of Elebeland) 2018. Interview by author, Elebe Village, Ogbomoso, Oyo State, Farmer, July 20.

Akanmu, Olayiwola (Asiwaju-Awo of Ogbomosoland) 2018. Interview by author, Arowomokun Compound, Ijeru, Ogbomoso, Oyo State, *Ifa* Priest, July 20.

Akanni, Olagoke Adio (Justice of Peace (JP), Araba-Oluawo of Ogbomosoland) 2018. Interview by author, Akede Compound, Abese Area, Okelerin, Ogbomoso, B.Edu. (Yorùbá), *Ifa* High Priest, August 3.

Akinade, Akanni Ojeniyi 2018. Interview by author, Alayede-Sokoto Compound, Ijeru, Ogbomoso, Oyo State, *Ifa* Priest, August 2.

Alamu, Oladejo (Akoda-Awo of Ogbomosoland) 2018. Interview by author, Akoda Compound, Ijeru, Ogbomoso, Oyo State, *Ifa* Chief Priest, July 17.

Awogbile, Awoniran 2018. Interview by author, Oko Township, Oyo State, *Ifa* Priest, July 18.

Awogbile, Ifatayo (Awoko-Orunmila and Araba-Awo of Oko Township) 2018. Interview by author, Oko Township, Oyo State, *Ifa* Chief Priest, July 18.

Awolade, Abayomi Olujide 2018. Interview by proxy and author, Ilashamaja, Lagos State, M.Div. (Theology), M.A (Theological Studies), PhD (In View), Clergyman with Background in Native Medicine and *Yorùbá* Magic, August 2.

Fakorede, Aderemi G. 2018. Interview by proxy, Bethel Baptist Church, Idimu, Lagos State, M.Th. (OT Lang. & Lit.), PhD (Lang. & Lit.), Clergyman with Background in *Ifa*, August 9.

Fasola, Adekunle 2018. Interview by author, Ogidi Compound, Ijeru, Ogbomoso, Oyo State, *Ifa* Priest, July 17.

Fasola, Mootemilawo (Bashorun-Awo of Ogbomosoland) 2018. Interview by author, Ogidi Compound, Ijeru, Ogbomoso, Oyo State, *Ifa* Chief Priest, July 17.

Ifadele, Gbadegesin Olokun (Oba Olomitutu & Elewi-Awo of Ogbomosoland) 2018. Interview by author, Arowomole, Ijeru, Ogbomoso, Oyo State, Osun High Priest in Ogbomosoland and Ifa Priest, August 10.

Jokotoye, Awolade Bankole (Adifala of Ogbomosoland) 2018. Interview by author, Olukan Compound, Arowomole, Ijeru, Ogbomoso, Oyo State, *Ifa* Chief Priest, August 10.

Ladigbolu, Ayo (Archbishop Emeritus and Prince) 2018. Interview by author, Apewo Villa, Ladigbolu Area, Oyo Alaafin, Oyo State, M.A (Mass Com.), M.Th., Retired Clergyman and Elder Statesman, August 7.

Ogunkanbi, Isaac Oluwale 2018. Interview by proxy, First Baptist Church, Olorunsogo, Ijaye-Ojokoro, Lagos State, C.Th., Dip.CRS, B.A/B.Th., MATS, D.Min., Clergyman, July 28.

Ogunmodede, Samuel Tunde 2018. Interview by proxy, Faith Baptist Church, Mologede, Meiran Road, Lagos State, M.A (Religious Studies), D.Min. (In View), Clergyman, August 4.

Ogunmola, M.O. (Otun-Alaafin) 2018. Interview by author, Akeetan, Oyo-Alaafin, Oyo State, M.A (English and History) in Manchester, Retired School Principal and Elder Statesman and Former Nigeria's High Commissioner to the Republic of Zambia and Malawi (Late 1981-Early 1984), August 7.

Oladayo, Olalere Sunday 2018. Interview by author, Mosadinwin Village, Ogbomoso, M.Th. (World Religions), PhD (World Religions), Clergyman, August 10.

Olopade, John Atilola 2018. Interview by proxy, NBTS, Ogbomoso, M.Th. (World Religions), PhD (World Religions), Lecturer, August 1.

Olugbon, Awogbade (President-General of Awo in Ogbomosoland) 2018. Interview by author, Olugbon Ibere Compound, Apake, Ogbomoso, Oyo State, *Ifa* Chief Priest, August 1.

Oyelami, Israel (Egbeji of Osun State, Akogun of Elebe and Aroni-Ifalase of Lagos) 2018. Interview by author, Elebe Village, Ogbomoso, Oyo State, Native Doctor, July 20.

INTERVIEW GUIDE

INSTRUCTION
Kindly answer the questions below as appropriate to you and comment briefly where necessary.

PERSONAL PROFILE
Name: _____
Town of Residence: _____
Gender: (a). Male   [   ]   (b). Female   [   ]
Profession: _____
Educational Qualifications: _____

QUESTIONS
1. Kindly explain what *Ifa* Corpus says about sanctity of human life in the *Yorùbá* understanding of life._____

_____

_____

_____

_____

_____

2. Mention some ideas, proverbs or wise sayings that express the worth of human life in *Yorùbá* vocabulary_____

_____

_____

_____

3. In your own view, what is sacredness of human life? _____

_____

_____

_____

4. Mention some of the practices of the *Yorùbá* people that depict the worth of human life _____

_____

5. List some of the factors that are promoting violations of the sacredness of human life among *Yorùbá* people _____

_____

_____

6. Mention types of violation to the sanctity of human life among *Yorùbá* people ____

_____

_____

_____

7. State some effects of the violations to sanctity of human life on the following:

(a). Victims: _____

_____

_____

(b). Family: _____

_____

_____

(c). Society: _____

_____

_____

(d). Younger generation: _____

_____

_____

8. Mention some responses of the following bodies to the violations of the worth of human life within the context of the *Yorùbá* people:

(a). Governments: _____

_____

_____

(b). Religious bodies: _____

_____

_____

(c). Family: _____

_____

_____

9. What measures do you think are appropriate to curtail violations of the sanctity of human life? _____

_____

10. What other information do you have on the sacredness of human life in *Yorùbá* worldview? _____

_____

_____

APPENDIX 4

LIST OF PICTURES OF SOME INTERVIEW RESPONDENTS

Picture 1: The Researcher with Archbishop Emeritus Ayo Ladigbolu,
Methodist Church, Nigeria

Picture 2: The Researcher with High Chief M.O. Ogunmola
(Otun-Alaafin of Oyo)

Picture 3: Chief Olagoke Adio Akanni, J.P (Justice of Peace)
(Araba-Oluawo of Ogbomosoland)

Picture 4: Chief Israel Oyelami (Egbeji of Osun, Akogun of Elebe & Aroni-Ifalase of Lagos)

Picture 5: Chief Ifatayo Awogbile (Awoko-Orunmila & Araba-Awo of Oko Township)

Picture 6: Olayiwola Akanmu (Asiwaju-Awo of Ogbomosoland)

Picture 7: Chief Mootemilawo Fasola (Bashorun-Awo of Ogbomosoland) with his son Mr. Adekunle Fasola

Picture 8: Chief Awolade Bankole Jokotoye (Adifala of Ogbomosoland)

Picture 9: Mr. Awoniran Awogbile (*Ifa* Priest at Oko Township)

BIBLIOGRAPHY

BOOKS

A., Vani Kesari. *Sanctity of Human Life in the Context of Human Genetic Research*. Thesis Submitted to the Cochin University of Science and Technology for the Award of Doctor of Philosophy in the Faculty of Law. Kerala: School of Legal Studies, 2015.

Abimbola, Wande. *Ifa Divination Poetry*. Trans., & Ed. Wande Abimbola. New York: NOK Publishers, 1977.

_____. *Sixteen Great Poems of Ifa*. Niamey: UNESCO and Abimbola, 1975.

Abrams, M.H. *A Glossary of Literary Terms*. Seventh Edition. Australia: Heinle & Heinle, 1999.

Akande, S.T. Ola. *Miracles, Mysteries, Death and Dying, and Other Supernatural Events in Nigeria*. South Carolina: CreateSpace Independent Publishing Platform, 2013.

Akintola, Akinbowale. *Yoruba Ethics and Metaphysics: Being Basic Philosophy Underlying the Ifa System of Thought of the Yoruba*. Ogbomoso: Valour Publishing Ventures Limited, 1999.

Alcorn, Randy. *Why Pro-Life? Caring for the Unborn and Their Mothers*. Sandy: Eternal Perspective Ministries (EPM), 2004.

Alexander, Ralph H. "עָבַד " *Theological Wordbook of the Old Testament*. ed., R. Laird Harris, Gleason L. Archer, and Bruce K. Waltke. Chicago: Moody Publishers, 1980.

Armstrong, Robert G. "The Etymology of the Word 'Ogun'." In *Africa's Ogun: Old World and New*. Eds., Sandra T. Barnes, Charles S. Bird, Ivan Karp, Thomas O Beidelman, James Fernandez, Luc de Heusch, John Middleton, and Roy Willis. Indianapolis: Indiana University Press, 1989.

Awolalu, J. Omosade. *Yoruba Beliefs and Sacrificial Rites*. United Kingdom: Longman Group Ltd, 1979.

Barnes, Sandra T. "Introduction: The Many Faces of Ogun." In *Africa's Ogun: Old World and New*. Eds., Sandra T. Barnes, Charles S. Bird, Ivan Karp, Thomas O Beidelman, James Fernandez, Luc de Heusch, John Middleton, and Roy Willis. Indianapolis: Indiana University Press, 1989.

Barnes, Sandra T. & Paula Girshick Ben-Amos. "Ogun, the Empire Builder." In *Africa's Ogun: Old World and New*. Eds., Sandra T. Barnes, Charles S. Bird, Ivan Karp, Thomas O Beidelman, James Fernandez, Luc de Heusch, John Middleton, and Roy Willis. Indianapolis: Indiana University Press, 1989.

Bel, Catherine. *Ritual Theory, Ritual Practice*. Oxford: Oxford University Press, Inc., 1992.

Benyon-Payne, Danielle Margaret Ramsey. "The Suicide Question in Late-Victorian Gothic Fiction: Representations of Suicide in their Historical, Cultural and

Social Contexts." *A Thesis Submitted for the Degree of Doctor of Philosophy at the University 2 of Leicester.* Leicester: University of Leicester, 2015.

Blevins, Dean G., Stanley J. Bodes, John E. Seaman, Terry S. Sowden & David P. Wilson, eds. *Church of the Nazarene Manual, 2013 - 2017: History Constitution Government Ritual.* Kansas City: Nazarene Publishing House, 2013.

Block, Daniel I. "Ezekiel 11:1-21." In *The New International Commentary on Old Testament."* Eds., R.K. Harrison, Robert L. Hubbard, Jr. Grand Rapids, Michigan\ Cambridge, U.K.: William B. Eerdmans Publishing Company, 1997.

Bradshaw, Robert I. "Tyre." *Biblical Archaeology.* Grand Rapids: Zondervan, 1998.

Bright, John. *A History of Israel: With an Introduction and Appendix by William P. Brown.* Fourth Edition. Louisville, Kentucky: Westminster John Knox Press, 2000.

Brotzman, Ellis R. *Old Testament Textual Criticism: A Practical Introduction.* Forw., Bruce K. Waltke. Grand Rapids, Michigan: Baker Book House Company, 1994.

Brown, William P. *The Ethhos of the Cosmos.* Grand rapids: Eerdmans, 1999.

Church Educational System, ed. *Old Testament Student Manual: 1 Kings –Malachi.* Utah: The Church of Jesus Christ of Latter-day Saints, 2003.

Clements, R.E. ed. *The World of Ancient Israel: Sociological, Anthropological and political Perspectives.* Cambridge: Cambridge University Press, 1989.

Coppes, Leonard J. "קָעַל " *Theological Wordbook of the Old Testament,* ed., R. Laird Harris, Gleason L. Archer, and Bruce K. Waltke. Chicago: Moody Publishers, 1980.

Constitution of the Federal Republic of Nigeria, 1999.

Dada, O.A. *Critical Introduction to the Old Testament.* Ibadan: University of Ibadan Press, Distance Learning Programme, n.d.

Davis, F. Daniel. "Human Dignity and Respect for Persons: A Historical Perspective on Public Bioethics." *In Human Dignity and Bioethics: Essays Commissioned by the President's Council on Bioethics,* ed., The President's Council on Bioethics, 2 19-36. Washington, D.C: The President's Council on Bioethics, 2008.

Denk, Daniel J. *Created in God's Image (Genesis 1-3).* Illinois: *Intervarsity Christian Fellowship,* 2013.

Drewal, Margaret Thompson. *Yoruba Ritual: Performers, Play, Agency.* Eds., Charles S. Bird, Ivan Karp, James Fernandez, Luc de Heusch, John Middleton, and Roy Willis. Indianapolis: Indiana University Press, 1992.

Düwell, Marcus. "Human Dignity and Human Rights." *In Humiliation, Degradation, Dehumanization: Human Dignity Violated,* eds., Marcus Düwell, Paulus Kaufmann, Hannes Kuch, Christian Neuhauser, & Elaine Webster. Library of Ethics and Applied Philosophy Volume 24 (2011): 215-230.

Elebuibon, Yemi. *Ifa: The Custodian of Destiny.* Bodija: Penthouse Publications (Nig.), 2004.

_____. *Invisible Powers of the Metaphysical World: A Peep Into the World of Witches*. Ibadan: Creative Books for Ancient Philosophy Institute, 2008.

_____. *Iyere Ifa (Tonal Poetry, the Voice of Ifa): An Exposition of Yoruba Divinational Chants*. 1st edition. San Bernardino, California: Ile Orunmila Communications, 1999.

_____. *The Healing Power of Sacrifice*. Illustrated edition. Henrietta: Athelia Henrietta PR, 1999.

Ellis, Robert Ray. *Learning to Read Biblical Hebrew: An Introductory Grammar*, Revised Edition. Texas: Baylon University, 2003.

Enslin, John Victor. "Kant on Human Dignity: A Conversation among Scholars." *A Dissertation Submitted for the Degree of Doctor of Philosophy at the Graduate School of Arts and Sciences*. Boston: Boston College, 2014.

Finkelstein, Israel. *The Forgotten Kingdom: The Archaeology and History of Northern Israel*. Ed. Ehud Ben Zvi & Roxana Hammini. Atlanta: Society of Biblical Literature, 2013.

Finnegan, Ruth. *Oral Literature in Africa*. World Oral Literature Series: Volume 1. Cambridge: OpenBook Publishers, 2012.

Friends of the Sabbath Australia. *Chronology of the Exodus and the Israelite Conquest of Canaan*. Vol. 7, No. 2 (April-June 2004): n.p.

Fuchs, Christian. *A Contribution to Critical Globalization Studies*. Working Paper (CSGP) 09/8. Peterborough: Centre for the Critical Study of Global Power and Politic, n.d.

Hamilton, Victor P. "שָׁמַשׁ " *Theological Wordbook of the Old Testament*, ed., R. Laird Harris, Gleason L. Archer, and Bruce K. Waltke. Chicago: Moody Publishers, 1980.

Hasel, Michael G. "Merenptah's Reference to Israel" Critical Issues for the Origin of Israel." *Critical Issues in Early Israelite History*. Ed. Richard S. Hess, Gerald A. Klingbeil, and Paul J. Ray, Jr. Winona Lake, Indiana: Eisenbrauns, 2008.

Healey, Joseph and Donald Sybertz. *Towards an African Narrative Theology*. Nairobi: Pauline's Publications Africa, 2000.

Holladay, William L. *A Concise Hebrew and Aramaic Lexicon of the Old Testament: Based upon the Lexical Work of Ludwig Koehler and Walter Baumgartner*. Leiden: Brill, 2000.

Hunting, Harold B. *Hebrew Life and Times*. New York: Nashville, MCMXXI.

Idowu, E. Bolaji. *Olodumare: God in Yoruba Belief*. Ikeja: Longman Nigeria Plc, 1996

Imasogie, Osadolor. *African Traditional Religion*. Ibadan: University Press, 1985.

Johnson, Samuel. *The History of the Yorubas: From the Earliest Times to the Beginning of the British Protectorate*, ed., O. Johnson. Lagos: C.M.S. Bookshop, 1937.

Kaiser, Walter C., Jr. Peter H. Davids, F.F. Bruce & Manfred T. Brauch. *Hard Sayings of the Bible*. Downers Grove, Illinois: InterVarsity Press, 1996.

Kalland, Earl S. "קדד" *Theological Wordbook of the Old Testament*, ed., R. Laird
    Harris, Gleason L. Archer, and Bruce K. Waltke. Chicago: Moody Publishers,
    1980.

Kaufmann, Paulus, Hannes Kuch, Christian Neuhauser & Elaine Webster. "Human
    Dignity Violated: A Negative Approach – Introduction." *Humiliation,*
    Degradation, Dehumanization: Human Dignity Violated, eds., Marcus
    Düwell, Paulus Kaufmann, Hannes Kuch, Christian Neuhauser, & Elaine
    Webster. Library of Ethics and Applied Philosophy Volume 24 (2011): 1-5.

Lemche, Niels Peter and Frederiek Cryer, Trans. "Israel, History (Archaeology and
    the Conquest)." *The Anchor Bible Dictionary*, Volume 3. Ed. David Noel
    Freedman. New York: Doubleday, 1992.

Mbiti, John S. *Concepts of God in Africa*. Nairobi: Action Publishers, 2012.

McCain, Danny. *Notes on Old Testament Introduction.* Revised Edition. Bukuru:
    African Christian Textbooks (Acts), 2002.

Morris, Benny. *The Birth of the Palestinian Refugee Problem Revisited.* Cambridge:
    Cambridge University Press, 2004.

Nakhai, Beth Alpert. *Archaeology and the Religions of Canaan and Israel.* Vol. 7, ed.
    Victor Matthews. Boston: The American Schools of Oriental Research, 2001.

National Consortium for the Study of Terrorism and Responses to Terrorism
    (START). *Global Terrorism Index 2016: Measuring and Understanding the*
    Impact of Terrorism. Sydney: Institute for Economics & Peace, 2016.

Neimark, Philip John. *The Way of the Orisa: Empowering Your Life Through the*
    Ancient African Religion of Ifa San Francisco: Harper Publishers, n.d.

Ogunmola, M.O. *A New Perspective to Oyo Empire History: 1530-1944.* Alagbon
    Oyo: Samuel Ayoade Reformed Press, 1985.

Oladejo, Olusayo B. *Life and Death in the Old Testament and Yoruba Worldview:*
    Reading Ecclesiastes in an African Context. Saarbrucken: Lap Lambert
    Academic Publishing, 2012.

Parrinder, Geoffrey. *West African Religion: A Study of the Beliefs and Practices of*
    Akan, Ewe, Yorùbá, Igbo and Kindred Peoples. London: Epworth Press, 1978.

Payne, William. "Sanctity of Human Life." *Message Preached a Trinity Baptist*
    Church. Burlington, ON: n.p., 2007.

Peek, Philip M. "The Study of Divination, Present and Past." In *African Divination*
    Systems: Ways of Knowing. Eds., Philip M. Peek et al. Indianapolis: Indiana
    University Press, 1991.

Schniedewind, William M. and Joel H. Hunt. *Ugaritic Language, Culture, and*
    Literature. Cambridge: Cambridge University Press, 2007.

Scott, William R. *A Simplified Guide to BHS: Critical Apparatus, Masora, Accents,*
    Unusual Letters & Other Markings, Third Edition. Richland Hills: Bibal
    Press, 1995.

Simango, Daniel. "The Image of God (Gen 1:26-27) in the Pentateuch: A Biblical-
    Theological Approach." *A Dissertation Submitted for the Degree of Magister*
    Artium in Old Testament at North-West University, 2006.

Smick, Elmer B. "מצבה" *Theological Wordbook of the Old Testament,* eds., R. Laird Harris, Gleason L. Archer, and Bruce K. Waltke. Chicago: Moody Publishers, 1980.

Smith, Mark S. *The Early History of God: Yahweh and the Other Deities in Ancient Israel.* Second Ed. Grand Rapids, Michigan/ Cambridge, U.K: William B. Eerdmans Publishing Company, 2002.

Stigers, Harold G. "הדר" *Theological Wordbook of the Old Testament,* eds., R. Laird Harris, Gleason L. Archer, and Bruce K. Waltke. Chicago: Moody Publishers, 1980.

The President's Council on Bioethics, ed. "Letter of Transmittal to The President of The United States." *In Human Dignity and Bioethics: Essays Commissioned by the President's Council on Bioethics,* ed., The President's Council on Bioethics, xi-xii. Washington, D.C: The President's Council on Bioethics, 2008.

UNODC. *Global Report on Trafficking in Persons 2016.* Vienna: United Nations Publication, 2016.

Vermes, Geza. *The Complete Dead Sea Scrolls in English.* Revised Edition. 80 Strand, London: Penguin Books Ltd, 2004.

Waltke, Bruce K. "The Textual Criticism of the Old Testament." In *Biblical Criticism: Historical, Literary and Textual.* Eds., R.K. Harrison, B.K. Waltke, D. Guthrie, and G.D. Fee. Grand Rapids, Michigan: Zondervan Publishing House, 1978.

Whiston, William A.M., trans. *The Works of Josephus,* Complete and Unabridged. New Updated Edition. Peabody: Hendrickson Publishers, Inc., 1987.

White, William. "צדק" *Theological Wordbook of the Old Testament,* eds., R. Laird Harris, Gleason L. Archer, and Bruce K. Waltke. Chicago: Moody Publishers, 1980.

Wilson, Marvin R. "מכר" *Theological Wordbook of the Old Testament,* eds., R. Laird Harris, Gleason L. Archer, and Bruce K. Waltke. Chicago: Moody Publishers, 1980.

_____. "נכה" *Theological Wordbook of the Old Testament,* eds., R. Laird Harris, Gleason L. Archer, and Bruce K. Waltke. Chicago: Moody Publishers, 1980.

Wiseman, Donald J. "הלל" *Theological Wordbook of the Old Testament,* eds., R. Laird Harris, Gleason L. Archer, and Bruce K. Waltke. Chicago: Moody Publishers, 1980.

Wolf, Herbert. "זכר" *Theological Wordbook of the Old Testament,* eds., R. Laird Harris, Gleason L. Archer, and Bruce K. Waltke. Chicago: Moody Publishers, 1980.

Zimmerli, Walther. *Old Testament Theology in Outline,* trans., David E. Green. Edinburgh: T & T Clark Ltd, 1978.

DICTIONARIES, COMMENTARIES, ENCYCLOPEDIAS AND LEXICONS

Adams, Sean. "Feminist Interpretation." *In Dictionary of Biblical Criticism and Interpretation*, ed., Stanley E. Porter. London: Routledge: Taylor and Francis Group, 2007.

Adeyemo, Tokunboh, ed. "Numbers 35:9-34 Cities of Refuge." *Africa Bible Commentary (ABC Commentary): A One-Volume Commentary written by 70 African Schola*rs. Nairobi: WordAlive Publishers, 2006.

Brown, F., S. Driver, and C. Briggs. *The Brown-Driver-Briggs Hebrew and English Lexicon: With an Appendix containing the Biblical Aramaic*. Peabody, Massachusetts: Hendrickson Publishers, 1906.

Henry, Matthew. *Concise Commentary on the Bible*. Grand Rapids, MI: Christian Classics Eternal Library, n.d.

_____. "Num. 35:9-35 – The Cities of Refuge. (B.C. 1452.)," *Matthew Henry's Commentary on the Whole Bible*, Electronic Database. Biblesoft, Inc., 2006.

Hess, Richard S. "Cultural Relationships in the Old Testament Period." *In Dictionary of Biblical Criticism and Interpretation*, ed., Stanley E. Porter. London: Routledge: Taylor and Francis Group, 2007.

Lemche, Niels Peter and Frederick Cryer, trans. "Israel, History (Archaeology and the Conquest)." *The Anchor Bible Dictionary*. Volume 3 ed., David Noel Freedman. New York: Doubleday, 1992.

Longman Active Study Dictionary. ed., s.v. "Sanctity."

Mattingly, Gerald I. "The Book of Numbers*." In New Living Translation (NLT) Study Bible*. Second Ed., eds., Sean A. Harrison, et al. Carol Stream, Illinois: Tyndale House Publishers, Inc., 2008.

Marsh, John & Albert George Butzer. "Exegesis of Numbers 35:9-34." *In The Interpreter's Bible*, eds., George Arthur Buttrick, Walter Russell Bowie, Paul Scherer, John Knox, Samuel Terrien, and Nolan B., eds. Harmon. Nashville: Abingdon Press, 1953.

Olson, Dennis T. *Dictionary of the Old Testament Pentateuch*, eds., T. Desmond Alexander and David W. Baker. Leicester: InterVarsity Press, 2003.

Richards, Lawrence O. *New International Encyclopedia of Bible Words*. Grand Rapids, Michigan: Zondervan, 1991.

_____. *Bible Reader's Companion*. Colorado Springs: Cook Communications Ministries, 2004.

Ryken, Leland, James C. Wilhoit, Tremper Longman III, Colin Duriez, Douglas Penney & Daniel G. Reid. "Adam." *Dictionary of Biblical Imagery*. England: InterVarsity Press, 1998.

Schenker, A., A. Alt, O. EiBfeldt, P. Kahle ediderat, R. kittel, adjuvantibus H. Bardtke, W. Baumgartner et al, eds. "Numbers 35:9-34." *Biblia Herbraica Stuttgartensia* (BHS). Nordlingen: Deutsche Forschungsgemeinschaft, 1997.

Shaw, Ian. "Ugarit," eds., Ian Shaw and Robert Jameson. *A Dictionary of Archaeology*. Cowley Road, Oxford: Blackwell Publishers Ltd, 1999.

Vine, W.E. Merrill F. Unger and William White, Jr. "To Kill." *In Vine's Complete Expository Dictionary of Old and New Testament Words,* eds., Merrill F. Unger and William White. Electronic Version.

JOURNALS ARTICLES

Afe, Adedayo Emmanuel. "Taboos and the Maintenance of Social Order in the Old Ondo Province, South-western Nigeria." *African Research Review: An International Multidisciplinary Journal* Vol. 7 No. 1 (January 2013): 95-109.

Allison, Charles S. "The Significance of Blood Sacrifice in the Old Testament." *African research Review: An Interdisciplinary Journal, Ethiopia* Vol. 10 (1), S/No 40 (January 2016): 46-60.

Anderson, J. Kerby. "Cloning, Stem-Cell Research, and the Bible." *Bibliotheca Sacra* 159 (October-December 2002): 462-72.

Barako, Tristan J. "Philistines and Egyptians in Southern Coastal Canaan during the Early Iron Age." *In The Philistines and Other Sea Peoples" in Text and Archaeology,* eds., Ann E. Killebrew and Gunnar Lehmann. *SBL* No. 15 (2013): 37-52.

Barrick, William D. "Penal Substitution in the Old Testament." *TMSJ* 20/2 (Fall 2009): 1-21.

Bloch-Smith, Elizabeth. "Israelites Ethnicity in Iron I: Archaeology Preserves What is Remembered and What is Forgotten in Israel's History." *JBL* 122/3 (2003): 401-425.

Brems, Eva. "SAS v FRANCE: A Reality Check," eds., Helen O'Nions & Janice Denoncourt. *Journal of Nottingham Law School* Vol. 25 (2016): 58-72.

Clapper, John. "The Sanctity of Human Life and Abortion." *WRS Journal* 5/2 (August 1998):31-45.

Cohan, John Alan. "Homicide by Necessity." *COHAN.DOC* Vol.10, No.119 (2006): 119-186.

Committee on Doctrine of the USCCB, ed. "Ethical and Religious Directives for Catholic Health Care Services." *USCCB.* Fifth Edition (November 2009): 1-43.

Ekeke, Emeka C. and Ephraim A. Ikegbu. *The Sanctity of Human Life in the Twenty First Century: The Challenge of Euthanasia and Assisted Suicide.* Educational Research Vol. 1(9) (October 2010): 312-318.

Fejes, Pal. "The Eessa-Exodus in the Paleolitic Age (An Epigraphic and Historical Study)." *Migration & Diffusion* Vol. 1, Issue No. 5 (2001): 6-29.

Gushee, David P. "Can a Sanctity of Human Life Ethnic Ground Christian Ecological Responsibility." *Notre Dame Journal of Law, Ethics & Public Policy* Vol. 23:2 (2009): 471-495.

Joffe, Alexander H. "The Rise of Secondary States in the Iron Age Levant." *JESHO* 45:4 (2002): 425-467.

Killebrew, Ann E. and Gunnar Lehmann. "The World of the Philistines and Other "Sea Peoples." *The Philistines and Other Sea Peoples" in Text and*

Archaeology. Ed. Ann E. Killebrew and Gunnar Lehmann. *SBL* No. 15 (2013): 1-17.

Knights, Samantha. "Face Veils and the Law: A Critical Reflection." Ed. Helen O'Nions & Janice Denoncourt. *Journal of Nottingham Law School* Vol. 25 (2016): 97-104.

Lewis, Shaun. "What is Man? Or, The Image of God." *Journal of Dispensational Theology*, eds., Christopher B. Cone, Ron J. Bigalke, and Gary E. Gilley. Volume 16, Number 48 (August 2012): 13-26.

Naaman, Nadav. "Habiru and Hebrew: The Transfer of a Social Term to the Literary Sphere." *Journal of Near Eastern Studies*. Vol. 45, No.4 (Oct.1986): 271-288.

Oladejo, Olusayo 'Bosun. "Household Gods in Jewish Cosmology and the Challenges of Syncre-Fetish Practices among Yoruba Christians." *International Journal of Research in Humanities and Social Studies* Vol. 2, Issue 12 (December 2015): 57-64.

Olarinmoye, Omobolaji Ololade. "Yoruba Politics 1999-2003." *African Journal of Political Science and International Relations* Vol. 1 No. 2 (November 2007): 020-027.

Omobola, Odejobi Cecilia. "An Overview of Taboo and Superstition among the Yoruba of Southwest of Nigeria." *Mediterranean Journal of Social Sciences* Vol. 4 No 2 (May 2013): 221-226.

Rowley, Matthew. "The Epistemology of Sacralized Violence in the Exodus and Conquest." *JETS* 57/1 (2014): 63-83.

Ruse, Cathy Cleaver & Rob Schwarzwalder. "The Best Pro-Life Arguments for Secular Audiences." *Family Research Council* (2011):1-9.

Simeone, Joseph J. "Survivors" of the Eternal Sea: A Short True Story *ST. LOUIS U.L.J* 45 (2001): 1123, 1140-41

Singer, Itamar. "The Philistines in the Bible: A Short Rejoinder to a New Perspective." *In The Philistines and Other Sea Peoples" in Text and Archaeology*, eds., Ann E. Killebrew and Gunnar Lehmann. *SBL* No. 15 (2013): 19-28.

Thomas, Rillo. "Pope Francis' Encyclical asks for Environmental Stewardship." *Benedictine Oblate*. Ed. Mary Jeanne Schumacher Vol. 21:4 (Fall 2015): 4-5.

Ujomu, Philip Ogo & Felix O. Olatunji. "The Value of Human Life and a Philosophy of National Security for Nigeria: Some Theoretical Issues." *Annales Philosophici* 6 (2013): 47-67.

West, Stuart A. "The Nuzi Tablets: Reflections on the Patriarchal Narratives." *Dor Le Dor* Vol. VIII No.1 (Fall 1979):12-20.

Wenham, Gordon. "Pentateuchal Studies Today." *Themelios: An International Journal for Students of Theological and Religious Studies* 22.1 (October 1996) 3-13.

BIBLE SOFTWARE

Clarke, Adam. "Numbers 35:31." *Adam Clarke's Commentary*. Electronic Database. Biblesoft, Inc., 2005.

Eaton, R.S. "Num. 35"9-34 (The Cities of Refuge)." *The Biblical Illustrator: Old Testament Volumes*. Electronic Database. Ed. Joseph S. Exell. Ages Software, Inc. and Biblesoft, Inc., 2006.

Jamieson, Robert, Andrew Robert Fausset, and David Brown. "Num. 35:11." *Jamieson, Fausset, and Brown Commentary*. Electronic Database. Grand Rapids, Michigan: William B. Eerdmans Publishing Company, 2006.

Keil, C.F. and F. Delitzsch. "Numbers 35:9-11." *Commentary on the Old Testament*. Electronic Database. Trans. James Martin. Peabody: Hendrickson Publishers, Inc., 1996.

Marsh, John and Albert George Butzer. "Exegesis of Numbers 35:9-34." *In The Interpreter's Bible*, eds., George Arthur Buttrick, Walter Russell Bowie, Paul Scherer, John Knox, Samuel Terrien, and Nolan B. Harmon. Nashville: Abingdon Press, 1953.

Richards, Lawrence O. "Expectation: Numbers 26-36 - Cities of Refuge," *The Teacher's Commentary*. Electronic Database. Wheaton, Illinois: Victor Books [A Division of Scripture Press Publications Inc.], 1987.

Roberts, W. *The Biblical Illustrator: Old Testament Volumes*. Electronic Database. Ed. Joseph S. Exell. Ages Software, Inc. and Biblesoft, Inc., 2006.

Winterbotham, R. "Num. 35:9-34 – The Cities of Refuge." *The Pulpit Commentary*. Electronic Database. Ed. H.D.M. Spence and Joseph S. Exell. Biblesoft, Inc., 2006.

Walvoord, John F., Roy B. Zuck, Kenneth L. Barker, Eugene H. Merirll and Stanley D. Toussaint, eds. *Bible Knowledge Commentary/Old Testament*. Electronic Database. Colorado Springs: Cook Communications Ministries, 2000.

Wiersbe, Warren W. *The Bible Exposition Commentary/Pentateuch*. Electronic Database Colorado Springs: Cook Communications Ministries, 2001.

INTERNET SOURCES

"History of Racism and Immigration Time Line: Key Events in the Struggle for Racial Equality in the United States," *https://www.google.com.ng/url?sa=t&-source=web&rct=j&url=http://cw.routledge.com/textbooks/9780415892940/data* (accessed April 30, 2018).

"The Sanctity of Life." *Religion and Early Life.* http://www.whitworth.lancs.sch.uk/userimages/website/Mock%25201%2520Revision/RS/Early%2520Life.pdf (accessed August 23, 2017).

Amnesty International. "Nigeria: Impunity for political violence in the run-up to the 2007 elections" (April, 2007). *Under "Settings."* https://www.amnsety.org/download/Documents/60000/afr440042007en.pdf (accessed on September 11, 2017).

Anderson, Kerby. "Capital Punishment: A Christian View and Biblical Perspective. Ed. Probe Ministries" (1992). *http://www.probe.org/capital-punishment/%3Fprint%3Dpdf* (accessed August 23, 2017).

Booth, F.L. *"Old Testament Wilderness Wanderings and the Conquest of Canaan"* (2015) *www.padfield.com/acrobat/booth/OT-Y1-Q4.pdf* (accessed September 2, 2017).

Campbell, Courtney S. "Cloning Human Beings: Religious Perspectives on Human Cloning." *Commissioned Paper.* *https://www.scribd.com/mobile/document/320925944/CC4-pdf* (accessed October 20, 2017), D-25.

Carnell, Steven W. "Does Scripture Support the Death Penalty?" *Millersville Bible Church.http://www.millersvillebiblechurch.org/_files/live/Does%2520Scriptur e%2520Support%2520the%2520Death%2520Penalty.pdf* (accessed August 23, 2017).

Cassidy, Keith. "Interpreting the Pro-Life Movement: Recurrent Themes and Recent Trends." *Life and Learning IX. http://www.uffl.org/vol%25209/cassidy.pdf* (accessed September 2, 2017).

COLF. "Choose LIFE: A Summary of the Encyclical Evangelium Vitae." *http://www.cccb.ca/site/Files/CHOOSE_brochure.pdf* (1997) (accessed September 5, 2017).

Dachen, Isaac. "8 notorious criminals Nigerians can never forget." *https://amp.pulse.ng/gist/pulse-list-8-notorious-criminals-nigerians-can-never-forget-id5731535.html* (accessed September 11, 2017).

Denk, Daniel J. "Created in God's Image (Genesis 1-3)." *Intervarsity Christian Fellowship* (2013). *https://www.%3A%2F%2Fcollegiateministries.intervarsity.org%2Fsites%2Fc ollegiateministries%2Ffiles%2Fresource%2Ffile%2FCreated_in_God%2527s _Image.pdf* (accessed August 29, 2017).

Focus on the Family. "Valuing Life from the Start: Age Specific Lessons and Activities for Kids, 2012." *http://www.thrivingfamily.com/~/mediaThriving/1-articles/PDFs/valuiing-life-tool-kit.pdf* (accessed August 23, 2017).

General Presbytery of the Assembly of God, ed. "Sanctity of Human Life: Abortion and Reproductive Issues." *http://abortion.procon.org/sourcefiles/sanctity-of-human-life-abortion-and-reproductive-issues.pdf* (accessed August 23, 2017).

Gilders, William K. "Sacrifice in Ancient Israel." *SBL.* Emory University, Atlanta, Georgia. *https://www.sbl-site.org/assets/pdfs/TBv2i5_Gilders2.pdf* (accessed August 31, 2017).

Gloria Dei Lutheran Church. "Sanctity of Human Life Sunday Bulletin." *Life Sunday 2016. http://www.gloriadeilcms.org/bulletins/160117_bulletin.pdf* (accessed August 23, 2017).

Gushee, David P. "The Old Testament and the Sanctity of Life." *Bioethics & Human Dignity. Trinity International University. https://cbhd.org/content/old-*

testament-and-sanctity-life&ved (February 2008) (accessed September 21, 2016).

_____. "The Sanctity of Life: An Evangelical Exploration," 2004. *https://www.uu.edu/programs/pew/Pew%2520Application%2520Gushee%252 02005.pdf* (accessed September 2, 2017).

John, E.C. "The Old Testament Understanding of Death." *https://biblicalstudies.org.uk/pdf/ijt/23_1-2_123.pdf* (accessed September 5, 2017).

Lemke, Steve W. "The Intelligent Design of Humans: The Meaning of the *Imago Dei* for Theological Anthropology." *A Paper Presented at the Southwest Regional Meeting of the Evangelical Theological Society Meeting in Houston, Texas. http://www.nobts.edu/faculty/itor/LemkeSW-files/PersonhoodETSpaper.pdf* (accessed August 23, 2017).

Map of Yorubaland_Cultural_Area_of_West_Africa (accessed February 15, 2018).

Mark, Joshua J. "Israel." *Ancient History Encyclopedia. http://www.ancient.eu/israel/* (accessed April 13, 2017).

Merrill, Eugene H. "Ai and Old Testament Chronology: Who cares?" *A Paper Delivered at an Archaeological Conference.* Houston Baptist University (2014).*http://www.hbu.edu/publications/museums/Dunham_Bible_Museum/D BM_ArchaeologicalConference_AiOTChr.pdf* (accessed August 31, 2017).

Michigan State University and Death Penalty Information Center. "Arguments for and Against the Death Penalty" (2000). *https://deathpenal-tycurriculum.org/student/c/about/arguments/arguments.PDF* (accessed September 3, 2017).

Na'aman, Nadav. "The Shephelah according to Amarna Letters." *http://mail.bibleinterp.com/PDFs/Naaman.pdf* (accessed September 30, 2015).

NRLC, Inc., ed. "The State of Abortion in the United States" (2014). *http://www.nric.org/upload/communications/stateofabortion2016.pdf* (accessed September 2, 2017).

NYA International: Crisis Prevention and Response, ed. "Global Kidnap Report-November 2016." *http://www.nyainternational.com/sites/default/files/nya-publications/161201_O-NYA_Global_Kidnap_Report_November_2016_652.pdf* (accessed September 11, 2017).

_____. "Global Kidnap Review, 2016." *http://presswire.com/pr/nya/160203-NYA-January-Kidnap-Review.pdf* (accessed September 11, 2017).

Olagunju, Olugbenga. "The Relevance of Historical-Critical Method of Biblical Interpretation for the Church in Africa." *American Journal of Biblical Theology.http://www.biblicaltheology.com/Research/Olagunju005.pdf* (accessed September 5, 2017).

Omipidan, Teslim Opemipo. "The Real Story of Ishola Oyenusi-Nigeria's Deadliest Armed Robber." *https://oldnaija.com/2017/03/23/the-real-story-of-ishola-oyenusi-nigerias-deadliest-armed-robber/* (accessed August 9, 2018).

_____. "The Death of Dele Giwa on October 19, 1986." *https://oldnaija.com/2015/10/30/the-death-of-dele-giwa-on-october-19-1986/amp* (accessed September 11, 2017).

Payne, William. "Sanctity of Human Life." *Message Preached at Trinity Baptist Church, Burlington, ON"* (2007). *httpwww.trinity-baptist-*

church.comdownloadsanctity.pdf%20(Sept%2019,%202016).pdf (accessed August 25, 2017).

Pentecostal Assembly of the Indies International, ed. Position Papers on Euthanasia, Capital Punishment, Homosexuality and Abortion (2010). *http://pawi-online.org/wp-content/upload/2012/11/General_Conference_Compendium_2010.pdf* (accessed August 23, 2017).

Ribera, José de. "Mosaic Authorship." *https://en.wikipedia.org/wiki/Abraham_in_History_and_Tradition* (accessed March 1, 2016).

Right to Life of Michigan: The Educational Fund, ed. "Sanctity of Life." *Discussion Guide*. *http://www.rti.org/church_school/pdf/GeneralDiscussionGuide.pdf* (accessed August 23, 2017).

_____. *2015 Annual Report http://www.rti.org/aboutus/pdf/AnnualReport_web.pdf* (accessed September 3, 2017).

Singer, Peter. "Unsanctifying Human Life: Essays of Ethics," ed., Helga Kuhse. *http://www.karlin.mff.cuni.cz/~holub/soubory/Singer.pdf* (accessed September 3, 2017).

Spindelbock, Josef. "The Catholic Church and the Sanctity of Human Life." *http://spindelboeck.net/sanctity_human_life.pdf* (accessed August 31, 2017).

Stibbs, A.M. "The Meaning of the Word 'Blood' in Scripture." *The Tyndale New Testament Lecture*, (1947). *httptheologicalstudies.org.ukpdfblood_stibbs.pdf%20(Sept%2019,%202016).pdf* (accessed September 20, 2016).

Wade, Roe V. "Sanctity of Human Life: Suicide, Physician-Assisted Suicide, and Euthanasia." (Adopted by the General Presbytery in Session August 9-11,2010*). http://ag.org/-/media/AGORG/Beliefs/Topics-Index/PP_Sanctity_of_Human_Life_Suicide_Euthanasia.pdf* (accessed August 23, 2017).

Wagner, William, comp. "Pope John Paul II - Evangelium Vitae: The Gospel of Life" (1995). *http://1178.sites.ecatholic.com/documents/2015/3/Evangelium%2520Vitae.pd* (accessed August 31, 2017).

NEWSPAPERS

Adedayo, Festus. "Nigeria: Fatherland as murderland." Nigerian Tribune, September 24, 2017.

UNPUBLISHED MATERIALS

Oladejo-Babalola, Olafimihan Solomon. "Leadership Failure in Ezekiel 11:1-15 and Its Implications for the Nigerian Context." M.Th. Thesis Ogbomoso NBTS, 2015.

Olopade, John Atilola. "Respecting the Dignity and God's Image in every Human Being: An Afrelists' Perspective." A Paper presented at WAATI Conference, Accra, 2017.

Printed by Books on Demand GmbH, Norderstedt / Germany